I0570212

Publishing E-Books FOR DUMMIES®

by Ali Luke

WILEY

John Wiley & Sons, Inc.

Publishing E-Books For Dummies®

Published by
John Wiley & Sons, Inc.
111 River Street
Hoboken, NJ 07030-5774

www.wiley.com

Copyright © 2012 by John Wiley & Sons, Inc., Hoboken, New Jersey

Published by John Wiley & Sons, Inc., Hoboken, New Jersey

Published simultaneously in Canada

No part of this publication may be reproduced, stored in a retrieval system or transmitted in any form or by any means, electronic, mechanical, photocopying, recording, scanning or otherwise, except as permitted under Sections 107 or 108 of the 1976 United States Copyright Act, without either the prior written permission of the Publisher, or authorization through payment of the appropriate per-copy fee to the Copyright Clearance Center, 222 Rosewood Drive, Danvers, MA 01923, (978) 750-8400, fax (978) 646-8600. Requests to the Publisher for permission should be addressed to the Permissions Department, John Wiley & Sons, Inc., 111 River Street, Hoboken, NJ 07030, (201) 748-6011, fax (201) 748-6008, or online at http://www.wiley.com/go/permissions.

Trademarks: Wiley, the Wiley logo, For Dummies, the Dummies Man logo, A Reference for the Rest of Us!, The Dummies Way, Dummies Daily, The Fun and Easy Way, Dummies.com, Making Everything Easier, and related trade dress are trademarks or registered trademarks of John Wiley & Sons, Inc. and/or its affiliates in the United States and other countries, and may not be used without written permission. All other trademarks are the property of their respective owners. John Wiley & Sons, Inc. is not associated with any product or vendor mentioned in this book.

LIMIT OF LIABILITY/DISCLAIMER OF WARRANTY: THE PUBLISHER AND THE AUTHOR MAKE NO REPRESENTATIONS OR WARRANTIES WITH RESPECT TO THE ACCURACY OR COMPLETENESS OF THE CONTENTS OF THIS WORK AND SPECIFICALLY DISCLAIM ALL WARRANTIES, INCLUDING WITHOUT LIMITATION WARRANTIES OF FITNESS FOR A PARTICULAR PURPOSE. NO WARRANTY MAY BE CREATED OR EXTENDED BY SALES OR PROMOTIONAL MATERIALS. THE ADVICE AND STRATEGIES CONTAINED HEREIN MAY NOT BE SUITABLE FOR EVERY SITUATION. THIS WORK IS SOLD WITH THE UNDERSTANDING THAT THE PUBLISHER IS NOT ENGAGED IN RENDERING LEGAL, ACCOUNTING, OR OTHER PROFESSIONAL SERVICES. IF PROFESSIONAL ASSISTANCE IS REQUIRED, THE SERVICES OF A COMPETENT PROFESSIONAL PERSON SHOULD BE SOUGHT. NEITHER THE PUBLISHER NOR THE AUTHOR SHALL BE LIABLE FOR DAMAGES ARISING HEREFROM. THE FACT THAT AN ORGANIZATION OR WEBSITE IS REFERRED TO IN THIS WORK AS A CITATION AND/OR A POTENTIAL SOURCE OF FURTHER INFORMATION DOES NOT MEAN THAT THE AUTHOR OR THE PUBLISHER ENDORSES THE INFORMATION THE ORGANIZATION OR WEBSITE MAY PROVIDE OR RECOMMENDATIONS IT MAY MAKE. FURTHER, READERS SHOULD BE AWARE THAT INTERNET WEBSITES LISTED IN THIS WORK MAY HAVE CHANGED OR DISAPPEARED BETWEEN WHEN THIS WORK WAS WRITTEN AND WHEN IT IS READ.

For general information on our other products and services, please contact our Customer Care Department within the U.S. at 877-762-2974, outside the U.S. at 317-572-3993, or fax 317-572-4002.

For technical support, please visit www.wiley.com/techsupport.

Wiley publishes in a variety of print and electronic formats and by print-on-demand. Some material included with standard print versions of this book may not be included in e-books or in print-on-demand. If this book refers to media such as a CD or DVD that is not included in the version you purchased, you may download this material at http://booksupport.wiley.com. For more information about Wiley products, visit www.wiley.com.

Library of Congress Control Number: 2012946056

ISBN 978-1-118-34290-9 (pbk); ISBN 978-1-118-35202-1 (ebk); ISBN 978-1-118-35203-8 (ebk); ISBN 978-1-118-37278-4 (ebk)

Manufactured in the United States of America

10 9 8 7 6 5 4 3 2 1

WILEY

About the Author

As well as publishing e-books on behalf of clients, **Ali Luke** has published much of her own work in digital form — ranging from specialized non-fiction guides to a novel trilogy-in-progress. She has an MA (Cantab) in English Literature from Cambridge University, and an MA in Creative & Life Writing from Goldsmiths College, University of London. Her blog Aliventures.com covers writing, blogging, and self-publishing, and she can also be found writing for many large writing- and blogging-related sites. She lives in Oxford in the UK with her wonderfully supportive husband Paul.

Author's Acknowledgments

My parents, Gill and Geoff Hale, have been a huge support to me throughout my life. My mother fostered my love of writing; my father showed me that you can do what you love and make a living at it — and neither of them have ever suggested that I should stop this writing lark and get a "real" job! I'm incredibly grateful to them.

Paul, my husband, has been eternally patient and understanding of deadlines and writerly mood swings. I wouldn't be able to do what I do without him. His confidence in me helps me rise to new challenges — and he's always there for me as a very practical support in so many ways (from cooking dinner to organizing my accounts).

Without my wonderful friends in the blogging world, this book wouldn't have happened. Huge thanks to Rick Calvert, Dave Cynkin, and Deb Ng for accepting my speaking proposal for BlogWorld in November 2011 — and to Nathalie Lussier for invaluable proposal-writing tips. I had no idea that my one-hour session on e-books would lead to Wiley commissioning *Publishing E-Books For Dummies* . . . but I'm very glad that it did.

Of course, I didn't simply get to speak at BlogWorld (now New Media Expo) without any prior experience. Four people, in particular, helped me get there: Srinivas Rao and Sid Savara, who founded BlogCast FM and interviewed me several times, and Pace and Kyeli Smith, who had me as a speaker on their online World-Changing Writing Workshop in 2011.

Many people have held a torch to light me on my journey through blogging into e-book-writing: some knowingly, many simply through their own blog posts, e-books, or books. Especially thanks to Rachel Abbott, Brian Clark, Naomi Dunford, David Gaughran, Kelly Kingman, Joe Konrath, Steven Lewis, Holly Lisle, Dave Navarro, Joanna Penn, Darren Rowse, Daniel Scocco, and Sonia Simone.

Through my blog, Aliventures, and my writing teaching site, Writers' Huddle, I've been blessed with a wonderful community of up-and-coming writers. The warmth and support of so many people has encouraged me to write more blog posts, more e-books, and more e-courses. I'm particularly grateful to Bill Polm and Doogie Glassford for their support, both emotional and practical.

Last, but most certainly not least, I want to thank the fantastic people who've had a hand in taking this book from initial idea to finished product: Amy Fandrei, Kim Darosett, Becky Whitney, Christopher Speckman, and Sheree Montgomery. I've been hugely impressed by your ability to be professional and meticulous whilst also being friendly and fun to work with. Thank you!

Publisher's Acknowledgments

We're proud of this book; please send us your comments at http://dummies.custhelp.com. For other comments, please contact our Customer Care Department within the U.S. at 877-762-2974, outside the U.S. at 317-572-3993, or fax 317-572-4002.

Some of the people who helped bring this book to market include the following:

Acquisitions and Editorial

Senior Project Editor: Kim Darosett

Acquisitions Editor: Amy Fandrei

Copy Editor: Rebecca Whitney

Technical Editor: Christopher Speckman

Editorial Manager: Leah Michael

Editorial Assistant: Leslie Saxman

Sr. Editorial Assistant: Cherie Case

Cover Photo: © Yunus Arakon/ iStockphoto.com

Cartoons: Rich Tennant (www.the5thwave.com)

Composition Services

Project Coordinator: Sheree Montgomery

Layout and Graphics: Joyce Haughey, Corrie Niehaus

Proofreaders: Melissa Cossell, Kathy Simpson, Rob Springer

Indexer: Dakota Indexing

Publishing and Editorial for Technology Dummies

    Richard Swadley, Vice President and Executive Group Publisher

    Andy Cummings, Vice President and Publisher

    Mary Bednarek, Executive Acquisitions Director

    Mary C. Corder, Editorial Director

Publishing for Consumer Dummies

    Kathleen Nebenhaus, Vice President and Executive Publisher

Composition Services

    Debbie Stailey, Director of Composition Services

Contents at a Glance

Table of Contents

Part V: Marketing Your E-Book 205

Chapter 15: Marketing Your E-Book via Amazon and Other Online Stores 207

Chapter 16: Promoting Your E-Book on Facebook and Twitter 217

Chapter 17: Promoting Your E-Book on Goodreads 231

Introduction

O ver the past few years, e-books have established a firm position in the mainstream market: Amazon is now selling more electronic editions than paperbacks, and in the United States, net revenue from e-book sales has exceeded net revenue from hardback sales. Whether you want to make your short stories available to online shoppers, find an audience for your novel, or sell a nonfiction book, the e-book world is ready and waiting for you. You can even publish your e-book and spend *no* money. Many authors are turning to self-publishing — and doing it well. *Publishing E-Books For Dummies* holds everything you need to know to get your e-book written, published, and marketed to a worldwide audience.

About This Book

This book is the one that I wish had been on my desk four years ago. I had to find out the hard way how to publish an e-book, by tracking down bits and pieces of information online, trying out different strategies, and making a fair number of mistakes. I've collected in one handy location everything I know about e-book publishing so that you can get your e-book in front of readers with a minimum of fuss and expense.

This book is designed so that you can dip in and out. Every chapter stands on its own, and you can use the table of contents (or index) to find whatever you need to know right now. I write in a down-to-earth, friendly style, as though we're chatting (over a pot of tea — I'm British) about your plans to write and publish an e-book. I hope you'll enjoy *Publishing E-Books For Dummies,* but most of all, I hope that before long, I'll see your finished e-book on the virtual bookshelves.

Conventions Used in This Book

To help you understand the information you see in this book, I use a couple of simple conventions — **bold** text for characters you type and *italics* to highlight definitions. (I explain these definitions as we go along, too.) Every piece of HTML code and every URL (web address) are presented in "old-. school" monofont:

```
www.aliventures.com
```

Foolish Assumptions

I've made a few assumptions about you:

- ✔ You write English capably, and you aren't seeking advice on grammar, spelling, or sentence structure. You've already written a few short stories or articles, though you need a hand in completing an e-book.

- ✔ You're comfortable with using computers, and you have basic experience in using word processing and e-mail. Though you definitely don't need to be technically minded, you need to be willing to try out new programs.

- ✔ You're publishing your own e-book, under your own steam. You may or may not be willing to hire freelance editors, designers, or technical experts to help.

Of course, even if all these assumptions don't quite fit you, you can still benefit from *Publishing E-Books For Dummies.* Use the table of contents (or the index) to find the parts or chapters that apply to your specific situation. For example, if you're setting up as a contractor working with independent e-book authors, you can find plenty of useful tips on formatting and publishing e-books in Parts II and III.

How This Book is Organized

Publishing E-Books For Dummies is split into six parts, and each one is divided into chapters. The parts guide you through the entire e-book publishing process, from your first inkling of an idea to marketing your engaging finished product. Here's the lightning-fast tour.

Part 1: Getting to Know E-Books

Part I walks you through the basic tasks involved in publishing e-books, giving you a quick overview followed by case studies and success stories to inspire you — and to give you some workable ideas of your own. You also get a few crucial tips for writing your e-book — an important prerequisite to publishing it.

Part 11: Creating Your E-Book

Part II, which shows you how to turn your manuscript into an e-book file, covers every step you need to take, from creating a clean manuscript in Microsoft Word to producing EPUB, MOBI, and PDF files. (Don't worry if those file formats look like gobbledygook now. I describe them in Part II.) This part also explains cover design because, like it or not, people tend to judge books by their covers.

Part 111: Creating Your Website

Part III spells out everything you need to know in order to set up a basic website. This online home or storefront is a crucial part of your author platform (your ability to reach readers). Many writers struggle to set up their websites and update them, so Part III lays out a simple way to create a site that you can easily maintain and update yourself. This part also looks at a crucial sales tool, particularly for nonfiction e-books — your sales page.

Part 1V: Selling Your E-Book

Part IV starts with an explanation of pricing strategies, because unless you plan to give away your e-book (which is a perfectly valid option), you need a way to sell and distribute it. The rest of the part tells you how to sell your e-book from your own website, from the Amazon.com site, and from other online stores via Smashwords — with step-by-step instructions for each one.

Part V: Marketing Your E-Book

Part V explains how to promote your e-book online, without spending hundreds of dollars. The first key step is to optimize your e-book's presence on Amazon and in other stores. You can also find out about the effective use of key social media sites, such as Facebook, Twitter, and Goodreads, and read tips for using blogging to promote your e-book — not only on your own website, but also by borrowing the much larger audience of other blogs.

Part VI: The Part of Tens

The Part of Tens gives you three bonus chapters that supply quick tips to help you solve common problems, edit and proofread effectively, and enhance your e-book sales (or even your career). These chapters tell you how to get going again when you're stuck, what to do when no one is buying your e-book, and how to use your e-book to start a digital product empire. You also find plenty of other handy advice.

eCheat Sheet

To give you a quick overview of the key points in this book, I've created an eCheat Sheet, which you can find online at www.dummies.com/ cheatsheet/publishingebooks. The eCheat Sheet gets you up to speed as quickly as possible — and serves as a useful reminder of the material presented in this book. It gives you crucial tips for publishing and marketing your e-book, and it lists several useful websites that I mention throughout this book.

Icons Used in This Book

To focus your attention on special pieces of information, keep an eye out for these icons in the margin as you're reading:

Throughout the book, these useful tips will help save you time and money — and, possibly, your sanity.

This icon highlights key points that I want you to be sure to keep in mind (no pop quiz necessary).

You don't have many ways to make huge mistakes in the e-book world — after all, the Undo command exists for a reason — but occasionally one false move can cause serious problems. The Warning icon alerts you to potential disasters, so read them carefully.

You can safely skip these paragraphs. I've included them in this book for anyone who (like me) wants to "geek out" occasionally and delve into all the boring details.

Where to Go from Here

Turn the page and start reading, or if you prefer, take a peek at the table of contents and then turn to any chapter you want.

If you've already written your e-book manuscript, jump in at Part II. If you have a finished e-book for sale already, you can head straight to Part V to try out some marketing ideas. Or turn to Part III to get your website up and running, if you haven't done so already.

The e-book world moves *fast*. If you want to stay in touch with me for up-to-date information, you can find me online:

Website: www.aliventures.com

E-mail: ali@aliventures.com

Facebook: www.facebook.com/aliventures

Twitter: www.twitter.com/aliventures

Occasionally, we have updates to our technology books. If this book does have technical updates, they will be posted at www.dummies.com/go/publishingebooksupdates.

Part I
Getting to Know E-Books

The 5th Wave   By Rich Tennant

"You want to know why I'm mad? I suggest you download my latest novel called, 'Why an Obsessive Control-Freak Husband Should Never Pick out Bathroom Tiles Without Asking His Wife First.'"

In this part . . .

You're about to start your journey toward publishing an e-book. To give yourself and your book a good shot at success in the exciting, fast-moving world of e-book publishing, you need to be confident about the basics of publishing and marketing an e-book — and you need to know that you can write it successfully, too.

In Chapter 1, I give you an overview of the e-book world: what readers want, how to publish and market your e-book, and what to expect from various e-reader devices. You can read in Chapter 2 about a few inspiring e-book authors — established writers who've had print deals and new authors who've seen huge online success. In Chapter 3, I give you all my best tips for planning and writing an e-book, maximizing your motivation and time management, and tackling common problems.

Chapter 1

Introducing E-Book Basics

In This Chapter

▶ Setting yourself up for success

▶ Selling your e-book on different sites

▶ Putting the word out about your e-book

▶ Examining e-book readers

Welcome to the world of e-books. It's an exciting, dynamic place with lots of opportunities just waiting to be grasped. Whatever type of e-book you're considering writing — whether it's a specialized nonfiction guide, a fast-paced thriller, or a simple freebie to build your readership — you have a fascinating journey ahead of you. I'm honored to be your guide.

In this chapter, I give you a quick overview of everything you need to know about e-books. First, I help you give your e-book a good chance of being enjoyed (and even loved) by readers. Next, I tell you about the key ways in which you can sell your e-book online so that you can start evaluating the options you might choose. I briefly explain attention marketing and then end this chapter with a look at the most popular e-book readers on the market.

Creating a Successful E-Book That Readers Will Love

Regardless of why you're writing (or planning to write) an e-book, your success will be at least partially defined by the number of readers you draw. You need readers if you want to:

✔ Make money

✔ Build an online platform

✔ Convey your message to a wide audience

A successful e-book isn't necessarily one that makes a lot of money for its author — it's one that is useful or enjoyable for a number of readers. To give your e-book a good chance of success, you should know your intended audience and then tailor your content and your writing style to them.

When you write fiction, you should be familiar with your chosen genre. Writers sometimes make the mistake of trying a genre that's popular, such as crime or romance, without first reading enough books from that genre to have a good grasp of common conventions (and done-to-death plots). Pay attention to market trends, of course, but also choose a genre that you as a reader enjoy. You'll produce a much better book, and you'll be less likely to abandon it in frustration when you're only halfway finished.

If you want to write nonfiction, focus (ideally) on a subject for which you already have an audience. If your blog or website has an existing readership, you can easily produce an e-book that's of interest to those people. If you don't already have a web presence, you can find out more in Chapter 9 about establishing yourself online.

As you write or edit your e-book, keep your readers in mind. For real success, you need their reviews and testimonials, so be sure to give them what they want. In fiction, it's strong characters, a gripping plot, and (perhaps most important) a strong climax and conclusion. In nonfiction, it's easy-to-digest information, with chapters in a logical order, and with extra material such as exercises, examples, and further reading lists to help your readers fully understand your topic.

Your e-book should be well written and well presented, whatever its subject matter. Obviously, a literary novel must meet different standards from a straightforward, factual e-book — but both must be carefully constructed, edited, and proofread to ensure that your book offers a fulfilling and engaging reading experience. You may have written a deeply moving novel or an extremely useful nonfiction book, but if it's riddled with typos and awkward sentences, readers will give up after a few pages (and leave you negative reviews).

These suggestions for creating a successful and enjoyable e-book may seem intimidating — and with millions of e-books in the world, you may suspect that many of them don't necessarily meet these standards. Sadly, plenty of poor-quality e-books exist. (Some of them even manage to be successful.) But if you want your e-book to stand out from the crowd, keep your readers in mind throughout the writing, editing, and publishing process.

Publishing Your E-Book on Different Platforms

The e-book market has grown rapidly over the past few years, which has brought a sometimes bewildering array of ways to sell your own e-book. You can sell copies of the same edition of a print book in multiple bookstore chains, but you'll find that different stores and publishing platforms require differently formatted e-book files.

This section presents an overview of the ways in which you might want to sell your e-book. I cover all of them in more detail in Part IV of this book.

Hosting your e-book with E-junkie

One simple way to sell your e-book is to use a shopping cart site. It hosts your e-book file for you and, when a reader buys your book, delivers it automatically. You can choose among dozens of shopping cart sites and solutions, but I recommend E-junkie because it's easy and inexpensive.

If you sell your e-book via E-junkie, you don't even need a website of your own. You can reach potential readers on Facebook or Twitter or by e-mail and give them the link to buy your e-book.

Turn to Chapter 12 to find out more about using E-junkie.

Selling your e-book from your own website

Many authors choose to sell their e-books from their own websites. This option is helpful if you have a blog, because your readers are likely to become loyal customers. Selling your e-book from your own website also means that you keep all profits — no retailer takes a cut. You can also provide your e-book in any file format you want, and you can even package extras (such as MP3 recordings) with it.

In the online marketing world, a specialized e-book is commonly sold from a sales page. This type of page, which typically explains the scope of the e-book and the benefits of reading it, often includes testimonials from satisfied customers. If you've written an expensive e-book for a specialist audience, this is a useful way to sell it.

Turn to Chapter 9 to find out how to set up your own website. Chapter 10 explains how to create a sales page for your e-book.

Getting your e-book onto Amazon

Amazon, the largest retailer of e-books, actively encourages self-publishing authors to upload their own books in its Kindle Direct Publishing (KDP) program, and the process is relatively straightforward.

I don't necessarily mean that Amazon is the perfect fit for you, though. If you write a specialized e-book with a small potential audience but a high retail price (more than $9.99), you'll make much more money selling it from your own website, due to Amazon's royalty structure and customer expectations. However, if you're writing fiction or general nonfiction, you have nothing to lose by selling your e-book from Amazon.

Amazon pays 70 percent royalties on e-books priced between $2.99 and $9.99 and pays 35 percent royalties on e-books outside this price range. If you aren't a citizen of the United States, your royalties are subject to withholding tax; if your country has a tax treaty with the United States (many do), you can fill in a form to ensure that this withholding tax isn't applied to your royalties.

E-books sold via Amazon can be read only on the Amazon Kindle or on a device with the Kindle app installed. (You can find Kindle apps for the PC, Mac, iPad, and iPhone and for Android devices.) Kindle e-books cannot be read on the Kobo, NOOK, or Sony Reader.

Check out Chapter 8 to find out how to turn your manuscript into a MOBI file, which is the file format that Amazon uses. In Chapter 13, I explain how to upload your e-book file to Amazon.

Distributing your e-book to other stores via Smashwords

Of course, Amazon isn't the only e-book store: Apple, Barnes & Noble, Kobo, and Sony all have online stores too. Every store has different, often complex, requirements. (Barnes & Noble requires you to have a U.S. bank account in order to collect royalties.) Rather than submit your e-book to every site individually, distribute it via Smashwords (www.smashwords.com) to save time and effort.

Smashwords handles the file conversion, so you provide only a Microsoft Word document, formatted according to the site's precise guidelines. You must also add *Smashwords edition* (or similar wording) to the copyright page; if you're uncomfortable doing so, choose a different method of distribution.

Your e-book will be available via the Smashwords site for readers to buy in a number of different formats. Smashwords pays 85 percent royalties, minus a small transaction fee, for sales via its site, and it pays 60 percent of the retail price for most sales via other stores. For more on Smashwords, see Chapter 14.

Marketing Your E-Book Online

After you've written and published your e-book, the hard work isn't over. (In fact, many authors feel that this point is where it truly begins.) Of course, you've completed a fantastic task — your own book is out there on the virtual shelves — but chances are good that you won't believe it's a success until you have at least attracted interested readers.

You need to market your e-book, even if it's available for free. Many authors shy away from marketing and its frequent association with pushy car salesmen, annoying cold calls, or scammy online websites. But your marketing effort doesn't need to conjure up these unsavory images. In fact, you'll be much more successful if you focus on sharing your message and giving valuable information to people who come across your marketing materials — even if they don't eventually buy your e-book.

One popular concept in the online marketing world is attention marketing, which means using valuable content to draw readers to you instead of using ads and other forms of interruption marketing. This valuable content can be almost anything: a free sample of your e-book, a funny or compelling video, a Twitter account where you share useful tips and interesting quotes, or a blog or podcast where you cover topics related to your e-book.

In addition to being more effective than traditional advertising, attention marketing has the huge advantage of being cheap or even free. Though it costs you nothing to set up and maintain a Twitter account, Facebook page, or simple blog for your e-book, they all take time, of course — so know how to use that time effectively.

In Chapter 9, I cover setting up your own blog or website. Part V of this book offers tips for promotion via Facebook, Twitter, and Goodreads (a social networking site for readers), and through blogging.

Comparing Different E-Book Readers

Before publishing your e-book, become familiar with at least one e-book reader, and preview your own book to ensure that it displays correctly. You can also see how the device operates and how to purchase e-books directly from the relevant online store.

If you don't already own an e-book reader, consider buying for your own use one of the devices I describe in the following sections. Doing so is a helpful way to test your e-book, and you gain crucial experience in seeing how readers interact with online stores and with the books they sell. I recommend the Kindle because it's the most popular and it has a 3G version (handy for travel). Any other brand of black-and-white e-reader gives you a similar reading experience. A basic e-reader costs about $120. All the major e-reader brands use some form of *e-ink* technology, which means that the display is designed to mimic the experience of reading on paper. This means that e-readers are much easier on the eyes than reading on a computer screen.

Whichever e-reader you have, sample (or buy) at least a few e-books on it to gain a sense of how e-books look, what information is best placed at the start of your e-book to form part of the sample, and what sort of material is currently popular in your genre or niche. In Chapter 2, you can read success stories about independent authors who have sold hundreds of thousands of e-books.

Amazon Kindle

The Kindle is the most popular e-book reader on the market — millions of these devices have been sold worldwide. Several different Kindle models are available, including the Kindle Fire (a tablet computer), the Kindle DX (a larger version of the original Kindle), and standard Kindles with — or without — these features:

- ✔ Keyboards
- ✔ Advertising
- ✔ Wireless only
- ✔ Worldwide 3G

In addition to being sold via Amazon, the Kindle is sold in certain stores. Because many Kindle models have worldwide 3G access, readers can buy and download books from almost any location; cheaper versions are Wi-Fi only. Check how your e-book's Amazon page looks on the Kindle itself, because not all buyers purchase from the Amazon site on their computers. The description of your book, for example, displays on only a few lines on the Kindle. You may also find that your e-book looks slightly different on the device itself than it does on your computer.

Most users now have standard Kindles rather than the Kindle Fire or Kindle DX, so preview your e-book and its sales page on the standard model.

Barnes & Noble NOOK

The NOOK, produced by Barnes & Noble, is a direct competitor to the Kindle. Like the Kindle, it comes in several different forms:

- **NOOK Simple Touch:** A basic, Wi-Fi–only (no 3G), black-and-white reader with a touchscreen
- **NOOK Color:** An inexpensive tablet computer
- **NOOK Tablet:** A tablet that is pricier than the NOOK Color and has extra features

One key difference between the NOOK and the Kindle is that the NOOK reads EPUB files and the Kindle reads MOBI and AZW (the Amazon proprietary format) files.

Although a reader can purchase books directly from the NOOK Simple Touch, the device must be connected to a Wi-Fi network in order to do so.

Kobo eReader

Like the NOOK, the Kobo e-reader (produced by Kobo Books, an e-book-only retailer) uses the EPUB file format. The Kobo comes in these flavors:

- **Kobo Wi-Fi:** A black-and-white e-reader with Wi-Fi but no 3G
- **Kobo Touch:** A touchscreen Kobo, also in black-and-white and also Wi-Fi only
- **Kobo Vox:** A tablet Kobo

Kobo e-books have no digital rights protection, so you can read them on any compatible e-reader (any device that can view EPUB files). Kobo focuses on the social experience of reading, and Reading Life (which integrates with Facebook and lets readers achieve "awards" in a gamelike fashion) keeps its customers engaged, with free reading apps for computers, smartphones, and tablets.

Sony Reader

The Sony Reader comes in one of three colors (red, black, or white), and it claims to be the world's lightest e-reader. It has a touchscreen and Wi-Fi but no 3G. Like the other major e-readers, it has a black-and-white e-ink display.

Sony doesn't produce a tablet version of its Reader device. Like the Kobo and the NOOK, the Sony Reader uses EPUB files.

Chapter 2

Joining the E-Book Revolution

*T*he increase in the number of e-book publications — and in e-book sales — has been incredibly rapid. It isn't much of a stretch to say that the e-book is the biggest shake-up in the publishing world since the Gutenberg press.

In the 1990s, if you wanted to publish a novel, you had to find and work with agents and publishers or pay to print thousands of copies. Around the turn of the century, you could publish electronically, but readers would almost certainly have had to read your novels on their computer screens — and many people saw the e-book as part of the geeky realm, not as an everyday reading experience.

Plenty of regular people (and book lovers) now own e-reader devices, and many of them have bought e-books by self-published authors, perhaps without even realizing it. These independent authors are taking control of their writing careers by publishing their own novels, nonfiction books, short story collections, poetry, and more. E-books have opened the publishing world to anyone who has a computer and an Internet connection.

In this chapter, I describe the choice you have to make between traditional publishing and self-publishing, present case studies of successful self-publishing authors, and finish with tips for making your own e-book a true success.

I hope that you're feeling excited about e-publishing. You have many different possibilities, and whatever your goals and dreams as a writer, you're fully in control of reaching them. I know that this task can be daunting as well as exciting (the thought of self-promotion can still make me want to hide under my duvet), but throughout the rest of this book, I help you work toward your goals. Believe me: It's well worth the journey.

Choosing Between Traditional Publishing and Self-Publishing

You can take one of two broad routes to publication: traditional publishing or self-publishing:

- ✔ **Traditional, or legacy:** You write a proposal (or an entire book, if you're writing a novel) and find an agent or a publisher to represent you. You maintain the copyright over your work but sign over certain other rights. In return, you (usually) receive an advance and, eventually, royalties.

- ✔ **Self, or indie:** You complete the work on your own — a task that many writers find exciting and daunting in equal measure. You write your book, and when it's finished to your satisfaction, you publish it. You keep all rights to your book. You receive no advance, but you have the opportunity to earn a higher profit per unit sold. You retain full control — and full responsibility — over pricing, cover design, and marketing.

The rapid rise of self-publishing has divided the industry. Some agents, publishers, and traditionally published authors have raised concerns about the quality of self-published books, and though the stigma of self-publishing is no longer nearly as strong as it once was, it lingers. Several prominent authors, though, have spoken out on behalf of self-publishing; J.A. Konrath (whom I discuss later in this chapter) is a notable example.

At this point, the scales are balanced. Traditional publishing has certain advantages; self-publishing has others. In the past, traditional publishing was by far the most sensible option; in the future, self-publishing may well win out. For now, though, decide which form of publishing will work best for you and your book.

Consider traditional publishing if

- ✔ Your book is unlikely to sell well as an e-book — for example, if it's aimed at a technophobic market or it's a coffee-table book.

- ✔ You're writing a book to help position yourself as an expert within your field, and you want to be associated with the name of a well-known publisher.

- ✔ You want to skip the time you would have to spend acquiring the skills necessary to self-publish successfully.

Self-publishing is likely the best route if

- ✔ You like the idea of retaining full control over your work.

- ✔ You have an existing online audience that you can market to or you're willing to build this type of audience. (See Part V for tips on marketing.)

- ✔ You hope to make a living from your writing, so you need flexibility in pricing and promotion and in publishing on your own time scale.

If you're unsure, give self-publishing a go. It doesn't need to cost you much. You aren't required to be a computer expert or to have any publishing knowledge: In this book, I walk you step-by-step through every task you need to complete.

Self-Publishing Case Studies and Success Stories

Plenty of self-publishers are doing quite well for themselves from e-books, by selling hundreds of thousands of copies of them via Amazon (www.amazon.com). No number officially signifies a bestseller, though 10,000 copies is a common rule of thumb.

The authors who succeed in self-publishing have varied backgrounds: Some have had long careers as authors working with traditional publishers, and others started out in self-publishing and quickly found success. What they all have in common is an initial online audience (not necessarily a *large* audience) and the willingness to experiment.

Following the example of established authors who are embracing self-publishing

Savvy authors are turning away from the traditional publishing world to make more money on their own by self-publishing e-books. Two examples are the genre authors J.A. Konrath, who writes thrillers and crime novels, and Holly Lisle, who writes fantasy and science fiction. Both have published multiple novels via traditional channels, and both have turned to e-books in recent years.

J.A. Konrath's thriller and crime novels

If you haven't yet come across J.A. Konrath's popular and outspoken blog, A Newbie's Guide to Publishing, give it a look. Figure 2-1 shows the site's home page, and you can find the site online at `http://jakonrath.blogspot.com`.

I find Konrath's tone acerbic at times, but at least he isn't afraid to speak his mind — that traditional publishing definitely isn't in an author's best interest and that self-publishing is a much better option.

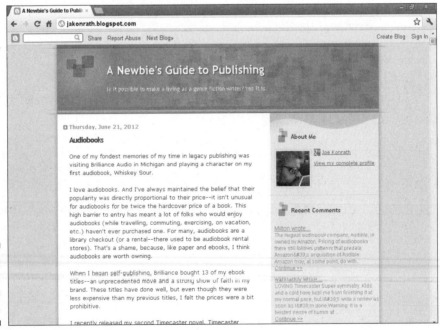

Figure 2-1: J.A. Konrath's blog.

This prolific author has 18 self-published e-books available, plus several more in print with traditional publishers (the Jack Daniels series). In January 2012, he said that he had sold a total of almost 700,000 e-books.

Consider following Konrath's example in these three key principles:

- ✔ **The more books you can write, the better.** If readers buy and love one book you've written, they're likely to go on and buy another, especially if your books are inexpensive. Most of Konrath's e-books are priced between 99 cents and $2.99.

- ✔ **Have the courage to self-publish.** A book that publishers have rejected (such as Konrath's *The List* or *Origin*) may be a hit with readers.

- ✔ **Self-publishing can bring in much more money than traditional publishing does.** You receive more royalties per copy sold — 70 percent via Amazon rather than the typical 17.5 percent from a publisher. Konrath often emphasizes this point on his blog.

Holly Lisle's fantasy and science fiction

Like Konrath, Holly Lisle has an established online fan base and a history of traditional publishing — 32 novels in print from major publishing houses. In 2011, Lisle announced that she would self-publish her fiction, for reasons that are similar to Konrath's: Dissatisfied with the publishing world, she wants the freedom to sell her books in her own way.

Writers can find lots of useful, free advice on Lisle's website (`www.holly lisle.com`), shown in Figure 2-2. Read her blog (`http://hollylisle. com/weblog`) to follow her journey with fiction and nonfiction independent publishing.

Keep Lisle's example in mind as you follow these key principles:

- ✔ **Making a living from a string of midlist (non-bestselling, but economically viable) novels is difficult, if not impossible.** Before Lisle's recent move into self-publishing fiction e-books, she wrote a number of nonfiction e-books and created self-study e-courses (with text, video and forums) on the craft of writing.

- ✔ **Retaining your publishing rights after you've sold a book to a traditional publisher can be quite difficult.** It's difficult even if your book is out of print. Lisle has written about her six-month battle to retrieve her rights on her novel *Talyn*.

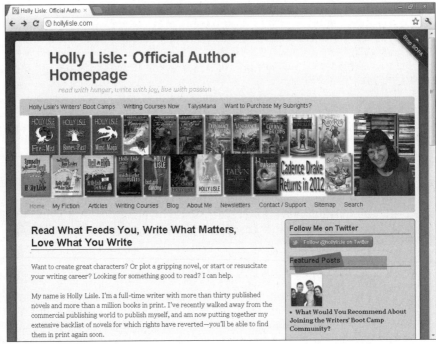

Figure 2-2:
Holly Lisle's
website.

Following the lead of new authors who are embracing self-publishing

Though J.A. Konrath and Holly Lisle are authors with decades of experience in traditional publishing, plenty of other, successful e-book authors started out with little or no experience, as described in the following three sections.

Amanda Hocking's paranormal romances

Amanda Hocking has become something of a poster girl for the world of self-publishing, and you may well have come across her name in the news. Her story is certainly an inspiring one: At the beginning of 2010, Hocking was writing at night while working a low paid day job. Wanting to raise cash for a trip, she decided to self-publish as e-books her unpublished novels (which then numbered 17).

Hocking uploaded her first e-book to Amazon in April 2010. By January 2011, she was selling more than 100,000 e-books per month. You can find her blog, shown in Figure 2-3, online at www.amandahocking.blogspot.com.

Like many other self-published authors of trilogies, Hocking often prices the first book of three at 99 cents, to encourage impulse buyers.

This list details helpful advice from Hocking:

- **Find time for writing, and stay focused on it.** Hocking claims to write a novel draft in two to three weeks. This goal isn't a realistic one for most authors, but writing a thousand words a day means that you finish a draft about every four months.

- **Study other self-publishers to benefit from their advice.** Hocking followed Konrath's blog and followed his tips to help her publish and distribute her books through Smashwords.

- **Remember that your goal is larger than simply self-publishing an e-book.** Hocking has now signed a print deal (for a reported $2.1 million) with St. Martin's Press, stating that she wants to focus only on writing.

Figure 2-3:
Amanda
Hocking's
blog.

John Locke's crime novels and westerns

John Locke originally struggled with self-publishing in print: No store would stock his self-published books, and though he bought advertising, hired a publicist, and distributed press releases, he became frustrated at the amount of money he had invested in a poor result.

After Locke e-published his novels, though, he managed to sell a million of them in only five months, with a strong eye on self-promotion and marketing via blogging and social media, and with bargain-basement prices — many of his e-books are 99 cents. You can find his website, shown in Figure 2-4, at www.donovancreed.com.

To benefit from Locke's experience, follow this advice:

- **One well-crafted blog post that grabs attention is much more valuable than daily posts that no one reads.** Locke was selling only 50 e-books per month before writing a blog post that drew 5,000 hits in a day — and sales of his book then snowballed.

- **Take the time to invest in strong relationships with readers.** Locke outlines a strategy for this task using a website, a Twitter account, and e-mail in his e-book for writers, *How I Sold 1 Million eBooks in 5 Months!*

Figure 2-4:
John Locke's website.

✔ **Series of genre fiction books draw repeat buyers.** Locke has a series of thrillers (the Donovan Creed novels) as well as a Western series (Emmett Love Westerns).

Darren Rowse's e-books on blogging and photography

Though Darren Rowse has a published print book (*ProBlogger: Secrets for Blogging Your Way to a Six-Figure Income*, co-authored with Chris Garrett) and an e-book produced by the established publisher SitePoint *(31 Days to Build a Better Blog),* he has also self-published a number of e-books on blogging and photography, for his sites `www.problogger.net` and `www.digital-photography-school.com`.

Consider these suggestions from Rowse:

✔ **An established online audience is helpful when marketing e-books.** A blog is an excellent way to build up readership, as discussed in Chapter 18.

✔ **You can repurpose existing content into an e-book:** Rowse's *31 Days to Build a Better Blog* was based on a monthlong series of posts on his blog.

✔ **You can move between traditional publishing and self-publishing or seek out a collaboration.** This statement applies especially if you have a strong online platform and an attractive proposition for a publisher; it isn't necessarily an either-or choice.

✔ **Don't go it alone.** If you're short on time, expertise, or inclination, you can bring someone else on board to write or co-write your e-books. Most of the e-books offered by Rowse are written by other people.

Making Your E-Book a Bestseller

Some e-books sell extraordinarily well. Others sink without a trace. Many fall somewhere between these two ends of the spectrum. If you want to nudge your e-book toward bestsellerdom, think carefully about the type of book you're writing and how you can increase its chances of doing well.

Rather than try to hit a particular sales number, think about what the term *bestseller* means in relation to your book. If you're writing genre fiction, for example, it might well mean selling 10,000 copies or more of your e-book. If you're writing specialist nonfiction with a high price tag, however, selling as few as 200 copies can mean a handsome reward for your time spent writing.

Successful e-books fall into two broad categories:

✔ **Mass market:** Genre fiction and popular nonfiction

✔ **Specialist:** Nonfiction that appeals to a niche audience

Notice that these categories omit plenty of possible forms, such as memoir, literary fiction, and academic works. It isn't impossible to succeed with these types of books — but if your focus is on sales and money, you should either aim squarely at the mass market or build a specialist audience that's willing to spend a significant amount of money on a highly targeted e-book.

Choosing genre fiction or popular nonfiction for a wider potential audience

If you're aiming to sell lots of books, concentrate on genre fiction or popular nonfiction. In the fiction genre, crime, thrillers, and romance are all well-represented on the bestseller lists. In nonfiction, chatty, accessible self-help e-books are popular, as are straightforward how-to guides. Money (from investing to frugality) is a hot topic, too.

To maximize your chances of success with genre fiction, follow this advice:

✔ **Play to your strengths.** Don't try to write in a particular genre just because it's popular — but consider which of your favorite genres might give you the best chance of success.

✔ **Make the reader want to continue turning the pages.** Have plenty of conflict, action, and dialogue. Yes, good writing matters, but pages of beautiful prose where nothing much happens won't reach a wide audience.

✔ **Create strong characters.** Readers tend to be drawn in by characters, not by clever plots (with the exception of mystery novels), and a compelling central character, or group of characters, helps you sell the next book in a series.

These suggestions can help maximize your chance of success in promoting popular nonfiction:

✔ **Choose a broad area that you're familiar with, not simply one that you believe will sell.** Within this area, consider what sort of advice the majority of people want — it's likely quite basic. You might want to ask your friends or Twitter followers for their questions or problems.

✔ **Write in an accessible way.** Use conversational, everyday language, even if you're talking about quite complex topics. Explain any jargon or acronyms.

✔ **Pay particular attention to the title and subtitle of your e-book.** You might not have the title set in stone when you start to write, but you definitely should test out a few possibilities on your friends, family, or online audience before you publish the e-book. When shoppers search on Amazon, for example, the only elements of your e-book that they see are its title, cover, star rating, and price.

Choosing specialist nonfiction for a higher price point

If you're planning to publish e-books for money rather than for fame, consider writing specialist books to market to niche audiences. These publications typically cost a lot more than genre fiction and popular nonfiction e-books. (A price of $97 isn't uncommon, though most cost between $20 and $50.) You might believe that their high prices will make them hard to sell — but these e-books can be easier to market because you have a specific sales pitch and a clearly defined audience.

A good example is *ProBlogger's Guide to Blogging for Your Business* (written by Mark Hayward), which costs $49.99. Figure 2-5 shows the start of the sales page for this e-book at www.problogger.net/business-blogging. Note the use of the 3D book graphic to help shape the digital product physically in the reader's mind, and the bold text, subheaders, and bullet points that clearly lay out the benefits of buying the e-book.

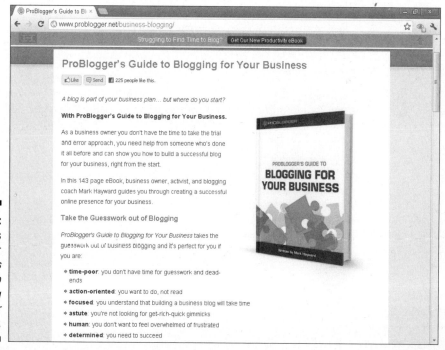

Figure 2-5: The sales page for *ProBlogger's Guide to Blogging for Your Business.*

You might think that $49.99 is a lot of money for an e-book, but readers happily pay for information that's specific to their situations and easy for them to put into action. This statement applies to more than simply books about blogging, of course: Any specialist e-book that can help readers progress in their careers, side businesses, hobbies, or personal lives can carry a high price tag.

This list describes techniques for maximizing your chance of success in producing high-priced, specialist nonfiction:

- ✔ **Build up an online audience for your topic.** You can do it by starting either a blog or an e-mail newsletter. Readers generally need to know and trust you before they're willing to spend $20 or more on an e-book.

- ✔ **Find out exactly what your audience wants to know.** Which problems are they struggling with? Which questions continually crop up about your particular area?

- ✔ **Write a strong sales page that makes clear the benefits of reading your e-book.** You may even want to invest in paying a professional copywriter and designer to help. Chapter 10 explains how to craft your own sales page.

- ✔ **Sell your e-book via your own website rather than third-party sites such as Amazon.** The high price tag makes it unlikely that you'll attract readers who are only browsing. In addition, Amazon pays only 35 percent royalties on e-books priced over $9.99.

- ✔ **Consider offering a money-back guarantee.** This can give readers enough confidence to buy an e-book with a high price tag, because they'll know they can return it if it turns out to be unsuitable. If you don't offer a money-back guarantee, supply a sample of your e-book for free download (perhaps the first three or four chapters).

- ✔ **Consider adding extras to your e-book.** For example, you can include audio interviews or video demonstrations to add extra "perceived value" for your readers.

Chapter 3

The Minimum You Must Do to Write an E-Book

Writing an e-book can be a daunting task. Your e-book may be the most challenging writing project you've ever embarked on — and you probably have concerns about whether you'll ever finish it. All writers feel this way (even experienced ones) when they start a major, new project. Worries, doubts, and the occasional crisis of confidence are completely normal. It's also normal to feel unsure about where to start or how best to move forward.

The good news is that whatever your circumstances, you can complete your e-book — and it will be worth the journey. Take a moment to imagine your finished e-book (with *your* name on it) on the virtual shelves at the Amazon site (www.amazon.com), with readers posting glowing reviews, money coming into your bank account, and the phrase *The author of . . .* as a highlight in your e-mail signature. All this is well worth working for.

In this chapter, I walk you through the crucial tasks you need to complete in order to write an e-book. My tips apply whether you're working on fiction or nonfiction and whether your e-book is a short, snappy read or a huge, complex tome. I explain how to find out what your audience wants — and how to deliver it to them. I also tell you how to make time to finish your e-book and how to overcome common writing problems (also touched on in Chapter 19).

Discovering What Your Audience Wants

Whether you have yet to start writing your e-book or you've stalled partway, you need to find out exactly what your audience wants. Ideally, your e-book sits at the point where your own areas of interests and expertise match up with the wants and needs of your audience. Though you might have a good idea of what you're capable of writing about, you might not be as sure of what people want to read.

Follow these suggestions, discussed in the following two sections, to figure out what readers want:

- ✔ Look in-depth at popular e-books in your genre or field.
- ✔ Request help from your existing audience.

Researching popular e-books in your genre or field

Even if you don't yet have much of an audience or a platform (see Part V for tips on how to build them), you can still do market research. You can form a reasonably accurate picture of what your potential audience wants by looking at existing e-books that are selling well. Here are a couple of suggestions:

- ✔ **Go to the listing of Kindle e-books at Amazon (**www.amazon.com/Kindle-eBooks**), and find your chosen genre or topic area.** Look at the ten or so best-selling e-books, and consider their common characteristics. Download samples to examine their tables of contents (if they have them) and their first few pages.
- ✔ **If you're writing specialist nonfiction, look at prominent blogs in your field.** Which e-books are they selling or promoting? You may want to read customer testimonials, to not only get a feel for which e-books are most popular but also gain insight into reader demographics, such as the age and gender of typical readers.

Create a list of five to ten popular e-books that have subjects similar to one you want to write about. Copy their book descriptions and any other information (such as an author biography) from the Amazon site, or key information (such as bullet points describing the e-book's contents) from their sales pages on websites.

Ask yourself these questions about your list of popular e-books:

- ✔ Which are the shortest and longest? What is their median length?

- ✔ How would you describe the writing style of each e-book (conversational, formal, irreverent, or down-to-earth, for example)? Look for common stylistic features in several of the books.

- ✔ Who are the target audiences for these e-books? Look for indications of their expected age, gender, education level, social status, and current level of expertise in the area.

- ✔ What topics or themes crop up again and again? In nonfiction, these might indicate vital information that readers need; in fiction, they may suggest popular genre conventions.

 Avoid slavishly creating a distilled version of all popular e-books — it would be no fun to write and would likely be perceived poorly by readers. Instead, learn from what's being done well, and figure out how to improve on it. Ditch anything that feels clichéd or less than useful. If a particular topic or theme comes up a lot, don't simply look for ways to include a similar topic in your own e-book — try to take the idea further.

Getting help from your existing audience while you write

If you have a blog, an e-mail list, a Twitter account, or a Facebook page (for example), you already have an audience. Granted, it might be small now, but it can still be a useful source of support as you develop and write your e-book.

One simple way to tap into the desires of your existing audience is to run a survey. You can ask your audience anything you want, though you'll find that surveys are most effective when you keep them short and to the point. That way, you receive more responses. This strategy is especially useful for nonfiction, but you can also use a survey to find out about your readers' interests in fiction.

Here are some examples of helpful questions (with sample topics in angle brackets) to ask your audience:

- ✔ What books or e-books have you read, and enjoyed, about <photography>?

- ✔ What are your biggest struggles with <time management>?

- ✔ What frustrates you most about standard <writing> advice?

- ✔ Which of these chapters would be useful to you? Check all that apply.

- ✔ Which of these extra features would you find helpful? Check all that apply.

If a survey feels too formal for your audience, you can simply write a blog post, an e-mail, a tweet, or a Facebook update that invites readers to respond to one question. If you have several possible e-book ideas, let your audience vote to find out which is most popular with them.

Let your audience help you as you're writing your e-book. If you get stuck partway, share some of your work-in-progress on your blog, and ask readers whether it's clear or whether it raises more questions that you need to answer. If you choose to publish your e-book as a serial while you're writing it, you can solicit feedback on new chapters before committing too much time to a particular direction — an idea that can work for both fiction and nonfiction.

Planning and Plotting Your Way to Success

If you're serious about writing and publishing an e-book, treat it as a business project: Have a plan for nonfiction or a plot outline for fiction. Even if you often write small, quick pieces (such as blog posts or short stories) without a plan, you need one in order to keep your e-book on track.

Think of your plan as the itinerary for a journey. By mapping it out in advance, you ensure that you can do and see all the attractions you want — and you can spot potential problems well ahead of time. You don't have to stick rigidly to the plan after your journey's underway (you may well find that you need to modify it), but you know that you always have the plan to fall back on if you run out of ideas or if you get stuck.

Mind mapping

One useful technique for planning your e-book is *mind mapping*, or generating ideas based on a central topic. In case you haven't yet come across this concept, Figure 3-1 shows an example of a mind map for an e-book about starting a blog. Notice that the provisional title of the e-book is in the center and that the ideas have been linked.

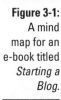

Figure 3-1:
A mind
map for an
e-book titled
*Starting a
Blog*.

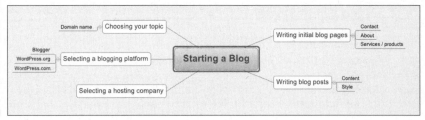

You can put your mind map on paper or use it with software such as XMind. The basic package is available for free at `www.xmind.net`.

Follow these steps to draw your own mind map:

1. **Write the title or topic of your e-book in the center of the page.**

2. **Jot down, around the edge of the page, any ideas that relate to the topic.**

   Write down *everything*. Consider all ideas at this stage, even if they initially seem silly or too difficult to manage. You can refine your ideas later.

3. **Draw lines to link related ideas.**

   You might like to use different shapes or colors as well.

4. **Relax.**

   You don't have to complete the entire mind map in a single session. Return to it after a few hours, or the next day, and see whether you can add any new ideas.

Mind mapping isn't simply a good way to capture existing ideas — it also helps you come up with new ones. As you write down key points for your e-book, you'll think of new pieces of information or new questions to explore. This is one reason why mind mapping works well, especially at the start of the planning process.

You can use mind maps for both fiction and nonfiction writing. In a fiction mind map, you might use the characters as the key points and then draw lines between them and briefly describe the relationship or link. This process can help you identify potential problems, such as one character who has little connection to everyone else in your story. You can also use a mind map to develop key scenes or plot points in your novel, or even to explore possible themes.

Index cards

Fiction writers sometimes use index cards and corkboards (or their software equivalents, such as Scrivener, available from www.literatureandlatte. com) to map out their novels. This method lets you shuffle scenes around with ease and try out different configurations until you're happy with the flow and progression of the plot. You can do the same with a short story collection by writing on cards the title and a brief description of every story and then rearranging the cards to try out different configurations.

You can also use the index card method with nonfiction. It's particularly useful if your e-book is composed primarily of stand-alone chapters. For example, if your e-book is a compilation of your best blog posts or essays, try different arrangements to see which one provides the best experience for the reader. Though readers often dip into and out of a book of essays or articles in print form, flicking through an e-book is more difficult — readers are more likely to read it linearly. After readers download a free sample of your book, they see the first few essays — which need to be especially well-written and engaging.

Chapter outline

For writing nonfiction in particular, a linear chapter outline is useful. It can be brief (only a list of chapter headings) or much more in-depth (chapter headings, subheadings, and brief notes on what you plan to add to every subsection). If you've already attempted and abandoned an e-book, try writing a more detailed plan this time to help you stay on track.

You can use a chapter outline for fiction, too. An author often plans the first few chapters, adds points of high drama throughout the rest of the book, and leaves the remainder blank, to be filled in after making progress on the story. It's up to you to decide how much planning to do.

Your plan isn't set in stone. You can adjust it as you go along.

Finding Your Motivation for Writing an E-Book

The question of why you want to write an e-book is important because the answer is the key to your motivation — and you need to stay motivated to move all the way from Page 1 to The End.

The most common reasons for writing an e-book are that you want to:

- ✔ Make money, as either an extra income stream or a key part of your small business

- ✔ Promote other products or services, such as small group courses or one-to-one consulting

- ✔ Establish your expertise in your field

- ✔ Place your writing in front of a large audience

- ✔ Prove to yourself that you can write an extended work

- ✔ Bolster your writing résumé before you approach agents or publishers to represent you

- ✔ Be able to say that you've written a book

You may well have more than one motivation; for example, your primary goal might be to gain an audience for your writing (though you may need money, too). There's no right or wrong reason to write, either.

If you're unsure exactly which reason motivates you, try journaling. Begin by writing "I want to write an e-book because . . ." and then finish the sentence in as many ways as you can. Determine which answers resonate most and then post only those responses in a visible location — perhaps on the wall behind your desk, where you can see them as you write.

As you work on your e-book, review your list of motivations whenever you're struggling to make progress. Remind yourself why writing your e-book is important and worthwhile.

Try to have multiple motivations so that if one of them doesn't particularly inspire you on a certain day, you can focus on the other. For example, if you're motivated primarily by the amount of money you might earn, but you're questioning whether your e-book will truly pay off, focus instead on your secondary motivation of establishing expertise in your field.

Setting Aside Time Regularly to Write Your E-Book

Writing is a high-resistance activity, so you'll easily find reasons not to write. One common excuse I hear when I'm teaching and coaching other writers is "I just don't have enough time to write."

If you want to be a successful writer — one who completes major projects — make time for your writing. Treat your e-book as a serious and important project, not one that you work on only if you happen to have a few hours to spare. (Honestly, does that ever even happen?)

To make time for your e-book, block out time in your diary. If you plan ahead and set aside a couple of evenings a week, or a full Saturday twice a month, you can safeguard your time against other commitments. Because you're also making a promise to yourself, you're less likely to convince yourself that you're not in the mood and skip writing.

Choosing the right place and time to write

Take control of when and where you write. You won't have a successful writing session if you try to sit down and work on your e-book after dinner, in front of the television, with your family seated nearby.

The best place to work on your e-book is a spot where you won't be disturbed or interrupted. It doesn't have to be quiet (though some writers prefer to work in silence). You might feel inspired when you're in a busy coffee shop instead. If you write at home, set up your writing space in a room that isn't used much by the rest of your household, such as your own office space or, more likely, a desk in the corner of your bedroom.

If it's difficult to focus at home, try other locations. Try writing during your lunch hour at work or taking your laptop to a public library. You can even ask to use a friend's house if she's away on vacation (and you can water her plants in return).

Finding the best time to write is also important. We all have different peaks and valleys of energy — some writers are morning people, and others work best in the late evening. You may need to experiment to find out what's right for you. What you'll find is that you can focus easily at certain times of the day (my peak occurs between 8:00 a.m. and 11:00 a.m.) but that you struggle to string together two coherent sentences at other times. (I often slump around 4:00 p.m.)

If your peak time coincides with your paid employment, or another commitment, try shifting your working hours. If you're at your best between 7:00 a.m. and 9:00 a.m., for example, and your company allows flexible hours, consider working from 9.30 a.m. to 5.30 p.m. rather than from 8:00 a.m. to 4:00 p.m. Another option is to shift your "peak" slightly: Try getting out of bed an hour earlier and writing from 6:30 a.m. to 7:30 a.m. Don't forget the weekends — be sure to write during your peak hours, and leave chores and errands for other times of the day.

Avoiding distractions while you're writing

After setting aside three hours on Saturday afternoon to write, you head into your office with a mug of coffee in hand. Three hours later, you've written a single paragraph — and you've acquired an encyclopedic knowledge of web comics. You end your writing session feeling frustrated with yourself. Perhaps you even feel that you're just not cut out to be a writer — because you're not self-disciplined enough.

Every writer I know struggles at least a little with procrastination (myself included), and for some, it's a true problem. If you notice that you're spending lots of time surfing the web when you should be writing, it doesn't mean that you're not cut out to be a writer — you only need to follow a few tips and techniques for avoiding distractions the next time you sit down to write:

- ✔ **Give yourself a specific target.** *Write for an hour* is an acceptable goal, but — ideally — you want a goal that's related to the work itself. Modify the original version to *Write the first section of Chapter 3* or *Write the scene where Tom has a fight with James.*

- ✔ **Turn off any electronic devices or programs that might cause an interruption.** Switch off your mobile phone, close your e-mail inbox, close Skype — the world can cope without you for an hour.

- ✔ **Try using a full-screen writing environment.** If you normally write in Microsoft Word or another word processing program, you may realize that you're spending a lot of time fiddling with (or fighting with) its various features. A simple full-screen program such as Dark Room for the PC (http://they.misled.us/dark-room) or WriteRoom for the Mac (www.hogbaysoftware.com/products/writeroom) eliminates these distractions.

- ✔ **Set a timer.** You can use a kitchen timer or an online time. Set it to 20 minutes, and write until the timer goes off. You can check facts, answer text messages, make coffee, or tend to other tasks after the 20-minute period ends.

- ✔ **Turn off your Internet connection.** This advice might seem drastic, but if you find it truly difficult to stay focused, it can make all the difference. If you're distracted by particular websites, you can prevent yourself from having access to them. Most browsers let you list URLs of sites you want to block.

Being able to focus and write for an hour or two at a time is more about habit than self-discipline. If you always sit down and surf the Internet for 30 minutes before writing your first paragraph, you'll soon feel like you *need* that 30 minutes in order to write. You don't — it's simply a habit. If, instead, you sit down for a writing session and immediately write a page before you take a break, you'll soon form a new habit — and you'll find it much easier to write.

Solving Common Problems in Writing E-Books

On any lengthy, complex project such as an e-book, you inevitably run into a few sticky spots. Some originate from outside the work itself (your personal circumstances change, for example), and others originate from within the e-book (perhaps you realize that Chapters 10–12 are massively off-course). If you're up against a problem, look for a solution in this list:

- ✔ **I have several ideas, and I don't know which e-book to write first.** You might have a whole list of potential books to work on. In many cases, though, it doesn't matter much which e-book you tackle first — as long as you tackle only one and see it through to the end.

  Think hard about your goals and motivations for writing an e-book, and choose the idea that best fits. (For example, if you want a good income stream, choose whichever project has the strongest potential market.) If you're still unsure, tackle the smallest idea first — the one that will be the shortest e-book.

- ✔ **I thought I had enough material for a 25,000-word e-book, but I wrapped it all up in 10,000 words.** Some writers excel at conveying information and ideas concisely — an important skill, but one that can get in the way of writing an outstanding e-book. Show your shorter-than-expected e-book to a few people in your target audience. If they find it hard to follow, you may need to explain concepts in more detail. If they enjoy it as is, publish it — and use your spare writing time on a second e-book.

- ✔ **I've written half my e-book, and I've already reached the allowable word count.** This problem is the opposite of the one in the preceding bullet — you realize that if you continue following your plan, you'll have an e-book that's much too long for your intended audience. Use this problem as an opportunity to revise your plan, perhaps by splitting your e-book into two separate works, for example. You may also need to look at your existing material to see whether you've overwritten; perhaps you've included lots of information on side topics or you've repeated yourself.

✔ **I've completely lost my enthusiasm for my topic.** Sometimes, after adding a few chapters to your e-book, you find that every word feels like torture. You're bored and fed up, and you wonder what in the world possessed you to choose this subject in the first place. Perhaps you picked it for the potential financial rewards. In that case, you need to decide whether the money you'll make is worth the effort to continue. You may be able to salvage what you've already written, possibly by converting the content into a shorter e-book or even a series of blog posts.

✔ **I need to include information on X, but I don't know anything about the topic.** When you create your plan, it becomes clear that your e-book needs to cover a particular subtopic — unfortunately, it's not one that falls within your expertise. For example, you might write an e-book on how to set up a website and you want to include information on choosing a domain name — but you don't know anything about it.

You have two options:

- *Research the topic by consulting articles or books written by people who do know about the topic.*

- *Ask an expert to contribute a short passage for your e-book.* Sometimes, people do this in return for an acknowledgement and a mention of their products or services.

✔ **Several important commitments have come up in my life.** Sometimes, your e-book is chugging along and an external event, or a series of events, derails it. Maybe you end up busier than usual at work, or a family member falls ill. Whatever the cause, the result is the same: You suddenly have little free time (or energy) to work on your e-book. Several solutions are available:

- *If the crisis will be short-lived, consider putting your e-book on hold temporarily.* To be able to restart after life returns to normal, jot down a few notes to yourself about where you were when you stopped and what you were planning to write next.

- *If your new commitment is likely to last a long time (a new child in the family, for example, or a health problem), you may need to revise your e-book plan.* Try to convert the material you've already written to a shorter e-book, or bring a friend or colleague on board as a co-author to help finish.

- *If you want to stick to the plan, try to change the times or places in which you write.* For example, you might be able to fit in a half-hour of writing early in the morning, before work, if you're exhausted in the evening after a long day. If you're doing a lot of traveling, you might be able to write on the plane or scribble notes while riding the bus.

✔ **My family and friends are unsupportive.** It's quite discouraging when your spouse believes that you're wasting your time or your kids roll their eyes at you or your friends laugh at your dreams. Explain your motivations to them, and if they then realize what your e-book means to you, they might be more supportive. Sometimes, though, you need to seek support elsewhere, by looking for a group of writers locally or for an online forum to join.

Even if you have to modify your e-book plans, don't give up on your goal — focus on finishing your e-book and publishing it. Try to see your e-book not as your only shot at producing your magnum opus but, rather, as the first milestone on a hugely rewarding path.

Part II
Creating Your E-Book

The 5th Wave   By Rich Tennant

"You show a lot of promise in e-publishing. Your first novel was rich with gripping XHTML, breathtaking in its hyperlinks, and visionary in its cross-browser platform."

In this part . . .

With your finished manuscript in hand, you're ready to create an e-book. This project isn't as simple as uploading a Microsoft Word document to Amazon.com — your e-book must be formatted correctly so that every word of it looks good to readers.

The first step is to give your Word manuscript a spring-cleaning, as I describe in Chapter 4. In Chapter 5, I show you how to put in place an appealing and inexpensive cover design.

Next, you can create an instant e-book in PDF format by using the simple instructions in Chapter 6. If your book has lots of bells and whistles, such as video, turn to Chapter 7 to try out iBooks Author. Finally, in Chapter 8, I walk you through using the free software Calibre to create MOBI and EPUB files, which are compatible with all e-readers (MOBI for the Amazon Kindle and EPUB for other e-readers).

Chapter 4

Formatting Your E-Book Manuscript in Word

. . . .

In This Chapter

▶ Fixing poor formatting in your manuscript

▶ Working with styles in Microsoft Word

▶ Including headers and footers

▶ Adding section and page breaks

▶ Reformatting your document

. . . .

*T*o produce an e-book that can be easily read (but not edited) on a computer or an e-reader device, you need to convert your manuscript into a file in EPUB, MOBI, or PDF format (or all three). Don't worry if these terms don't mean much to you: I walk you through the conversion process later in this book. For now, simply ensure that your manuscript is formatted so that it's easy to convert.

In this chapter, I focus on Microsoft Word 2010, because this is the most recent version of the most popular word processing program. Word 2010 has all the features that you'll need (you'll find that Word 2007 is very similar, too). If you don't have Microsoft Word on your computer at home, you will probably be able to use it at work or in a library. The same principles apply to other word processing software, such as Open Office.

In this chapter, I describe the crucial tasks you must complete to ensure that your Microsoft Word manuscript is beautifully formatted. I tell you how to fix formatting problems and inconsistencies, and explain good practice to make your life easier. I show you how to use helpful features such as styles and page numbering in Word, and give you quick tips on setting up your manuscript correctly from the start, in case you have yet to begin writing your e-book.

Choosing your word processing platform

Your word processing program should be easy and comfortable to use while you write, and it should give you all the functionality you need when you prepare your manuscript for publication. Try the following platforms to see which one (or ones) you find easiest to work with:

Microsoft Word, which is widely familiar, may well already be on your home computer. Using its variety of useful features for e-book authors (as discussed in this chapter), you can easily save files in the PDF format. Word is pricey, however (up to $200 for a single-user business version), so if you don't already own it, you might consider other options.

Open Office, freely available for download at www.openoffice.org, includes a word processing application whose features and

functionality are similar to Word's, including being able to save PDFs. Though you can save and read files in the Word .doc format using Open Office, the Open Office learning curve may be steep if you're accustomed to using Word. Word may be useful for collaborating on documents with other authors, as Word is the most commonly used word processing software.

Google Docs (at https://docs.google.com) lets you work on your documents from anywhere that you have an Internet connection. If you're working with a co-author, you can even keep all your e-book material in one place. Though Google Docs (which is free) lacks many features of Word and Open Office, it lets you convert manuscripts as PDF files.

The features that I describe in this chapter benefit you in two primary ways:

- ✔ **You can quickly and easily adjust the style of your manuscript in Word, which is how it appears in PDF format.** For example, if you choose uppercase letters for chapter headings, you can adjust a single style rather than retype every heading.

- ✔ **You can easily convert documents to the MOBI and EPUB formats.** Because these file types use a form of HTML, poor formatting practices result in your having to make corrections. Good formatting means a good conversion result — for example, if you've set up headings to use styles, all your chapter headings are automatically set up as HTML headers when you convert the Word document into an HTML document (as described in Chapter 8).

These methods are fairly easy to grasp and can make your e-book writing life much easier in the long run. After you've used them a few times, they'll become second nature, so persevere in using these techniques even if you find them different from the ones you're used to.

Fixing Inconsistent Formatting in Your Current Manuscript

If you're like most writers, your finished manuscript isn't in perfect shape. Perhaps you've written your e-book in several separate document files, all with slightly different formatting. Even if everything in the document looks correct on your screen, all sorts of weird and wonderful formatting may be in effect — causing problems when you convert the Word document into an EPUB file or a MOBI file. (Formatting in a PDF file is less of an issue, but poor formatting can still create problems in an element such as the table of contents.)

A spring-cleaning is therefore *crucial* for your manuscript. Similar to spring-cleaning your house, you have to reach every nook and cranny rather than settle for a tidy-looking surface.

You may spot certain problems in your manuscript — and not know how to fix them efficiently. You might even believe that readers won't notice minor formatting inconsistencies. To help your e-book create a truly professional impression, format it as thoroughly and consistently as possible.

Before you begin, make a backup copy of your file — in case you run into problems and need to return to the original file.

Viewing formatting marks

To view the behind-the-scenes formatting of your manuscript, click the Show/Hide button on the Home tab of the Ribbon in Word. The button, which is in the Paragraph section, looks like the Paragraph symbol (a backward *P*), as shown in Figure 4-1. Click the button once to turn on formatting symbols, and click it again to turn them off. In Figure 4-1, you can see several Paragraph symbols (which indicate line breaks) and individual dots between words (these represent spaces).

Fixing punctuation marks

Keep an eye out for trouble spots related to these three punctuation marks:

- Quotation marks
- Periods (and the spaces that follow them)
- Dashes

Space   End of paragraph   Show/Hide button

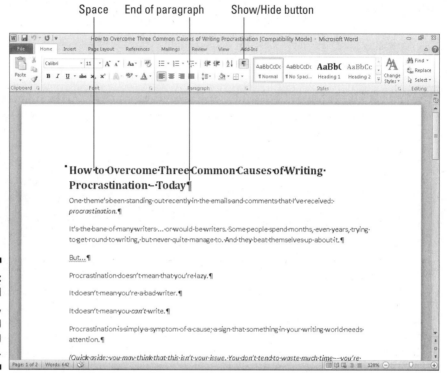

Figure 4-1:
Word
document,
showing
formatting
marks.

Quotation marks

If you're writing fiction, you'll almost certainly use quotation marks (or *quotes* or *inverted commas*) to indicate that a character is speaking; if you're writing nonfiction, you may well include direct quotes from experts in the field you're writing about. Keep in mind that in the United States, double ("double") quotation marks are standard; however, you may prefer to use the convention of your home country, or you may simply like the look of single ('single') quotation marks. Whichever type you use, the key is to be consistent.

If your e-book is compiled from various articles or chapters over an extended period, you may find that you've used quotation marks inconsistently. You can easily switch from double to single quotation marks by using the Find and Replace feature. Follow these steps:

1. **Press Ctrl+H to open the Find and Replace dialog box.**

2. **Type the double quotation mark (") in the Find What box, and type the single quotation mark (') in the Replace With box, as shown in Figure 4-2.**

   If you need to switch from single to double quotation marks, you must do this manually because Find and Replace also changes all apostrophes if you click Replace All.

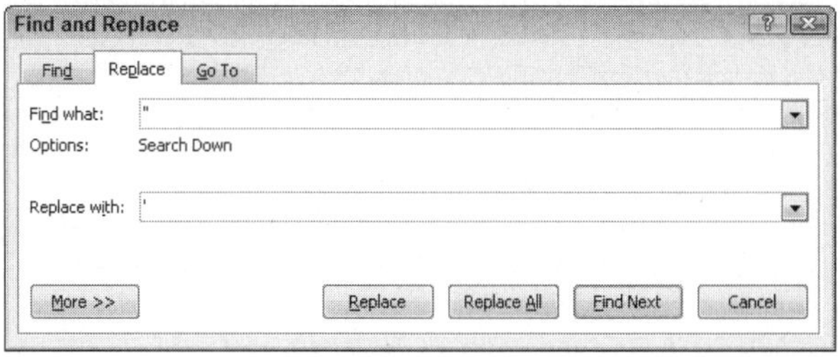

Figure 4-2:
Using Find
and Replace
to replace
double quo-
tation marks
with single
ones.

3. **Click the Find Next button to jump to the first instance of double quo-tation marks in your document.**

4. **Click the Replace button to replace the text (or Find Next again if you don't want to replace the selected text).**

5. **Repeat Steps 3 and 4 until you've finished replacing text.**

Spaces

Writers were taught traditionally to type two spaces after a period. Modern fonts make one space sufficient, so two spaces now look odd to many read-ers. You can easily remove any double spaces in your document by using Find and Replace: Simply press the spacebar twice in the Find What box and once in the Replace With box, and click Replace All. (If you want to test the process of finding double spaces, use the Find Next button.)

Dashes

The *dash* character, which can be used in several different ways within a sen-tence, is different from the hyphen, used to join or divide words or numbers. To complicate the issue, you have to choose which type to use — the en-dash or the em-dash (which is a little longer than the em-dash):

  ✔ **En-dash: –**
  ✔ **Em-dash: —**

To select these characters, choose Symbol from the Symbols group on the Insert tab, select More Symbols from the drop-down list, and in the Symbol dialog box, select General Punctuation from the Subset drop-down list. Alternatively, Word will, by default, autoformat two joined hyphens sur-rounded by spaces into an en-dash and two joined hyphens with no sur-rounding spaces into an em-dash. To change your autoformatting options, click the File tab and then choose Options⇨Proofing, click the AutoCorrect Options button, and then select the AutoFormat tab.

You can replace the dash in your document with another character by using Find and Replace. Remember to insert spaces too, if appropriate. Figure 4-3 shows how to convert the em-dash to an en-dash that has a space on both sides.

Figure 4-3:
Replacing
the em-dash
with the
en-dash.

If the dashes in your document appear as hyphens surrounded by spaces, you can also use Find and Replace to fix them. Simply type the spaces also on the Find What line; otherwise, Word replaces *all* hyphens with dashes.

Applying Styles in Microsoft Word

You might not know that Microsoft Word has a *styles* feature, allowing you to instruct the program to always format a certain type of text (such as a chapter header or a quotation) in a certain way, for every instance of that type of text. Many people use Word for years without experimenting with its incredibly useful styles. I'm one of those people. In fact, the first time I had to use styles, I couldn't quite see the point. Now I cannot imagine creating e-books, or even writing blog posts, without using styles.

The styles feature allows you to format paragraphs of text. (Note that these may be single lines, which is commonly the case with headers.) You can also format individual words or characters within your text using bold, italic, underline, and strikethrough formatting — this is separate from the paragraph styles feature.

Before you convert your document into a PDF, MOBI, or EPUB file, be sure that every paragraph is formatted as Normal text. You aren't deleting italic or bold formatting, but you are changing entire paragraphs to ensure that each one is formatted in the same consistent way, by removing any unusual fonts or line spacing. (For example, if some sections of your manuscript are double-spaced or in a different font, applying the Normal style will turn them all back to the default text.) To set everything to Normal, open your document and follow these steps:

1. **Press Ctrl+A to highlight the entire document.**

2. **On the Home tab, select the Normal style in the Styles gallery, as shown in Figure 4-4.**

   All the paragraphs in your document are now styled as Normal.

   If your document still seems to have several different types of formatting, take a look at the "Fixing a Disaster of a Manuscript by Reformatting the Entire Document" section, later in this chapter.

The following sections take a closer look at applying styles in Word.

Figure 4-4:
The Word Styles gallery, with the cursor positioned over Normal.

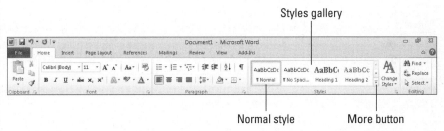

Using headings and subheadings to represent chapters and subsections

One helpful use of styles is to apply them to headings to create chapter titles (and subtitles with several heading sublevels) in your documents. If you normally format chapter titles individually, you have to click to set each one in a particular font or size. By using styles, you can create an already-formatted chapter title in a single click. Even better, if you change your mind about how you want things to look, you can change all chapter titles in your document at one time.

Follow these steps to apply a heading style to your chapter title in Word:

1. **Open your e-book manuscript, and find the first chapter title.**

2. **Click to position the cursor anywhere on that line.**

3. **In the Styles gallery (refer to Figure 4-4), click Heading 1.**

   The chapter title is now large and bold and (likely) in a different font from the one you were using. Depending on your version of Word, the title may also be a different color.

You can apply a style to an existing heading by highlighting it first (click and drag with the mouse), or to a new heading by first clicking to select the style in the Styles gallery before typing your heading text.

If the chapters in your document have subsections, you can use the Heading 2 style to distinguish them from Heading 1 paragraphs. The standard style has the same font as Heading 1 but in a smaller size. You can create sub-subsections by applying the Heading 3 style. If you see no Heading 3 style listed on the Styles menu, remember that it appears only after you create a subheading by applying Heading 2.

If your e-book is divided into parts, you may want to reserve the Heading 1 style for part titles and apply Heading 2 to chapter titles. This strategy lets you easily create a table of contents for your e-book. You can advance all the way to Heading 9, though you're unlikely to need that many heading levels.

All heading styles are correctly preserved when you convert your Word document into HTML format. In fact, if you've ever used HTML, the heading descriptions in this section might sound familiar. Heading 1 corresponds to the <h1> tag in HTML; Heading 2, to <h2>; and so on.

Modifying a style to change all instances in your document

You can tweak the default Word styles to suit your word processing preferences. For example, you can use the Change Styles drop-down menu (on the Home tab, select Change Styles from the Styles group) to select a style set or a color palette. The headers you've already styled automatically change to the selected style. For example, you can switch to the Modern style in Word 2010 to place white headings on a colored background, as shown in Figure 4-5.

Figure 4-5:
A Heading 1 in Word 2010's Modern style.

You don't have to stick with the built-in style or color combinations in Word, though. You can easily tweak a style by following these steps:

1. **Right-click the name of the style in the Styles gallery, and select Modify from the context menu, as shown in Figure 4-6.**

Figure 4-6:
Altering
a style in
Word.

The Modify Style dialog box appears, as shown in Figure 4-7.

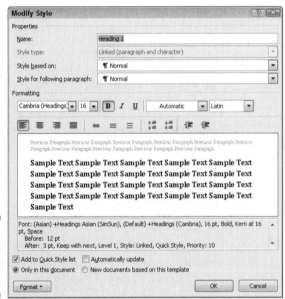

Figure 4-7:
The Modify
Style dialog
box.

2. **Change any aspect of the style that you want.**

   For example, choose a different font. Or, if you want to add extra spacing before or after a header, click the Format button in the lower-left corner and select Paragraph from the drop-down list. In the Paragraph dialog box that appears, make your changes.

3. **After you've made all the changes you want, click OK to save them.**

   Word updates all instances of that style in your document.

Styles aren't useful only for headers — you might want to format other sections in a particular way. For example, if your chapters begin with quotations, you can use the Quote style to emphasize them.

Indenting the first line of a paragraph without using tabs

Most documents and web pages have unindented paragraphs divided by blank lines. This formatting strategy can work for nonfiction e-books in PDF format, but most e-books should use indented paragraphs with no blank lines between them. This is what readers expect. (Pick up any book, or take a look at any e-book from a major publisher, to see how the paragraphs are formatted, and you'll find that they're indented in this way.)

Many authors create an indent by pressing the Tab key to start a paragraph or by pressing the spacebar several times. Both (somewhat inefficient) methods can cause problems in your e-book manuscript. Converting it into the MOBI and EPUB formats makes the tabs disappear. Extra spaces usually are preserved, but they make your manuscript look messy. Smashwords, a site that distributes your e-book in various formats (as explained in Chapter 14), displays an automatic error message if you use tabs, and your e-book may not display correctly in some formats, such as HTML.

If you need to remove tabs from your document, turn on the display of formatting marks (as described in the earlier section "Viewing formatting marks"), look in your document's text for the small right-pointing arrows (they're *tabs*), and delete them. Tabs positioned on a blank line rather than at the start of a paragraph can still cause problems when you convert your manuscript into an e-book document. Figure 4-8 shows an example of two paragraphs that begin with tabs, and it shows three tabs on a blank line.

Tab

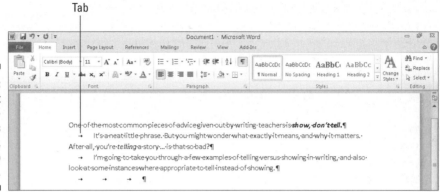

Figure 4-8:
A document with format-
ting marks
turned on,
showing tab
characters.

In Word 2010, you may find that single tabs at the start of paragraphs are automatically turned into indents for you. If this is the case, it's still a good idea to
set up the Normal paragraph style correctly (you may have missed some paragraphs, or you may experience conversion problems) — but you don't have to
find and remove tab characters.

To create indented paragraphs without using tabs, simply modify the Normal
style by following these steps:

1. **Right-click the Normal style in the Styles gallery, and select Modify
   from the context menu (refer to Figure 4-6).**

2. **In the Modify Style dialog box, click the Format button, and select
   Paragraph from the drop-down list.**

   The Paragraph dialog box appears.

3. **Change the style so that no space appears after the paragraph (set
   Spacing to After to 0pt).**

4. **Change the style to create a suitable indent at the start of each line
   (under Indentation, choose First Line from the Special drop-down list
   and then set the By option to the indent you want).**

   The exact indent size you choose depends on the font size, so try a few
   different positions. You can see an example of the changes you need to
   make in the Paragraph dialog box, shown in Figure 4-9, where the First
   Line option is set to 0.5 centimeters and the Spacing option is set to 0
   points before and after the paragraph.

5. **When you finish, click OK to save your changes and then click OK
   again to close the Modify Style dialog box.**

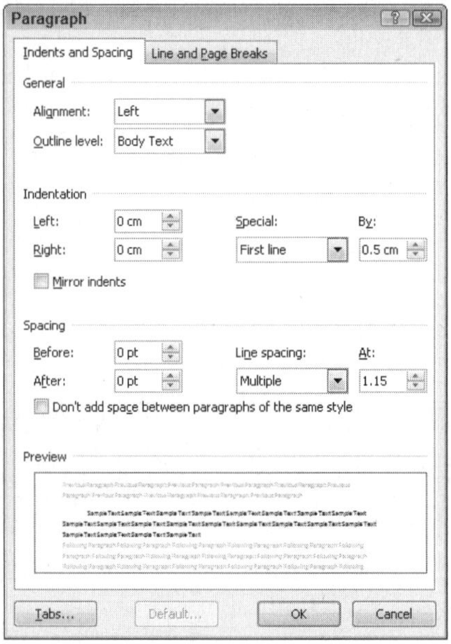

Figure 4-9:
Modifying
the Normal
style so that
paragraphs
are indented
with no
space
between
them.

Not indenting the first line of the first paragraph in a new chapter or section is standard procedure. You can create a custom style for these paragraphs, as described in the next section.

Creating a custom style for your manuscript

You can create as many styles as you like in a Word document. You may want to create an extra style to use for a particular purpose, which works well on the unindented first paragraph of a new chapter or on more complex styles. For example, you might specifically format an exercise at the end of every chapter of your nonfiction e-book or display different fonts in fictional news-paper reports or diary excerpts in your novel.

To create a style for the first paragraph, for example, follow these steps:

1. **Position the cursor within a snippet of text that's similarly formatted.**

   It's likely text formatted as Normal in your document.

2. **Click the More button in the Styles gallery, in the lower-right corner of the Styles section (refer to Figure 4-4).**

   Additional styles are revealed, as shown in Figure 4-10.

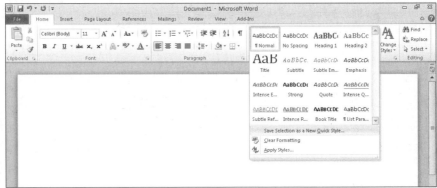

Figure 4-10:
Creating a
new style.

3. **Select the Save Selection As a New Quick Style option.**

   The Create New Style from Formatting dialog box appears, as shown in
   Figure 4-11.

Figure 4-11:
Naming and
previewing
your new
style.

4. **Type a name for your style.**

   Use either a single word or two words with no space between them to
   help in formatting your document as a MOBI file or an EPUB file. **First** or
   FirstLine works well, for example.

5. **Click the Modify button to set other features of this style.**

   To create your first paragraph styling, simply set the indentation to 0.
   For more complex styles, choose a different font or set italics, for example. You can even choose a border for the text.

6. **Click OK.**

   You should see your new style in the Styles gallery.

Now, whenever you want to format the first paragraph or a special section
of text, you can simply apply the custom style. You don't have to remember
how you originally created the section of text (and introduce inconsistencies
as a result), and you don't have to navigate the formatting menus every time.

Adding Headers and Footers

Headers and footers are useful if you're producing a PDF e-book. They can be used to show the title of your e-book, your name, your website's URL, or any other information you want to provide. It's an especially good idea to put a page number in either the header or the footer.

You may already know how to insert a header or footer into a document. If you've never done so, however, follow these steps:

1. **On the View tab, choose Print Layout in the Document Views group to change to Print Layout view.**

2. **Double-click in the white space above (or below) any page.**

   The header (or footer) appears.

   If the pages seem to run together (they have no blank space at the bottom or top) in Print Layout view, double-click the gray line that separates the pages. The blank space then opens.

3. **Type some text.**

   You see that the text now appears on every page.

If you prefer, you can also create a header or footer by choosing either Header or Footer in the Header & Footer group on the Insert tab.

If you're inserting text into a header or footer, it's often a good idea to make it smaller than the main text. You may also want to apply italics or specify a different font. That way, when you convert your document into a PDF file, the header or footer text is clearly distinguished from the main part of the page. Note that headers and footers aren't preserved when you convert your e-book into MOBI or EPUB files.

Creating Sections with Different Header and Page-Numbering Schemes

There's a good chance that you *don't* want a header or footer to appear on every single page of your e-book. Pick up any professionally published book, and you can see that no page number appears on the internal title page and that the table of contents, acknowledgements, and other elements in the front either have no page numbers or use Roman numerals rather than Arabic (modern) numbers. No page headers appear on these first few pages, either. (The page header often states the title of the book or chapter or the name of the author.)

When you use sections in Word, the header, footer, and page numbers in your document (or any combination of them) can appear for the first time on the first page after the front material in your e-book. To create sections in your document, follow these steps:

1. **On the View tab, choose Print Layout in the Document Views group to change to Print Layout View.**

2. **Go to the final page of front matter (for example, the table of contents or any other element that appears before the main text of your e-book begins), and move the cursor to the end of the page.**

   You may need to add an extra line break to do this.

3. **In the Page Setup group on the Page Layout tab, choose Next Page from the Breaks drop-down list, as shown in Figure 4-12.**

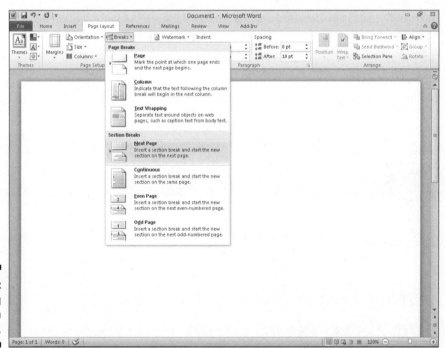

Figure 4-12:
Inserting a section break.

This step splits the document into two sections.

If you can't see the section break, turn on hidden formatting symbols by clicking the Show/Hide option (the paragraph symbol) on the Home tab of the Ribbon. You can see a section break here:

Section Break (Next Page)

You can now create different headers and footers for the two sections. To do so, you need to unlink the sections, as described in Step 4.

4. **In Print Layout view, open the header or footer on any page in Section 2, and then, on the Header & Footer Design contextual tab, click the Link to Previous button to deselect it (see Figure 4-13).**

The two sections are now unlinked.

Now you can type any text you want in the header or footer on any Section 2 page without affecting Section 1 pages. For example, to add a page number, click where you want to position the page number in the header or footer. Then, in the Header & Footer group on the Insert tab, choose Current Page from the Page Number drop-down list, and select the style you prefer.

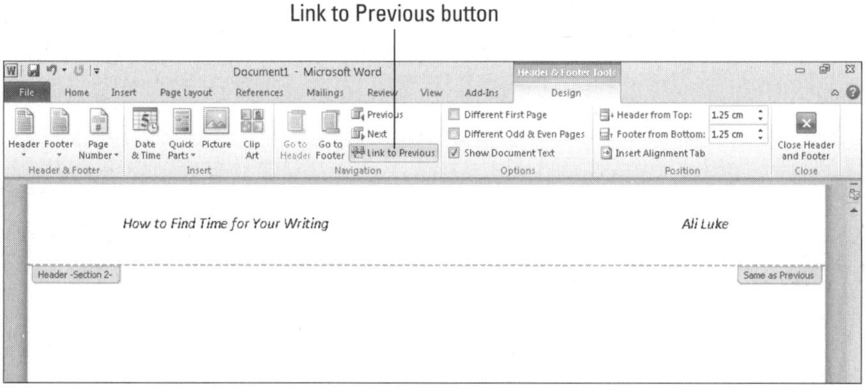

Link to Previous button

Figure 4-13: Unlinking the sections in a document.

Using Page Breaks to Separate Your Chapters

In almost any book, a new chapter begins on a new page. Your e-book is no exception. Many authors make the mistake of bumping a chapter to a new page by pressing the Enter key multiple times. This technique causes all sorts of problems, including one that you've almost certainly noticed: If you add material to, or remove it from, Chapter 2, for example, you have to add or delete line breaks in all remaining chapters to force every chapter to start at the top of a new page again.

All these extra line breaks cause other problems: They make the HTML code look messy, and they create huge gaps in the MOBI or EPUB files you create, making them difficult to read. (The page size on the Kindle, the Kobo, the iPad, and other e-readers is much smaller than on your computer screen.) Smashwords doesn't even accept e-book manuscripts that contain more than four consecutive line breaks.

Frustrating, right? The good news is that you can start text on a new page in a much easier way — by using the Page Break feature in Word. To add a page break, open your e-book, go to the end of a chapter, delete any extra line breaks, and then follow these steps:

1. **Position the cursor where you want to insert the break.**

   The easiest position is at the start of the chapter heading.

2. **On the Insert tab, choose Page Break from the Pages group.**

   The chapter heading "jumps" neatly to the next page.

To remove the break, you may need to turn on the display of hidden characters (using the Show/Hide button on the Home tab). You can delete the page break in the same way as you delete text.

This procedure might already seem like a time-saver, but you can make it even more efficient. If you want every chapter to start on a new page and you've formatted chapter headers as Heading 1, follow these steps:

1. **On the Home tab, go to the Styles gallery, right-click the Heading 1 style, and choose Modify.**

   The Modify Style dialog box appears (refer to Figure 4-7).

2. **Click the Format button and choose Paragraph.**

   The Paragraph dialog box opens.

3. **Click the Line and Page Breaks tab, shown in Figure 4-14.**

4. **Select the Page Break Before check box.**

5. **Click OK to close the dialog box, and then click OK again to modify the style.**

Now all chapters automatically start on a new page. You may need to review your manuscript and remove all the now-unnecessary line breaks. Turn on the hidden formatting marks to make them easy to spot and remove, as shown here:

Page Break

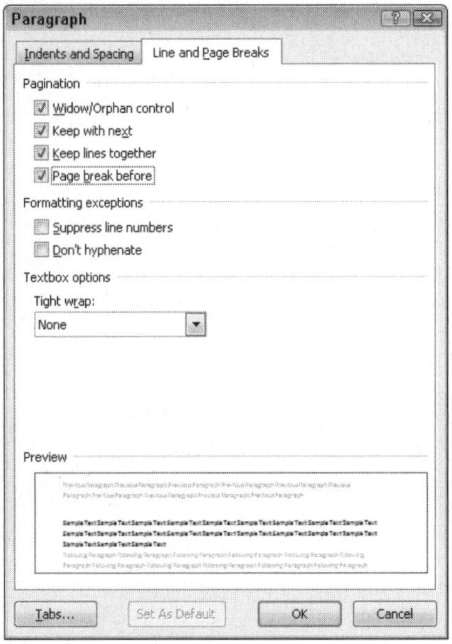

Paragraph

Indents and Spacing | Line and Page Breaks

Pagination

☑ Widow/Orphan control
☑ Keep with next
☑ Keep lines together
☑ Page break before

Formatting exceptions

☐ Suppress line numbers
☐ Don't hyphenate

Textbox options

Tight wrap:

None ▼

Preview

Tabs... | Set As Default | OK | Cancel

Figure 4-14:
The Line
and Page
Breaks
tab on the
Paragraph
screen.

Fixing a Disaster of a Manuscript by Reformatting the Entire Document

Perhaps you've written a novel in different types of files (such as Word documents, plain-text documents, and e-mail messages that you've sent to yourself) and you've gathered them all into one huge document. It's a mess of different fonts and different types of formatting.

In this case, you might choose what Smashwords refers to as "the nuclear option," which is a slightly scary way of saying "stripping out all the formatting from your document." This operation is most easily performed on an e-book that consists mainly of text, without much formatting. Novels are usually in this category.

Before you remove the formatting from your document, save a backup copy (or print the document). Highlight all formatting in the backup (or printout) — including all italics, bold text, large text, and bullet points. These will be lost when you take the next steps, so it's important that you can refer to them on paper or in the backup of your original document.

Follow these steps to save your document as a text file:

1. **Click File in the upper-left corner of the screen, and choose Save As.**

   The Save As dialog box opens.

2. **Select Plain Text (*.txt) from the Save As Type drop-down menu.**

3. **Click OK to save the file.**

Close the document (it should have the .txt file extension) and then reopen it in Word. (Otherwise, Word may try to retain certain formatting.) To format the entire document in the Normal style, follow these steps:

1. **Press Ctrl+A to highlight all text in the document.**

2. **In the Styles gallery, choose Normal.**

You can now review your document and restore the italic and bold text, the bullet points, or any other formatting that was removed. If the original document contained multiple line breaks, you still need to remove them.

Follow the other tips in this chapter to ensure that you format the rest of your document correctly. For example, use page breaks to start every chapter on a new page, and use styles to indent paragraphs.

Setting Up Formatting from Day One

If you're lucky enough to be reading this chapter before you've written your e-book, or if you're determined to format your next e-book perfectly from the start, follow these guidelines:

- ✔ **Always use the Normal style to style text.** If you want the text to appear in a larger font, for example, change the Normal style — avoid changing the text directly.

- ✔ **Create a new style for special paragraphs.** To format certain text differently (for example, to indent Normal paragraphs but not the first paragraph of a section), create a new style based on the Normal style.

- ✔ **Use the Heading 1 style for chapter titles.** You can apply the Heading 1 style to the chapter heading and apply Heading 2 to subheadings within the chapter.

- ✔ **Never use tabs to indent paragraphs.** Change the style instead.

✔ **Always use page breaks to start chapters on a new page.** Don't use line breaks.

✔ **Add a section break to separate the front matter (for example, the cover page, table of contents, and acknowledgements) from the main book text.** The section break lets you easily make headers, footers, and page numbers display correctly, with these elements removed (or different) in the front matter.

Chapter 5

Designing a Professional E-Book Cover (Without Spending a Fortune)

....

....

*Y*ou might wonder why an e-book needs a cover if it's simply a digital file, not a book in physical form that readers can pick up and hold in their hands. Readers will view your e-book on virtual bookshelves, however, and its "cover" is the digital image that appears on Amazon and in other electronic bookstores.

Your e-book *must* have an eye-catching, professional-quality cover. Like it or not, your e-book isn't judged by most shoppers on the quality of your writing. If its cover isn't attractive and well-designed, readers won't buy your e-book. (Even if you're giving it away, it still needs a cover that encourages people to download it and read it.)

In this chapter, I walk you through the steps in designing a cover, and I offer my advice for using inexpensive stock photography and the free Paint.NET software. I also give you tips for working with cover designers to produce a truly professional result.

Planning the Cover If You're Designing It Yourself

Before you get to work on designing the cover of your e-book, do some preparatory work. Don't launch the design process in a rush — you may end up scrapping your hard work or producing an e-book with a cover that's less than ideal.

One way to begin the planning process is to take a virtual shopping trip. Head to your favorite e-book store (www.amazon.com, for example), take a look at e-books in your genre or field, and ask, "Which covers grab my attention?" "Which covers look amateurish?" "Which e-books would I sample or buy?"

Make a list of features that entice you to click the title of an e-book for more information and ones that scream "Steer clear!" Don't worry if you're unsure *why* a particular cover works — I give you plenty of tips for attractive design later in this chapter.

This advice might seem to be a lot to consider before creating a single pixel of your e-book cover, but trust me — I know how frustrating it is to dive into a cover design only to realize that it isn't working. And you don't want to start buying stock photos, or spend hours shooting your own photos, without a clear idea about what the cover truly needs.

Knowing which elements to include on the cover

Whatever your e-book is about, its cover needs these vital features:

- ✔ An image
- ✔ A title
- ✔ Your name (or pen name)

These elements might seem obvious and hardly worth listing — but all these elements, even at small sizes, *must* be clearly visible on the cover.

Throughout the design process, keep the cover simple enough to display well at a small size. Although you can splash the cover — in full, high-resolution glory — across your own website, an e-book retailer shows only a *thumbnail* (a scaled-down version of the image) in search results and a fairly small image on the sales page for your e-book.

Depending on the genre of your e-book, consider adding other components to its cover. For example, a business e-book might well have a subtitle, and a book in the fiction genre often has a *tagline* (a compelling sentence or phrase to entice readers to buy the book). Plan from the start to add these elements so that you leave space for them. If your e-book has already received positive reviews from well-known names in your field, add a brief quote to the cover, too.

Knowing what not to include on the cover

After you know which elements the cover of your e-book should have, you should also know which ones it *shouldn't* have. Avoid using these elements in your e-book design:

- **Clip art:** It makes your design look amateurish and makes you look lazy.

- **The word *by* in front of your name:** It never appears on professionally published e-books.

- **Copyrighted images (without permission):** These images include company and website logos and images you might find by searching Google Images (`http://images.google.com`) or a similar search engine.

- **Too many images:** Most professional covers have a single key image, even if it has several different elements.

- **Too much text:** The text must be clearly visible at the standard size on your e-book's sales page.

Buying stock images

A *stock image* is a royalty-free piece of artwork (usually a photograph or graphical image) that you can purchase. Check the license terms and conditions of the site selling the stock image to ensure that you can use the image on the cover of an e-book you're selling. Sites have different rules about how their images can be used.

Follow these guidelines for picking stock images:

- **Choose a clear, professional image.** It should reproduce well at small sizes. That means looking for an image without a great deal of complexity or detail. A simple, quick way to check this is to look at the image on a search results page on the stock site; it will be shown at a small size.

Choosing a stock site

Dozens of sites offer stock photographs and images. Gives these three a try:

Getty Images (www.gettyimages.com), one of the best-known stock agencies, has a wide range of images (as well as video clips and music) and stricter quality standards than many other stock sites. You can use *royalty-free* images as many times as you want (rather than *rights-managed* images, with limitations on how often you can use them, or where and for how long). Depending on the size and type of image you want for the cover, you'll spend between $25 and $200. (Getty Images is now known for aggressively pursuing individuals who use its images without a license. Be sure to purchase the appropriate license for any image you use.)

iStockPhoto (www.istockphoto.com), owned by Getty Images but managed independently, has become one of the most popular stock photography sites on the web. Before purchasing images from iStockPhoto, keep its unique licensing structure in mind. Its images are often cheaper (starting at a few dollars) than those on Getty Images.

Shutterstock (www.shutterstock.com) uses a subscription-only package, so you can't pay for a single image. (iStockPhoto and Getty Images also offer subscriptions.) It's worth your time to look into a subscription if you plan to create lots of e-books or if you want to use stock images in other ways, such as on your website.

✔ **Use *watermarked* images in a preview.** These versions have a faded logo across the main part of the image, to prevent illicit use. Before spending money on images you find on a stock photography site, use their watermarked versions (the ones you see before making a purchase) to create a rough version of the cover.

✔ **Create a short list of potential images.** Search several stock photography sites to avoid buying the first image that looks suitable. (See the nearby sidebar "Choosing a stock site" for more on these sites.)

✔ **Consider using an artist's related images.** If you find an image that's almost but not quite right, see whether the artist has created other, similar images. A photographer, for example, might have a series of shots of the same model.

If you're on a tight budget, head over to Flickr (www.flickr.com) to search for images that are licensed under Creative Commons for commercial use. (Creative Commons is a non-profit organization that assists artists, authors, musicians, and other creative types in allowing their work to be shared whilst maintaining their copyright.) You have to credit the artist or photographer in your e-book. If you want to use an image that isn't available under Creative Commons, try contacting the artist. That person may be willing to let you use the image for a small fee or in return for promoting their work to your audience.

You can search for Creative Commons images licensed for commercial use on Flickr by using the advanced search at `http://flickr.com/search/advanced`. Ensure that you check the boxes Only Search Within Creative Commons-Licensed Content and Find Content to Use Commercially. When viewing an image, you can see its Creative Commons status (if any) under License on the right-hand side of the page: Run your cursor over the icons here to view the specifics of the license. If you want more information about Creative Commons, visit their website at `www.creativecommons.org`.

Using Paint.NET to Create the Cover

To create the cover of your e-book, use a graphics program that lets you easily manipulate images and text. I recommend Paint.NET, which is free and relatively simple to use (and available only in Windows).

Downloading and installing Paint.NET

To download Paint.NET, follow these steps:

1. **Go to** `www.getpaint.net/download.html`.

2. **Scroll down the page and click the Download Now button, shown in Figure 5-1.**

   The site has a number of other download buttons for different software, so be sure to get the right one.

3. **On the page that opens, click the link under the text** *Free Download Now* **in the upper-right corner.**

   The Save As dialog box appears.

4. **Navigate to the folder where you want to save the file and then click Save.**

Figure 5-1: Click the Download Now button to download Paint.NET.

Click here to download program.

5. **Open or unzip the file.**

   You should see the application (.exe) file.

6. **Double-click the application to install it.**

   You may need to select Run or Yes.

7. **Leave the default Quick Installation option selected, and click Next.**

8. **Select the I Agree radio button to agree to the license agreement, and click Next.**

9. **Wait for Paint.NET to install, leave the box Start Paint.NET checked, and then click Finish.**

   Paint.NET should load automatically, as shown in Figure 5-2.

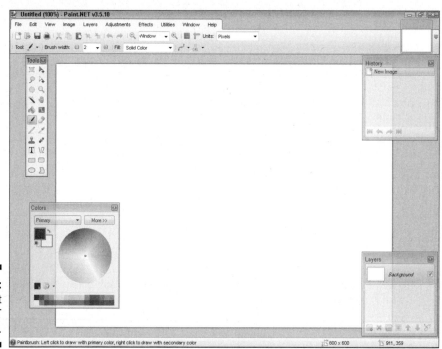

Figure 5-2:
The default
Paint.NET
interface.

Creating the canvas at the correct size

When you open Paint.NET, you see a number of buttons and menu options. First resize the *canvas* (the white area that you will create your cover upon). If you want to sell your e-book only on your own website, the canvas can be a square or a wide rectangle. If you're selling instead at an e-book retailer, such as www.amazon.com, make the canvas a standard shape and size. Amazon recommends a height-to-width ratio of 1.6, and the cover (and thus its canvas) has to measure at least 500 by 800 pixels.

Create a larger canvas, if you prefer — perhaps 750 by 1200 pixels. The ratio must stay the same.

To resize the Paint.NET canvas, follow these steps:

1. **Choose Image⇨Canvas Size.**

   The Canvas Size dialog box opens.

2. **In the Pixel Size section, enter the width and height that you want for the canvas.**

   Figure 5-3 shows an example of 500 (width) x 800 (height) pixels.

3. **Click OK.**

   The resized canvas appears onscreen.

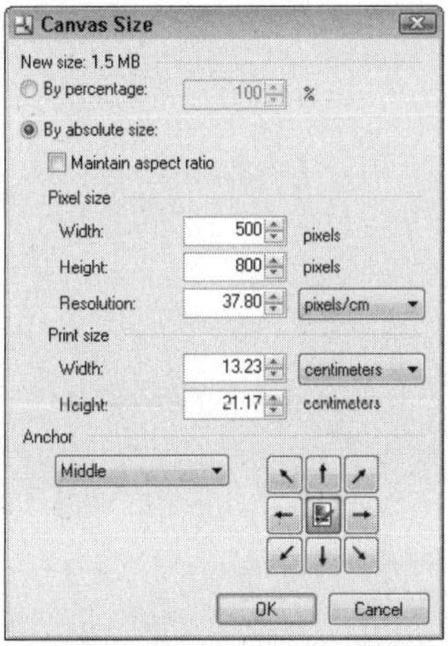

Figure 5-3:
Resizing the
Paint.NET
canvas.

Constructing the cover with separate layers

One of the most useful features in Paint.NET is the *layer,* which lets you easily adjust cover elements individually. Imagine that you're creating a cover by hand, using tracing paper, with a different element drawn on each sheet — layers work in a similar way. You can add as many layers as you want, and you can easily switch them on or off to add or remove, respectively, different parts of the cover, which is an easy way to try a variety of options, such as two possible title fonts.

The default canvas has only one layer. To create a new layer, click the Add New Layer button, which is the leftmost button along the bottom of the Layers window. (If the Layers window isn't open, choose Window➪Layers to open it.) After you add a layer, you should see it in the Layers window, as shown in Figure 5-4. The new layer is transparent, as indicated by its gray-and-white checkerboard background.

New layer

Figure 5-4:
Adding a
second
layer in
Paint.NET.

The cover of your e-book needs at least two layers: one for the main image and one for its title and your name. You may find it easiest to have the title and name on separate layers, too.

Adding an image to the cover

To add an image to the canvas, follow these steps:

1. **Open the cover image in Paint.NET, as shown in Figure 5-5.**

   To open the image, choose File➪Open, navigate to the image, and click Open.

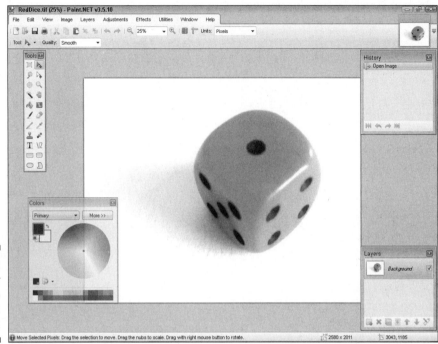

Figure 5-5:
The cover
image open
in Paint.
NET.

2. **Select the image by pressing Ctrl+A to highlight the whole image and then press Ctrl+C to copy it.**

If you want to copy only part of the image, use a Paint.NET selection tool to draw around the area you want to copy. The selection tools are represented by the first three icons in the leftmost column in the small Tools window (refer to Figure 5-5).

3. **Return to the original canvas (the white rectangle in the upper-right corner of the Paint.NET window), and select the Background layer in the Layers window (refer to Figure 5-4).**

4. **Press Ctrl+V to paste the image.**

You can see an example of a canvas with an image added in Figure 5-6. Note the rectangle around the image, which shows the area selected. The image can be moved by clicking and dragging.

If the image is larger than the canvas, you have to resize the image so that it's either smaller or the same size. To do so, go back to the image file, and choose Image⇨Resize from the Paint.NET menu bar. In the Resize dialog box, enter the new size for the image and click OK to save your changes. Then repeat Steps 2 through 4.

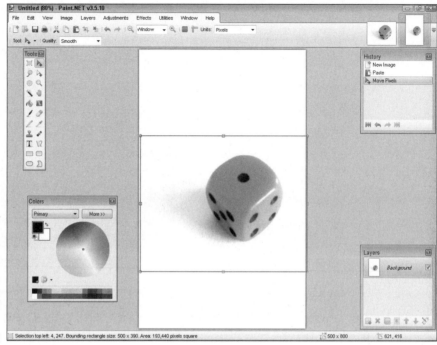

You can move the image around at this point. Just click and drag the image to move it around on the canvas. If you want to move the image again later, you can use the Paint.NET tools to select it and then click the Move tool (in the upper-right corner of the Tools window).

Paint.NET has loads of features to let you manipulate images. If you're happy with the way an image looks, leave it alone — but if you want to adjust colors, convert to black-and-white, add a cartoonish look or an oil-painting style, or take advantage of any other effects, try the options on the Effects menu. If you don't like a particular effect, simply click the Undo button on the toolbar.

Adding your name and the e-book title

To add the title of the e-book to the canvas, follow these steps:

1. **Select Layer 2 (which is the layer that you created).**

2. **In the Tools window, click the text tool (the T symbol).**

   If you can't see the Tools window, choose Window⇨Tools to open it.

3. **Click wherever you want to place the title on the canvas, and select a font and size from the toolbar.**

4. **In the Colors window, select your color.**

5. **Type the title.**

   If your text doesn't show up on the screen, ensure that you don't have a specific part of the cover selected. (To unselect part of the cover, click the Select tool in the Tools window and then click in the gray area outside the cover.)

   You can move the title around on the canvas by positioning the cursor below and to the right of it. When a small icon with arrows on it appears, click it to reposition the text. Note that this only works immediately after placing the title; if you wish to move it again, use the Select tool to select a rectangular area that includes the title.

   Experiment with placing the title below or above the image. If you want words of different sizes in the title (a feature of many e-book covers), add each word separately.

6. **To add your name, create a new layer, which makes it easy to reposition the title and your name separately, and then type your name.**

   You'll likely use the same font face as for the title, but in a smaller size. Try different positions for the title and name to see which position looks best. Though titles and authors' names are generally centered on book covers, you can experiment with different positions.

You can move the text later in the same way as you move an image: Use a selection tool (I recommend the Rectangle) to select it and then click the Move tool. You can now reposition the selected text by clicking and dragging.

Figure 5-7 shows the image from Figure 5-6 with the title and the author's name added. Note the use of different font sizes and the way the edges of the text align down the cover. To the right of the cover, you can see how the three layers have been combined.

Saving the cover

To save the cover, choose File➪Save. The file is saved in the Paint.NET
format (.pdn) so that you can easily edit it later.

When you're happy with the cover, save it as a file that can be used on the
web. The .jpg extension (file type) is a good choice because it loads quickly
on websites and is accepted by all major e-book retailers.

Always save the cover file in .png or .pdn format first, even if you don't plan
to edit it. These formats preserve the layers of the image and prevent your
having to start from scratch if you decide to make changes when you have
only the flat (single-layered) .jpg version.

To save the cover as a .jpg file, follow these steps:

1. **Ensure that all layers you want to include are active (their check
   boxes are selected in the Layers window).**

2. **Choose File➪Save As.**

3. **In the Save As dialog box, select JPEG from the Save As Type drop-down menu.**

   The Save Configuration dialog box appears.

4. **Select 100% quality, and click OK.**

   You see a warning to reduce the file to a single layer.

5. **Click Flatten.**

   The image is now saved.

Finding and Working with a Cover Designer

Creating your own cover might sound like a lot of work, especially if you (like me) would much rather write than struggle to make a decent-looking cover. Although I create my own covers for my free e-books, I pay a professional to design covers for my other e-books — and there's nothing stopping you from doing the same.

You don't necessarily need to spend a lot of money to produce a great-looking e-book cover, though it's worth the money to see it as an investment in your book. Here's a rough rule of thumb: Start with a $100 minimum for a straightforward cover design by a professional graphical designer — and plan to budget between $200 and $300.

If you can't afford this amount, consider one of these strategies to find someone to help:

- ✔ **Hire a freelance designer who's willing to work at a discount.** A recent graduate (or even a current student) who simply wants to gain experience may even be willing to work for free. You could e-mail local universities' design departments to see whether they can pass a message around to potentially interested students.

- ✔ **Swap skills with an experienced designer.** For example, the designer creates your cover, and you edit the copy on her website.

Offering the designer a percentage of sales rather than an up-front fee can cost you plenty of time and hassle, because you'll need to keep careful track of sales and arrange regular payments to your designer. And if your e-book sells well, you can easily pay far more than a few hundred dollars up front.

If a deal sounds too good to be true, watch out. You aren't likely to find some-one to create an inexpensive *and* professional-quality cover design. The result of choosing a bargain-basement e-book cover might well be a cover that looks amateurish or — worse — infringes copyright if the "designer" doesn't pro-vide original artwork.

Asking for recommendations from other writers

One truly effective way to find an excellent designer is by way of personal recommendation. If you know writers who've published their own e-books, for example, ask for their recommendations for a cover designer. Or check your social networks, such as Twitter or Facebook. Even if you don't person-ally know any self-published writers, your friends and other contacts may have useful connections.

Look for self-published e-books in your genre that have attractive covers, and seek out their designers. You might have to do some investigative work, such as downloading a free sample of the book to look for the designer's name in the acknowledgements or e-mailing the author to ask for it.

Knowing whether a designer is right for you

If you contact several cover designers to ask for price quotes, don't simply pick the cheapest option: Choose a designer you can work with easily and who can provide you what you need.

A qualified cover designer should have

- **A portfolio of completed e-book covers:** A person who has only print experience won't necessarily understand the vital features of an e-book cover. The text size is typically larger, for example, to ensure that it reproduces well at thumbnail size.

- **Clear communication skills:** Don't expect instant responses to your e-mail — good designers are busy people. If the person's replies are unclear (and therefore not helpful), find someone else to work with.

- **Testimonials from satisfied customers, especially from authors who appear to have books similar to yours:** Contact a couple of these people to ask about their experiences while working with the designer.

Before signing a contract or handing over payment, find out

- ✔ **Whether (or how) your use of the completed cover is limited:** For example, you may want to use the print version in your publicity materials.

- ✔ **How the revision process works:** For example, how much back-and-forth can you expect to take place between you and the designer? Obviously, you shouldn't expect to tweak the cover endlessly, but the designer should reasonably expect to make a few minor changes if you aren't sold on the first version.

- ✔ **The length of the design process:** If you need the cover in a hurry (to meet a launch deadline, for example), let the designer know — and ask whether the time scale is realistic. Don't be surprised if you need to pay extra for a rush job.

Supplying the cover designer with vital design information

To simplify the process for the person who designs the cover of your e-book (and to maximize the chance of your e-book sporting a great-looking cover that you love to look at), supply the person with all the information necessary to create the cover. Follow these helpful tips:

- ✔ **Assume that the designer *won't* read your e-book.** Unless you plan to pay for several extra hours of the person's time, provide the table of contents and the cover blurb (if your e-book is nonfiction) or a descriptive synopsis (if it's fiction).

- ✔ **State explicitly any information that's important to you personally.** For example, if you're determined that the cover feature the hunky male protagonist, let the designer know. If you want space for a quote from a reviewer, say so. After you've worked on your e-book a while, you can easily assume that other people see it the same way you do; remember that the designer has a fresh perspective.

- ✔ **Provide copies of covers from other authors' e-books as examples.** If you've seen e-book covers in your genre that you especially like — or especially dislike — show them to the cover designer.

- ✔ **Read all instructions and guidelines requested by the designer.** If the designer asks for specific information, do your best to provide it in a timely fashion. If you're unsure about something, speak up.

Designers speak out about common cover mistakes

A few skilled e-book cover designers have provided their tips for avoiding three common mistakes in e-book cover design:

Providing too much information

The most common problem I see in cover design is creating confusion. A book usually has a singular message, and the cover is the place to make that message clear with graphics, fonts, colors, etc. But the cover can't clarify that message if there are too many images, if the fonts aren't legible, or if the colors don't make sense.

—Charlie Pabst, www.charfishdesign.com

Adding all your main characters, their pets, a castle, the murder weapon, and a sunset, will make your cover noisy and confusing. What you need to do is consider who or what the story is focused around and the primary message of the book. Keep to one theme with one or two strong elements, and don't overcomplicate the cover image.

The buyer needs to understand, within just a couple of seconds, what the book is about and if it's going to be suitable for them. If the reader can't judge this quickly, they'll move on to something else.

—Anthony Puttee, www.bookcovercafe.com

Giving the wrong impression

I can't tell you how many times I've been disappointed as soon as I started reading a book. Why? Because the style of the cover held a hint or a promise of a certain voice — yet the tone of the book was nowhere near that promise.

Make sure the style of your cover mirrors your writing voice. A cartoon-like illustration on your cover wouldn't work for a serious, academic book — and diagrams and flow charts on the cover would clash with a lighter, more humorous tone.

That said, you can be playful with the image you choose. A single element that triggers a question or hints at the content is much more effective than trying to illustrate exactly what the title says (much like an apple or the tail of a snake would be a more enticing visual than the entire Garden of Eden).

—Lisa Valuyskaya, www.ideastylist.com

It's funny how we develop ideas about how things should be. An author sees a bestseller with an attractive cover and thinks, "I'll just make my cover like this — that will work." But notice something: The book he's looking at is a novel about the hijinks nannies get up to in New York City. His book is about retirement communities in the Southwest.

The author, caught up in a good-looking book from a big publisher, has forgotten that the people who will buy his book have almost no overlap with the people who buy the nanny book.

—Joel Friedlander, www.thebookdesigner.com

Using the wrong text size or positioning

A good e-book cover is like the curtain that parts at the beginning of a show: It sets the tone for everything that follows. E-book cover art is used all over, and at all different sizes. It might be a little thumbnail image on a black-and-white Kindle screen or a tiny image used in a web ad.

That's why it's crucial to make sure the most important text on your e-book cover is still readable even when reduced in size and converted to black-and-white. Don't lose [the] prospective buyer's interest because they can't read your book title or tagline.

–Pamela Wilson, www.ebookevolution.com

All too often the author's name is placed at the bottom right or left in very small text. This makes it almost unreadable when the cover is viewed at thumbnail size in the online store. It can also subliminally suggest a lack of confidence from the author.

Make sure your author name is large enough to be clearly read when viewed as a thumbnail: This shows you believe your book is worth buying. It will also help readers immediately identify your books, as you build your author brand.

–Anthony Puttee, www.bookcovercafe.com

A common reason for the amateurish look of many e-book covers is the various pieces of text that are positioned haphazardly. Draw vertical lines on your cover wherever any element begins or ends. The fewer lines you have to use, the cleaner and more organized the result looks.

The grid — or dividing the page into equal columns — is always used for professional page and cover layout. In simple layouts, three or four columns are enough. Your title, subtitle, byline, and any other elements should line up along these lines.

–Lisa Valuyskaya, www.ideastylist.com

Chapter 6

Creating an Instant E-Book Using a PDF File

*S*uppose that your e-book manuscript is now a nicely formatted Word document. Though you can, in theory, sell it to customers, I've never known an e-book author to do that. And here are a couple of reasons why you won't want to:

✔ **Word documents can be edited.** Someone else can easily steal your hard work and pass it off as their own (by changing your copyright page, for example).

✔ **Not all customers can easily view a Word document.** They might have different word processing programs installed, or they might want to read your e-book on an e-reader rather than on their computer.

You want to format your e-book as a read-only file that can be viewed on a wide range of computers and devices. A PDF is the simplest option.

In this chapter, I walk you through the steps to turn a Word document into a PDF file. I explain why you might want to create only a PDF file and why you might want to also create MOBI and EPUB versions of your e-book so that you can decide what will work best for you and your book.

Turning Your Microsoft Word Document into a PDF File

There's a good chance that Adobe Reader is already installed on your computer. This free and commonly used software program enables you to view PDF files. If you're using Windows, you should find it listed under Programs.

If you don't already have Adobe Reader, you can download it from `http://get.adobe.com/reader`.

If you're using Word 2010, you will already have the option to publish the file in PDF format. If you're using Word 2007, you may not yet have this option. To check, follow these steps:

1. **Open your e-book manuscript (or any Word document).**

2. **Click the Office icon in the upper-left corner of the screen.**

3. **Hover the cursor over the Save As option.**

    A menu should appear to the right.

4. **Look for the option labeled PDF or XPS.**

If the PDF or XPS option isn't present, you need to install an add-in for Microsoft Office. Download the add-in from the Microsoft site, and follow the instructions there to install it on your computer:

```
www.microsoft.com/download/en/details.aspx?displaylang
           =en&id=9943
```

To save your e-book as a PDF file using Word 2010, follow these steps:

1. **Open your e-book manuscript.**

2. **Click File in the upper-left corner of your screen.**

3. **Click the Save As option.**

    A Save As dialog box appears.

4. **Select PDF from the Save As Type drop-down list.**

5. **Select the Open File After Publishing check box.**

6. **Select the Standard radio button for the Optimize For option.**

    Figure 6-1 shows the Save As dialog box with standard optimization selected and the PDF file type shown on the Save As Type list.

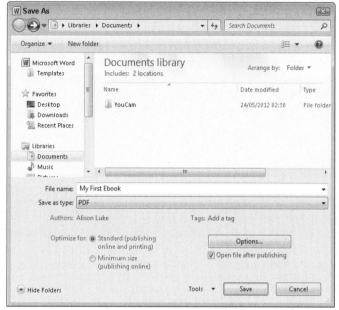

Figure 6-1:
The Save As
PDF dialog
box.

Choose the Standard optimization option rather than the Minimum Size option to create a high-quality PDF. Its slightly larger file is unlikely to be a problem for your readers. Choosing the Minimum Size option *compresses* images: The file doesn't look as good when a reader views it at a large size (such as on a computer monitor) or prints it.

7. Click Save.

After you save the PDF file, it should open automatically. (If you didn't select the Open File After Publishing check box, find the file in the folder where you saved it and open it.)

If you're using Word 2007, the process for creating a PDF file is very similar. The main difference is that you need to click the Office button in Step 2 rather than the File tab (which doesn't exist in Word 2007).

Check the PDF file to ensure that all formatting and elements, such as the table of contents, headers, and footers, have converted as expected. The file should look essentially the same as your Word document, though any grammar and spelling squiggles (the red, green, or blue underlines) will disappear. In Figure 6-2, you can see a Word document; Figure 6-3 shows its corresponding PDF file. Note that the formatting is preserved, though the squiggly line underneath the word *But* has disappeared.

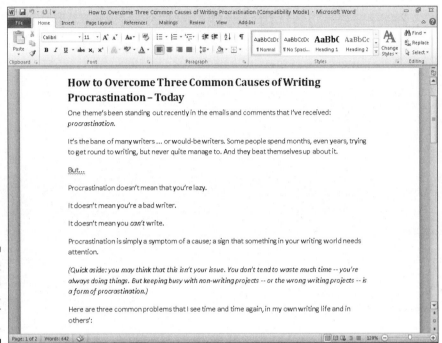

Figure 6-2:
A Word document, ready for conversion.

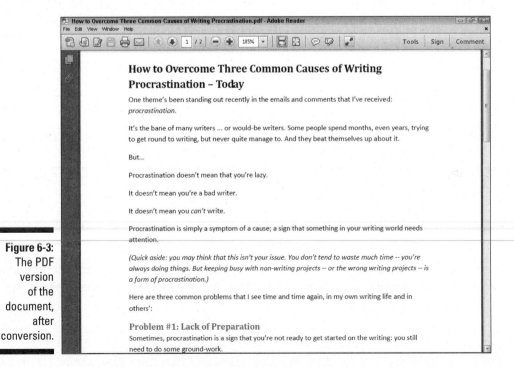

Figure 6-3:
The PDF version of the document, after conversion.

You need no special software for the PDF conversion process, and you can be confident that most potential readers will already be familiar with PDF files because many documents online are provided in this format.

Deciding Whether to Use Only the PDF Format

Some e-books are available only in PDF format, especially in the information marketing world — where e-books tend to carry high price tags and are often optimized to be read on computer screens. Depending on the type of e-book you've written and your goals for it, you may want to stick with only the PDF version.

If, like me, you're averse to doing more work than you need to (some people call it *laziness,* but I prefer to think of it as *efficiency*), the PDF file is a quick and simple way to create your e-book. For specialized nonfiction e-books, it may well also be the only option that your audience will expect, though as e-readers become more common, e-book customers are increasingly asking for MOBI and EPUB versions.

If you're writing a novel, however, a PDF file alone isn't your best option — in fact, you may want to skip the PDF file type entirely. You're unlikely to need the formatting features of PDF, and most readers don't want to print a whole novel or sit at their computers to read the entire thing. They'll want to read it on the Kindle, iPad, NOOK, Kobo e-reader, or another device.

Consider these key questions when you're deciding whether to use only the PDF format for your e-book:

- ✔ Does your e-book include color illustrations?
- ✔ Do you want to sell your e-book in online stores, such as Amazon?
- ✔ What format will your readers want?

Illustrating your e-book in full color

If your e-book involves a lot of illustrations (images, photographs, drawings, screen shots, or graphics, for example), you might prefer to publish it only in PDF format. Most e-reader devices remain black-and-white only, so your e-book may not be as easy and attractive for readers who are using them.

For an e-book with all the bells and whistles, try the Apple iBooks Author application to include full-color illustrations, video, and interactive elements. You can find out more about iBooks Author in Chapter 7.

An e-book that includes beautiful page design and layout, plus high-quality graphics, is easier to sell at a higher price point. It should work well as a PDF, without an accompanying MOBI or EPUB version.

Selling your e-book on Amazon or in other online stores

If you want to have your e-book in major online stores, such as Amazon or Barnes & Noble, you can't produce it only as a PDF file: These stores prefer e-books as MOBI files (Amazon) or EPUB files (most others). If you're aiming for the mass market, with general-interest nonfiction or a genre novel, you'll definitely want your e-book to be available in stores. After all, readers aren't likely to hunt around the web for their next e-book fixes: They'll head to Amazon or to their favorite online retailers.

When you distribute your e-book via Smashwords (see Chapter 14), all file conversions are done for you. Smashwords turns your Word document into several additional file types, including PDF, MOBI, and EPUB. The site puts your e-book into online stores for you, too. You can't, however, sell Smashwords files on your own site, and Smashwords doesn't distribute via Amazon.

Of course, there's no rule that your e-book has to be present in major online stores. In some cases, you'll do better by selling your e-book from your own website — a topic I discuss in more detail in Chapter 10.

Giving readers the format they want

You want to put your e-book into the hands of as many readers as possible — and that means making their lives easy. They may have format preferences: For example, if they own a Kindle, they need a MOBI file; if they like to read on their computers, in full color, they'll want a PDF.

If you're unsure what your readers prefer, ask them. Find out what other e-books they own and in which format they read them. If you don't yet have an audience, look at similar e-books produced by other authors: Which ones seem to be selling well? Which format (or formats) are they in?

Ultimately, the more file types you can provide, the more readers you're likely to reach. Unless you have a clear, focused target market already (such as a newsletter list or a lot of blog subscribers), create a MOBI file or an EPUB file — and if your e-book would be enhanced by interactive elements, consider using iBooks Author.

Turn to Chapter 7 for information about iBooks Author and to Chapter 8 to find out about creating MOBI and EPUB files.

Chapter 7

Creating an Interactive E-Book with iBooks Author

In This Chapter

▶ Downloading the iBooks Author app

▶ Adding the text and images for your e-book

▶ Including multimedia elements in your e-book

*I*f you want to create an e-book for the iPad, packed with such innovative elements as video clips and heavily designed pages, the iBooks Author application can be just what you need. But if you're writing a novel or a nonfiction e-book that consists mainly of text (with perhaps a few images), the app has more bells and whistles than you need and may overcomplicate things for you.

This chapter walks you through the process of installing iBooks Author on your Mac computer. (To use the app, you need OS X 10.7.2 or later. It isn't available for Windows.) You can see how to import your e-book manuscript, including text and images, into iBooks Author and how to add videos and Keynote presentations.

 The e-book you create in iBooks Author can be sold only from the Apple Store, not via other online stores or even your own site. However, you can export your e-book in the standard EPUB format and then sell it via any store or your own website. The EPUB version doesn't include all the same formatting and features, though.

Installing the iBooks Author App on Your Computer

Like other Mac software, the iBooks Author application is available from the Apple App Store. To download the app, follow these steps:

1. **Open the App Store on your Mac.**

2. **Search for *iBooks Author*.**

3. **Click the Free button.**

   The Free button turns into the green Install App button.

4. **When prompted, sign in to the App Store (or create a new account).**

   The download should begin immediately. The app installs automatically.

   After the installation is complete, you can open iBooks Author from the Launchpage menu or by using the Finder.

Importing the Text and Images of Your E-Book

When you open iBooks Author, you're shown six templates, as shown in Figure 7-1. Decide which one best suits your project.

After you choose a template, you see that iBooks Author has prepopulated it with a chapter, a section, and a page. The chapter, which is the highest-level element, can have multiple sections, and sections can have multiple pages. You can add pages directly to chapters, with no sections, if you prefer.

You can see the chapter, section, and page in Figure 7-2. The three elements are nested on the left side of the screen, to show their positions in the hierarchy.

If you choose to, you can write your e-book directly in iBooks Author by adding new pages and typing in their text boxes. You've likely already written your e-book manuscript (or at least part of it), though, so now you can import it.

Figure 7-1:
Choosing a
template.

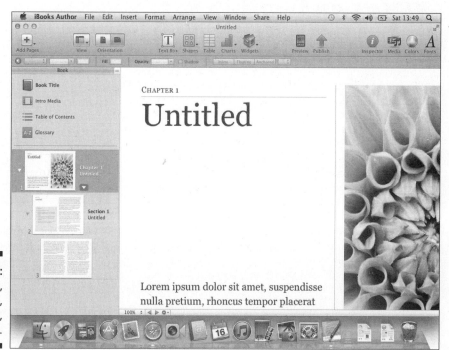

Figure 7-2:
A chapter,
section,
and page,
on the left.

The app lets you import files created in either the Microsoft Word or Apple Pages word processor, and it preserves both text and images (though you may notice stylistic changes, made during the import process).

To import your manuscript into iBooks Author, follow these steps:

1. **Choose Insert⇨Chapter from Pages or Word Document, as shown in Figure 7-3.**

   A Finder window appears.

2. **Browse your computer for your manuscript file, select it, and then click Insert.**

   You see two chapter layouts to choose between.

3. **Click one of the chapter layouts to select it.**

4. **Select the Preserve Document Paragraph Style check box.**

5. **Click Choose to confirm your chapter layout selection.**

   The dialog box closes, and your manuscript is imported. Note that it may take a minute or two for a full-length manuscript to be imported.

After your manuscript is successfully imported, iBooks Author may warn you that fonts have been changed or that the formatting has been removed, for example. Review these warnings so that you know which elements of your e-book to double-check.

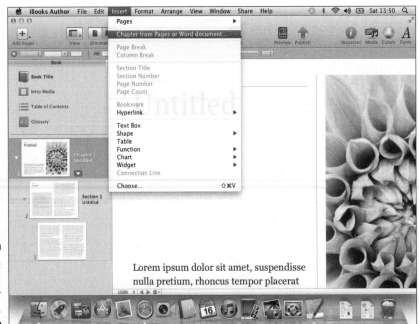

Figure 7-3: Importing your manuscript.

After the import operation, you should find all your text and images transferred into the iBooks Author file. You may need to make alterations, such as adding or removing chapter and section pages.

Review every page of the e-book you create in iBooks Author to ensure that it's correct. Pay special attention to the start of chapters or any pages with images.

If the source document contains several (unwanted) paragraph styles and needs to be cleaned up, follow the preceding steps, but leave Preserve Document Paragraph Style deselected in Step 4. iBooks Author automatically renders all paragraphs in the default style (no indent and with a blank space between paragraphs).

Adding Multimedia Elements to Your E-Book

In addition to using text and images, the e-book you create in iBooks Author can include multimedia, such as videos and presentations. Though you're more likely to use these elements for nonfiction e-books, if you're writing for young children, you might choose to include short videos.

To be added to your e-book, video files must be in MP4 format, and your presentations must be created in Keynote (not PowerPoint).

Video

To add a video to your e-book in iBooks Author, follow these steps:

1. **Open your book, and select the page where you want the video to appear.**

2. **Click the Widgets button and then click Media, as shown in Figure 7-4.**

   iBooks Author places a box, labeled Movie by default, on the page.

3. **Use the Finder to locate your video and drag it into the Media box, as shown in Figure 7-5.**

   You can reposition the video on the page by moving the Media box, and you can edit the title of the box and its text.

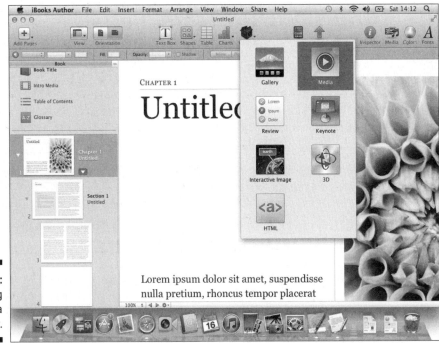

Figure 7-4:
Selecting
the Media
widget.

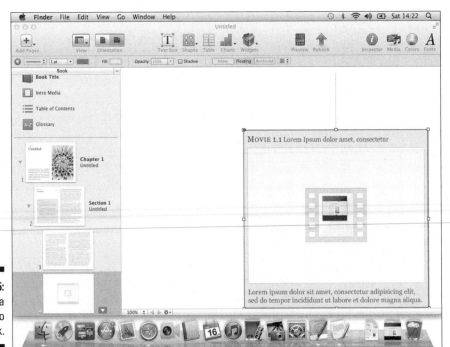

Figure 7-5:
Dragging a
video into
your e-book.

Adding videos to your e-book increases its final file size considerably. If you want to offer large videos as bonus content, you can host them on your website instead and provide readers with the link (and password, if you've protected the page) so that they can watch or download the videos at their leisure.

Presentations

Adding a presentation to your e-book in iBooks Author is similar to adding a video. You need Keynote version 5.1 or later installed in order to embed a Keynote presentation in your e-book.

Follow these steps in iBooks Author:

1. **Select the page in your e-book where you want the presentation to appear.**

2. **Click Widgets and then click Keynote.**

   iBooks Author creates the default Media box.

3. **Use the Finder to locate your Keynote presentation, and drag it into this box.**

   As with video, you can reposition the box on the page.

Chapter 8

Creating MOBI or EPUB Files with Calibre

. . . .

In This Chapter

▶ Saving your manuscript as an HTML file

▶ Turning your e-book into MOBI and EPUB files using Calibre

▶ Viewing your e-book on an e-reader

. . . .

Most e-readers can, theoretically, handle PDF files, but these files may not display well on the small, and often black-and-white, e-reader screen. The two most common file types that e-readers use are MOBI (for the Kindle and for MobiPocket reader software) and EPUB (for everything else).

The good news is that after your manuscript is ready to convert into MOBI format, you can simply convert it to EPUB format, too. Both file types are based on HTML code. The not-so-good news is that it takes a few steps to convert a Microsoft Word document into MOBI and EPUB files — it isn't quite as simple as PDF conversion (as described in Chapter 6).

Certain software programs, such as Adobe InDesign, allow you to save files in EPUB format, though you still need to use other software for the MOBI conversion. If you use Word, you have no option to save your manuscript as an EPUB file; instead, you save it as an HTML file and then convert it to both EPUB and MOBI by using another piece of software.

In this chapter, I walk you through the steps to save your Word document in HTML format, ready for conversion to MOBI and EPUB. I also explain how to use the free Calibre software to turn an HTML file into both a MOBI file and an EPUB file.

Turning Your Document into an HTML File

Before you can convert your e-book document into a MOBI or EPUB file through Calibre, you need to save it as an HTML file. To save your document as an HTML file, first open your e-book in Word. (Save a backup copy, in case something goes wrong.) Then follow these steps:

1. **Delete the table of contents from your file.**

   You remove the table of contents because Calibre (the software covered later in this chapter) automatically creates one for you when you convert the file. If you already have the table of contents in place, your HTML file will have unnecessary hyperlinks, which can cause problems. Use the table of contents produced specifically for the MOBI and EPUB files rather than the one generated by Word.

2. **Choose File⇨Save As.**

   The Save As dialog box appears.

3. **Select Web Page, Filtered from the Save As Type drop-down list, as shown in Figure 8-1.**

4. **Click Save.**

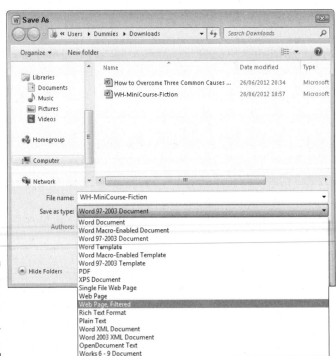

Figure 8-1:
Saving a
Word file
as an HTML
file.

You can open your file in Word or in a web browser to ensure that all elements look good. To see the HTML code, open the file in Notepad or another plain-text processor. To open it in Notepad, navigate to the folder where you saved the file, right-click the file, and choose Open With➪Notepad.

Installing Calibre on Your Computer

You have several different ways to create MOBI and EPUB files. The software that I recommend is Calibre. It's free, and it has versions for Windows, OS X, and Linux. You can find the Calibre website at

`http://calibre-ebook.com`

You don't have to complete every stage involved in the creation of an e-book by yourself. There are plenty of companies and individual experts who can convert your Word document into a MOBI and/or EPUB file for you. I recommend giving Calibre a try on your own, but if you get stuck or simply prefer to outsource this step of the e-book creation process, look online for help. You can normally expect to pay around $50 to $100 for manuscript conversion from Word to MOBI / EPUB, but note that the price will depend on the length and complexity of your manuscript.

For simplicity's sake, I assume that you're using Windows. (The Calibre site has instructions for Mac OS X and Linux users also.) To download and install Calibre, follow these steps:

1. **Go to** `http://calibre-ebook.com/download`.

2. **Click the Windows icon.**

3. **Click the Download Calibre link.**

4. **Navigate to the folder where you want to save the file and then click Save.**

5. **After the download is complete, double-click the downloaded file, and click Run to install the software on your computer.**

6. **Select the check box to accept the terms of agreement and then click Install.**

7. **During the installation process, leave the default options selected on each screen, whenever you are offered a choice.**

8. **When the installation is finished, click Finish.**

Calibre is also used by readers who want to convert and store e-books they've purchased, so certain options relate to reading rather than to the file creation process.

Converting Your E-Book Using Calibre

After your e-book is in HTML format and you've previewed it in a web browser to ensure that everything looks good, you're ready to import it into Calibre.

Open Calibre on your computer, and follow these steps:

1. **Click the Add Books button along the top of the screen.**

   The Select Books dialog box opens.

2. **Select the HTML file you created, and click Open.**

   The HTML file should have the extension `.html` or `.htm`.

   After you click Open, your file is added to the Calibre library, as shown in Figure 8-2.

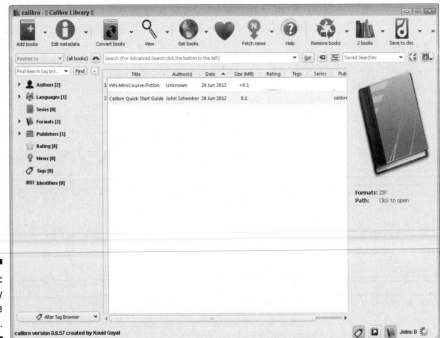

Figure 8-2:
A newly imported file in Calibre.

3. **Click to select the title of the file you added in Step 1 and then click the Convert Books button at the top of the page.**

   You should now see the Convert window, with nine tabs along the left side. (You can see eight of them in Figure 8-3.) The Metadata tab opens by default. The default input format, in the upper-left corner, is ZIP; the output format, in the upper-right corner, should default to MOBI. (If it doesn't, select MOBI or EPUB.)

4. **Enter all necessary data on the tabs (see the next section for details).**

5. **After you've set all the options for your e-book, click the OK button in the lower-right corner of the screen to start the conversion process.**

   The Convert window disappears, and a spinning wheel of spokes appears in the lower-right corner of the Calibre window. When the conversion is complete, the new MOBI or EPUB file is listed on the right side of the screen.

In the following sections, I discuss in detail what information you need to (or may want to) enter on the Calibre tabs and explain how to preview your new file.

Figure 8-3: The Convert window in Calibre.

Getting to know the Calibre tabs

Here are explanations of all the tabs and the options that you may want to select when converting your e-book.

To take advantage of the more advanced Calibre features, which are beyond the scope of this book, see the Calibre online manual at

`http://manual.calibre-ebook.com`

Metadata

The following list details the information you may want to include on the Metadata tab:

- **Title:** Enter your e-book's title.

- **Author(s):** Enter your name or pen name, as it appears on the cover of your e-book.

- **Author Sort:** This line should populate (fill in) automatically, with your surname first.

- **Publisher:** If your publishing company has a name, enter it.

- **Tags:** You don't need to enter anything here, because this is mainly used within Calibre itself. You will have the option to enter tags on Amazon for your e-book when you upload it (see Chapter 13).

- **Series:** If your e-book is part of a series, enter the series name.

- **Change Cover Image:** Browse for, and select, a cover image for your e-book. If the cover image is stored within a file, select the Use Cover from Source File check box.

You can see all these settings in the Metadata tab, shown in Figure 8-4.

Look & Feel

You can leave most of the default settings on the Look & Feel tab — though you may want to experiment with converting your e-book at different settings if the exact layout is important to you. The options in the following list are the ones you're likely to use:

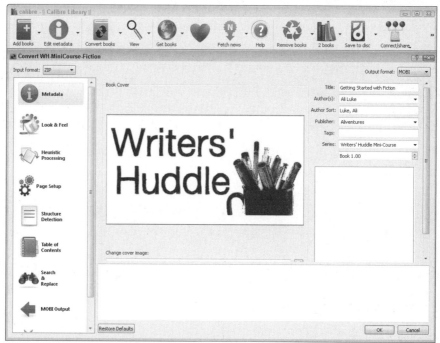

Figure 8-4:
The
Metadata
tab.

✔ **Remove Spacing Between Paragraphs:** By default, a blank line separates paragraphs in HTML. Select this check box if you want to indent
paragraphs instead.

✔ **Insert Blank Line Between Paragraphs:** If you want to insert a space
between paragraphs because they look too close together, select this
option. (Understandably, you can't select this option in tandem with the
Remove Spacing Between Paragraphs option.)

✔ **Smarten Punctuation:** Add smart ("curly") quotes and apostrophes to
your file, if you've used straight quotes and apostrophes.

✔ **UnSmarten Punctuation:** Change smart ("curly") quotes and apostrophes to straight quotes and apostrophes.

✔ **Extra CSS:** Enter styling code, if you want. You can easily adjust styles
and reconvert your file without needing to import your e-book again.

You can see all these settings in the Look & Feel tab, shown in Figure 8-5. The
example code shown on the Extra CSS tab, toward the bottom of the window,
places all `<h1>` and `<h2>` styled text in the center of the page. (Note that you
do not need to add any Extra CSS unless you wish to do so.)

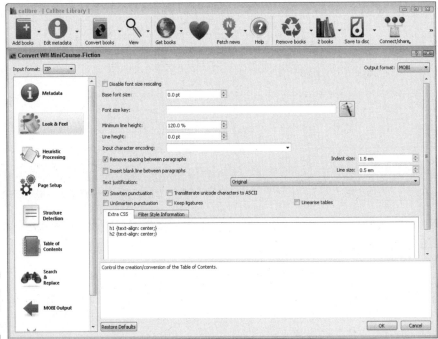

Figure 8-5:
The Look &
Feel tab.

Heuristic Processing

If you have followed the instructions in Chapter 4 and have a clean Word manuscript that uses styles, you are very unlikely to need this option. Refer to the Calibre manual if you want more information.

Page Setup

On the Page Setup tab, keep the default settings under Output Profile and Input Profile. Also, leave the margins at their defaults.

Structure Detection

For a standard e-book that's split into chapters (and assuming that your chapters are marked with H1 or H2 tags), you can leave all the settings alone on this tab.

If the chapter and section headings in your e-book contain only numbers or titles (and not the word chapter or section), remove the middle section of the Detect Chapters At (XPath Expression) code, indicated in bold type:

```
//*[((name()='h1' or name()='h2') and re:test(.,
       '\s*((chapter|book|section|part)\
       s+)|((prolog|prologue|epilogue)(\s+|$))', 'i'))
       or @class = 'chapter']
```

The code now reads this way:

```
//*[((name()='h1' or name()='h2')) or @class = 'chapter']
```

Table of Contents

Calibre automatically creates a table of contents, so you can leave this tab alone — unless your table of contents doesn't appear the way you want.

Search & Replace

Avoid using this tab, if possible. Edit the text in your original file instead.

MOBI Output

The MOBI Output tab is shown on the left side whenever MOBI is selected as the output format in the upper-right corner of the window.

Normally, you can leave all these options at their default settings. You might choose to place the table of contents at the beginning of the e-book — a good idea for nonfiction works or short-story collections. Otherwise, the table of contents will appear at the end. You may even want to remove the table of contents, which is appropriate for many novels.

EPUB Output

The EPUB Output tab is shown on the left side whenever EPUB is selected as the output format, in the upper-right corner of the window.

You can leave all the EPUB Output options at their default settings.

Debug

If you want to dig deeply into the technicalities of the conversion process, select a folder on this tab, and the debug output will be sent to this file.

Previewing your new file

When the conversion is complete, you see the new MOBI or EPUB format listed in blue on the right side of the screen, as shown in Figure 8-6. When you click the format link, Calibre opens an e-book viewer that lets you preview the file, as shown in Figure 8-7.

Figure 8-6:
The link
to the
MOBI file.

Authors: Ali Luke
Formats: MOBI, ZIP
Series: Book I of *Writers' Huddle Mini-Course*
Path: Click to open

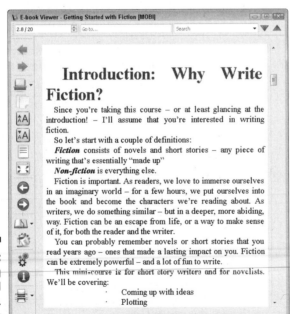

Figure 8-7:
Previewing
the MOBI
file.

Introduction: Why Write Fiction?

Since you're taking this course – or at least glancing at the introduction! – I'll assume that you're interested in writing fiction.

So let's start with a couple of definitions:

Fiction consists of novels and short stories – any piece of writing that's essentially "made up"

Non-fiction is everything else.

Fiction is important. As readers, we love to immerse ourselves in an imaginary world – for a few hours, we put ourselves into the book and become the characters we're reading about. As writers, we do something similar – but in a deeper, more abiding, way. Fiction can be an escape from life, or a way to make sense of it, for both the reader and the writer.

You can probably remember novels or short stories that you read years ago – ones that made a lasting impact on you. Fiction can be extremely powerful – and a lot of fun to write.

This mini-course is for short story writers and for novelists. We'll be covering:
- Coming up with ideas
- Plotting

View your file on an e-reader or at least on an e-reader app. You can download the Kindle app for free for your PC or Mac, for example. The Calibre previewer doesn't make page breaks clear.

After you've completed the conversion process once to create your first file, you can simply select your e-book and click the Convert Books button again (in the row along the top of the Calibre screen) to create the other type of file. All your selected options remain intact, as do all the text and code you've entered. Simply select EPUB (or MOBI, if you started with the EPUB version) in the upper-right corner of the screen, and change any necessary settings under EPUB Output (or MOBI Output). As before, you can preview the file in the Calibre e-book viewer, as shown in Figure 8-8.

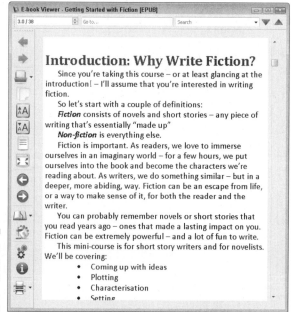

Figure 8-8: Previewing the EPUB file.

Note that the MOBI and EPUB files look slightly different from each other in Calibre. (In Figure 8-7, the MOBI file has indented headers, whereas the EPUB file in Figure 8-8 has none.) You may notice a few minor cosmetic differences like this, but all the fundamental formatting of your text (chapter headings, bold text, italics, and so on) will be the same in both files.

Saving and Viewing Your E-Book File on Your E-Reader

After you've previewed your file in the Calibre e-book viewer (as described in the preceding section), you want to save it so that you can transfer it to your e-reader. In your Calibre library, click to select the name of the e-book and then follow these steps:

1. **Click the Save to Disc button along the top of the screen.**

   The Choose Destination Directory dialog box opens.

2. **Choose the folder where you want to save the files and then click the Select Folder button.**

   Calibre automatically creates a folder (your surname is listed first, followed by your first name, as specified in the Author Sort option) and saves your MOBI or EPUB file there. The new folder opens automatically onscreen.

3. **Transfer the MOBI or EPUB file to your e-reader.**

   Your e-reader's user guide or manual should have instructions for transferring a file to your device.

   Use MOBI for the Kindle, and use EPUB for any other reader.

4. **Check your e-book for formatting issues.**

   Review the whole e-book, and make a note of anything you want to change. To fix problems, you need to edit and convert the file again.

Part III
Creating Your Website

The 5th Wave   By Rich Tennant

"Sometimes I feel behind the times. I asked my 11-year-old to build a website for my e-book, and he said he would, only after he finishes the one he's building for his ant farm."

In this part . . .

Your website, a crucial marketing and sales tool, acts as a salesperson who's available 24-7, always ready and waiting to greet potential new customers — from anywhere in the world. Because you may feel confused or overwhelmed by the idea of setting up a website, though, this part is designed to give you a simple, free way to get your own site online.

I cover how to set up a website using WordPress in Chapter 9, and I guide you to the types of pages you might want to include on your site and explain how best to write them. The most important page you create is the sales page; in Chapter 10, I explain what it is and how to get it right, by giving you tips on how to approach the text and formatting and showing you where to find images and other types of graphics.

Chapter 9

Using WordPress to Set Up a Website or Blog

In This Chapter

▶ Understanding why your author platform is important

▶ Getting your website set up on WordPress.com

▶ Customizing your website design

▶ Creating the pages for your website

▶ Considering the pros and cons of blogging

*I*f you don't already have a website or a blog, you need to set one up. You need to have a home on the web that potential readers can visit to find out about you and your books. Though Amazon and other online stores give you only limited space to explain your e-book, you can pack your website with useful information and interesting resources for your potential readers. You have full control over what you include — for example, you can serialize your e-book in blog form or give readers extra information about the subject matter of your nonfiction book or your novel's characters.

Many authors feel daunted by the prospect of setting up a website — but it doesn't have to be a complicated process. You certainly don't need to pay a huge sum to a web designer. In fact, you can get your site online for free, in less than an hour.

Even if you already have a blog or a website, skim this chapter, and look for anything that you're not yet doing or that you want to improve on. For example, you might want to add or update the pages on your site to make sure that potential readers can find out what they want to know.

In this chapter, I explain why your author platform is important and how your website works to engage prospective and current readers. I explain how to set up your website using WordPress.com (which is free), and I describe the crucial pages that your site needs. I also help you decide whether to include a blog on your site — though WordPress is designed for blogging, you can also use it for a regular site without a blog.

Establishing a Strong Author Platform with a Website

You often hear the phrase *author platform* in the publishing world. To me, it always sounds like I'm supposed to be standing on a soap box — though having an author platform simply means that you have the ability to reach people. For example, if your e-mail list has 2,000 subscribers — people who've specified (by opting in) that they want to hear from you regularly — you have a strong author platform of committed readers. You can easily send out an e-mail that reaches all those people.

Your platform is important, for two key reasons:

- **The platform helps you sell copies of your e-book.** If you have no online platform, you won't easily persuade anyone to notice your e-book; it's only one among hundreds of thousands. If you have a platform, though, even a fairly modest one, you can get some true momentum behind your e-book.

- **Agents and traditional publishers will be interested in your platform.** If your goal is to attract a prestigious publishing house to your book, they'll want to know whether you have a blog or an e-mail list with established fans.

Social media accounts can be a useful addition to your platform, but I recommend building your own website as a home base. That way, you're in full control, and you have a lot of flexibility in what you can provide. You can then use your Twitter account, Facebook page, or Goodreads profile to direct readers to your website. I cover social media marketing in Part V of this book.

Turning website readers into e-book customers

Most people who visit your website haven't read your e-book yet. They might not even know that you have an e-book for sale. If your site is supporting a nonfiction e-book (or a series of e-books), your visitors may be looking for information on a particular topic. If your site is supporting a novel or a short-story collection, visitors will likely have been directed there by a friend who has read your e-book — and might also be casually browsing.

You don't want visitors to visit your site once and leave instantly. You want them to stick around and, ideally, buy your e-book. (Even if they don't buy it straightaway, you want them to return until they're interested enough to purchase it.) Consider these suggestions:

- ✔ **Make your site design clear and attractive.** If you fill your site with neon text, flashing graphics, music that automatically plays, or nifty features that slow the site to a crawl, readers won't stay more than a few seconds. Create a good first impression.

- ✔ **Avoid sending visitors away from your site.** I know that it sounds obvious, but too many authors plaster their websites with ads, hoping to make a few dollars from visitors clicking them. It's not a good strategy — most people find ads annoying, and you add more money to your pocket if they buy your e-book instead.

- ✔ **Make your e-book clearly visible.** Not everyone who visits your site will know about the book. Include the cover graphic in your header or sidebar. (These elements appear on every page of your site.) Specify how visitors can buy your e-book, too; don't expect them to search at the Amazon site.

- ✔ **Provide value.** Offer visitors an item that's immediately useful or entertaining, such as a couple of free chapters, a series of blog posts that tie in with the book's subject matter, some short stories, articles about your research, or anything else that readers would enjoy.

Keeping readers involved after they've finished your e-book

Some of the visitors to your website will be readers who've already finished your e-book, especially if you've added a link to your site on the final page. Cater to these people, too: If they've bought one e-book from you, there's a good chance they'll buy more.

Don't let years go by before you update your site, because by then, those readers will have forgotten you. To keep them involved, make sure you have interesting content in place and that you have a way to capture their e-mail addresses so that you can contact them.

To achieve these goals, keep these principles in mind:

- ✔ **Update your site with new content regularly.** Blogs are helpful for this task because you can easily and regularly add new articles, photos, videos, or audio recordings. The most recent *post* (a piece of content) usually appears at the top of your home page or at the top of your blog's page.

- ✔ **Ideally, maintain a mailing list so that interested readers can leave their e-mail addresses, making it quick and easy for you to contact them.** If you're selling your e-book via E-junkie (see Chapter 12), you have the e-mail addresses of all the people who have bought it already, so you may not want to create a separate mailing list. Another option is to provide a sign-up spot for your blog so that readers can choose to receive new posts directly to their inboxes.

✔ **Consider ways to give readers extra value beyond your e-book.** For example, if you write fiction, you might include background details about the characters, related short stories, or a behind-the-scenes look at the writing process. For nonfiction, add useful lists of resources, reviews of related books, or in-depth articles about a particular aspect of your e-book.

Mark potential spoilers carefully — some of your site's visitors won't yet have bought your e-book.

Creating, updating, and maintaining a website might sound like a lot of work. But after your site is up and running, you can easily and simply add an update every week or two — and you'll build a loyal base of fans who'll be eager to buy your next e-book.

Keep things simple. In the rest of this chapter, I show you, step by step, how to set up and customize your first website.

Comparing WordPress.com and WordPress.org

WordPress makes powerful, free software for building websites — software that I now use on almost all my websites. (I even have a T-shirt bearing the WordPress logo. Yes, I'm a geek at heart.) WordPress comes in two flavors: WordPress.com and WordPress.org.

WordPress.com, the simpler version of WordPress, gives you a free domain name with the word *wordpress* in it (such as `aliluke.wordpress.com`), and you have lots of options to choose among for its design and for adding extras to your site, for example. WordPress hosts the site for you, making it available all around the world, day and night.

WordPress.org is more advanced. Rather than being run on the WordPress servers, this site lets you install the software on your own website that you're hosting elsewhere. The advantage is that you have full control over absolutely everything; the disadvantage is that it's more difficult to set things up, and you need to pay for a domain name and a web host. You sometimes hear this version as *self-hosted* WordPress.

Neither type is "better" — they're simply suited for different people and purposes. If you already have a web hosting package or a friend who can help you out with cheap web hosting, you might want to choose WordPress.org. For most writers, though, WordPress.com is the better option, at least to begin with. You can move a site from WordPress.com to WordPress.org, so it's not an all-or-nothing decision.

Setting Up Your WordPress.com Account

Creating a website might sound like a huge task. Maybe it's one that you've thought about for months or even years — but you've always put it off. The great news is that your website setup will be quick and easy. In fact, you can probably get it done in only 15 minutes. In this section, I walk you through the process.

To create your WordPress.com blog, follow these steps:

1. **Go to** www.wordpress.com, **and click the orange Get Started Here button.**

   You see a straightforward form to fill in, as shown in Figure 9-1. Note the instructions on the right side of the form — these should help you if you get stuck.

2. **Fill in the following fields on the form:**

   • *Blog Address:* You might want to enter your name or the title of your e-book. Try to keep your blog address short — remember that it also contains *wordpress.* If you type a name that already exists, WordPress prompts you to choose a different one.

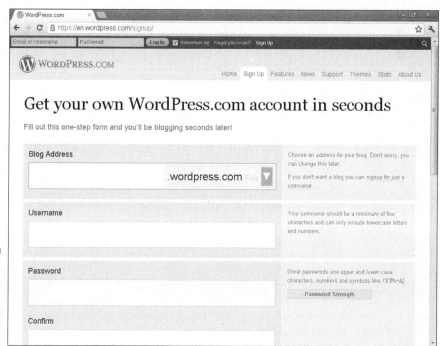

Figure 9-1:
The WordPress.com sign-up form.

By using the drop-down menu, you can omit *wordpress* from your blog's address by purchasing a domain name. If you choose to do this, I recommend choosing a .com address.

- *Username:* Like your blog address, your username must be unique. It doesn't show up to other users, so you can choose whatever you like.

- *Password:* Make your password strong (hard to break) by using a combination of letters, numbers, and symbols. Don't pick a familiar word.

- *Confirm:* Retype your password to confirm it, just in case you typed it wrong.

- *E-mail Address:* Enter an e-mail address that you have easy access to, because you need to access your e-mail to complete the blog setup. You can change your e-mail address later if you make a mistake.

- *What Language Will You Be Blogging In?* You're also prompted to choose your language.

- *Thinking about Upgrading?* WordPress.com has a bundle package on upgrades. You probably don't need it (and you can always buy individual elements of it later), so I recommend opting for the free sign-up.

If you want to read the Terms of Service, click the Fascinating Terms of Service link at the bottom of the page.

3. **When your form is complete, the Create Blog button turns orange; click this button.**

4. **Check your e-mail.**

   You should have a message from WordPress.com, asking you to activate your blog.

5. **Open the e-mail to see the blue Activate Blog button, and click it to open your blog.**

   If you can't click the button, you can copy and paste the link instead.

6. **Log in to your blog, using the username and password that you chose when you signed up.**

   You might not need to do this step, if WordPress logs you in automatically.

Congratulations! Your WordPress site is now fully set up. Type your blog's address into the address bar of your browser to take a look at the site, which uses a WordPress default theme. My site defaults to the Twenty Eleven theme, shown in Figure 9-2.

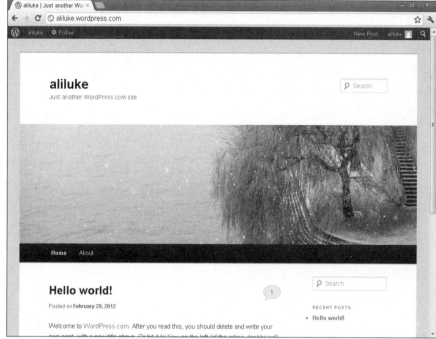

Figure 9-2:
A
WordPress
blog, with
the Twenty
Eleven
theme
design.

Changing the Design of Your Website

Your brand-new site is fresh out of the box, and it's using the default design.
You might be perfectly happy with it — or you might want to customize it.
(After all, a few thousand other blogs will also have the WordPress default
look.) You may want to add a fresh new look, add new pages, arrange the
menu differently, or change the elements that appear in the sidebar. All these
tasks are simple and straightforward in WordPress, and I describe how to do
them in the following sections.

Switching to a new WordPress theme

There's no need to be a technical or design expert to have a great-looking
blog: WordPress comes with lots of *themes*, or custom-made designs. You can
switch to a new theme with only a few clicks. When you change themes, all
your website content remains the same — everything you've written is still
there, even if it's in a different font or in a different place on the screen.

Follow these steps to change your WordPress theme:

1. **Log in to your site so that you can see the dashboard.**

2. **Hover your cursor over the Appearance link in the panel on the left and then select Themes.**

3. **Scroll down to see the available themes.**

   You can see a few in Figure 9-3.

4. **Choose a theme to try, and click the Activate link.**

   If you prefer, you can preview the theme using the Live Preview button. WordPress shows you how your site would look with the new theme, but it won't make any actual changes to your site. In the Live Preview, you can choose to Cancel or adopt the new theme by clicking Save & Activate.

5. **View your site to see the new theme in action.**

   Refresh the page if it's already open.

By default, themes are randomized. You can choose to sort them in a different order, or you can search them, which is useful if you're looking for a specific sort of design. For example, you might want to look for colorful themes or for designs with one sidebar.

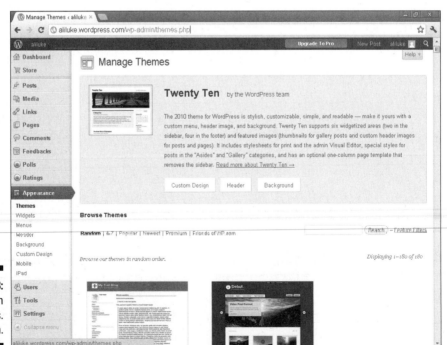

Figure 9-3:
Themes in
WordPress.
com.

Adding a new page

To add a new page to your site, follow these steps in the dashboard:

1. **Click Pages and then Add New.**

   The Add New Page page appears.

2. **In the text box at the top of the page, enter a title for your page.**

   You may want to create the suggested pages in the section "Planning and Writing Your Website's Pages," later in this chapter.

3. **Enter placeholder text in the Visual editor (which is the large box in the center of the screen).**

   At this point, you may find it easiest to enter a line of text like **Page coming soon**. If you prefer, you can start writing your pages, as described in "Planning and Writing Your Website's Pages."

4. **Click Publish in the column on the right.**

WordPress has many different options to allow people to use the software in lots of different ways. At this stage of creating your site, stay focused on getting a few pages in place. It's very easy to edit a page after creating it, and WordPress has comprehensive documentation online — so you can adjust and amend your website as you learn more.

Arranging your WordPress menu

After you've created the pages for your website (see the previous section), you see that those pages appear on the default navigation menu of your site. You might want to put them in a different order, though — and you may have pages that you don't want to include in the menu. (If you have a page that includes a copyright notice or disclaimer about your website, you might prefer to link to it from your footer or sidebar.)

For now, you might simply want to create blank pages to fill in later. (You can easily edit them by hovering your cursor over the Pages link and then clicking the All Pages link. You will see a list of your pages. Click the title of a page to edit it.) Later in this chapter, I cover the key pages that your site needs: About and Contact and a page for your e-book, perhaps named My Book or given the same title as your e-book.

To create a customized menu, follow these steps:

1. **On the dashboard, click the Appearance link and then the Menus link.**

   The Menus page appears.

2. **In the Menu Name text box, enter a menu name and then click the Create Menu button.**

   The name is for your own administrative purposes, so make it simple and descriptive. After you click Create Menu, the new menu appears on the right of the Menus page.

3. **In the Theme Locations panel, select your newly created menu from the drop-down list and click the Save button.**

4. **In the Pages panel, select the check boxes for the pages that you want to include in your navigation and then click the Add to Menu button.**

5. **Drag each page name on the menu to change its position.**

   Items at the top appear on the left side of the menu, if you have a horizontal navigation menu.

   You can also create subpages this way, by dragging one page so that it's indented beneath another.

Figure 9-4 shows a custom menu, with six pages. The Novels and Non-Fiction pages are subpages of the Ebooks page. Figure 9-5 shows that menu as it appears on the website.

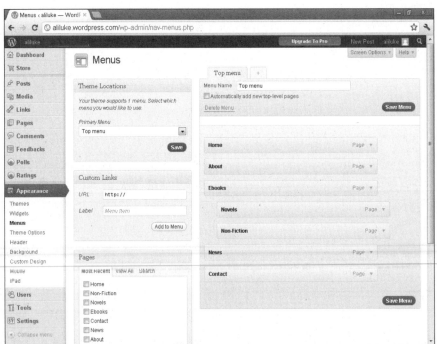

Figure 9-4:
Custom menu being created.

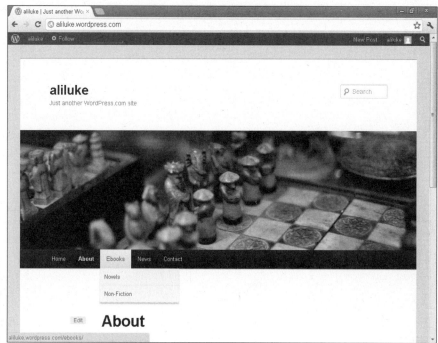

Figure 9-5:
Custom
menu on the
live website.

Modifying your sidebar

You may want to modify the sidebar of your site (or the footer, if your chosen theme has no sidebar). WordPress uses widgets to form the sidebar — each widget acts as a separate block, and you can easily omit or add widgets.

To add a widget, on the dashboard, click the Appearance link and then the Widgets link. You see the screen shown in Figure 9-6, with standard widgets in the center and your site's sidebar widgets on the right. You can drag and drop widgets to add or remove them or to change the order of the widgets within the sidebar.

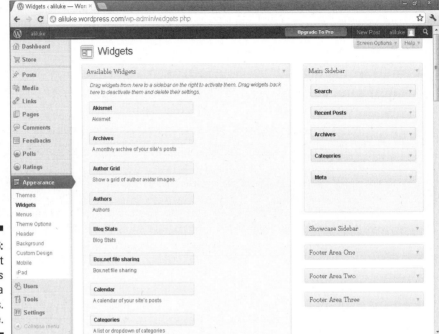

Figure 9-6:
The default
widgets
on a
WordPress.
com site.

Planning and Writing Your Website's Pages

After your great-looking design is in place, it's time to think about the basic content of your website. Though the point of a blog-style site, of course, is that you can easily add new posts (dated content) and pages (undated content, usually shown on the navigation menu) over time, you should have basic pages in place from the start.

An About page with details about you and your e-book

When visitors open a website, one of the first things they want to know is what the site is all about, such as who's behind it and its purpose. An About page answers these questions.

The About page is normally written in the first person, as in "I'm Ali Luke, a writer from Oxford in the United Kingdom," not "Ali Luke is a writer from Oxford in the United Kingdom." The About page can include these elements:

- **Biographical details about you, especially ones that are relevant to your e-book:** For example, if you have a relevant qualification or related work experience, that's definitely worth including — it helps inspire readers' confidence in your expertise.

- **Information about your e-book:** Not everyone who visits your site will know that you have an e-book for sale. Visitors might find you via a link on Twitter or a search engine such as Google. Don't go into too much detail about your e-book on the About page, though; save it for a focused sales page.

- **Information about your website:** Visitors will want to know what to expect from your site. For example, is it a resource to accompany a particular e-book, or is it a general author site where you have information about multiple e-books? How often will you update it? Where should new visitors begin?

- **Photographs, images, and video:** Some authors feel uncomfortable putting photographs of themselves on the Internet — but if you're willing to do it, it's a useful way to establish a stronger connection with visitors. You can even record video of yourself — many web users prefer watching videos to reading text. If you don't want to post a photo of yourself, you can have a designer create a cartoon-style avatar for you, or you can take photos that relate to the subject matter of your e-book.

A sales page for your e-book

On the About page of your e-book, you gently draw people into your website — you don't want to make them feel pressured into buying your e-book. Create a separate page for information about your e-book, especially if you're writing nonfiction. I cover sales pages in detail in Chapter 10.

A Contact page so that readers can get in touch

One of the best feelings in the world is receiving an e-mail that says, "I loved your e-book, and thanks so much for writing it!" By including a Contact page on your site, you make it easy for readers to get in touch with you. They might have questions or important feedback that you'll want to listen to.

Some people put their contact information on the About page of their websites, but I recommend having a separate Contact page to make these details easy to find. After all, it might not be only readers and potential readers browsing your site. What if a busy agent or publisher sees your page and wants to get in touch?

Your e-book's Contact page should be short and simple. Include, at minimum, your e-mail address. You might also want to add your phone number, particularly if your e-book is part of a larger business for you. Some authors also include their postal addresses. If you're active on sites such as Twitter or Facebook, you may also want to include links to your profiles there.

Deciding Whether to Include a Blog

E-book authors sometimes have blogs to maintain reader engagement and involvement; others prefer to simply have websites that give details of their book or books. WordPress makes it simple and easy for you to publish blog posts, if you want to do so. The decision comes down to whether it will be worth the time you invest in it.

Consider these factors when you decide whether to include a blog:

- ✔ **How much time you have:** If you have a full-time day job, you might struggle to keep up a blog *and* write that next e-book. If your job involves periods of work interspersed with weeks of vacation (if you're a teacher, for example), you might easily be able to write an e-book during a vacation, but you might struggle to keep up your blog all year round.

- ✔ **The type of book you've written:** A nonfiction e-book benefits more from a blog than a fiction one does, because you can draw in readers who are looking for information on a specific topic.

- ✔ **How many books you plan to write:** If you're publishing a series of novels, an author blog can be a great way to keep your readership up-to-date on your progress, and you can easily announce and promote every new book you release.

- ✔ **How long your e-book will be relevant:** It takes time to establish a successful blog with hundreds or thousands of readers. If your e-book is highly topical, think of other ways to promote it.

Calling your blog by a different name

If you decide to blog (and I definitely recommend giving it a try), you'll also want to think about whether the word *blog* means much to your current and prospective readers. For some readers, particularly those who aren't tech-savvy, the word *blog* can be off-putting or intimidating — they might believe that your blog is simply a personal diary or a geeky site with no relevance to them.

What else might you call your blog? Think about the sort of content you want to post there, and consider which words would be self-explanatory for your readers, such as these examples:

✔ News

✔ Writing diary

✔ Articles

✔ Resources

By default, your blog is simply the home page of your site. If you want to have your WordPress blog on a specific named page, follow these steps in the dashboard:

1. **In the left column, hover your cursor over the Pages link and then click Add New.**

   The Add New Page page appears.

2. **In the text box at the top of the page, enter a name for your new page (*Blog, News, Articles,* or whatever word or phrase you want to use); when you're finished, click Publish.**

3. **Repeat Steps 1 and 2 to add another new page for your home page, named Home or Welcome or whatever else you want.**

   If you prefer, you can omit the title.

4. **In the left column, click the Settings link and then Reading.**

   The Reading Settings page appears.

5. **Next to Front Page Displays, select A Static Page.**

6. **Select your front (home) page from the Front Page drop-down list, and select your Blog (or News, Articles, or whatever) page from the Posts Page drop-down list; when you're finished, click Save Changes.**

7. **In the left column, hover your cursor over the Appearance link and then click the Menus link.**

8. **If you're using a custom menu, add the new pages to your navigation menu.**

   If you're not using a custom menu, the new pages should automatically appear in your blog's navigation system.

What to include on your website

Several successful e-book authors (of fiction and nonfiction) have given me their top tips for elements to include on your website. Here are their suggestions:

A photo of yourself (from Joanna Penn; www. thecreativepenn.com): Include a picture of your face, preferably smiling and looking approachable — unless your brand is particularly hard-core. People connect with people, so having a human face on a site can make you stand out amongst millions of impersonal business and brand sites. It's important that people know, like, and trust you if they are to buy your e-book, and a photo goes a long way toward helping with this [goal]. [Consider] paying a professional photographer to [take a photo that] you like enough to use on the site. You can use the same photo in social media avatars as well as on business cards, and a smile can connect you across cultures.

A tagline or call to action (from Amy Harrison; www.harrisonamy.com): To attract your ideal reader, use a short tagline on your website which includes *who* should read the e-book, *why* they will love it, and *what* they need to do to get it. This explains why they should be interested and has them taking action within seconds.

For example: "Romance fans, if you love a tale of modern-day relationships (warts and all!), click the button to download your copy today."

Or, "If you're thrilled by dystopian novels with fast-paced action, click this link and find out more about [book title]."

Sean Platt (www.thedigitalwriter. net) also suggests having a specific call-to-action that tells your readers exactly what you want them to do. "If you want them to download a sample chapter of your e-book, give them the direction, and then tell them where and how to do it. Never assume your reader knows what you want them to do. Whether you want them to download a sample, buy the full book, or share it on social media, always give your reader clear, concise language that leaves little (if anything) to chance. And always be polite."

Special features for readers (K.M. Weiland; www.kmweiland.com): "I like to think of my author's website rather like the Special Features segment on a DVD. The website is where I get to share with my readers all the extra goodies that didn't make it into the book itself: deleted scenes, further reading, behind-the-scenes info about my writing process and inspirations, interviews, Easter eggs, and sneak peeks at upcoming projects. The point of the website is to augment the books and allow me to form a more personal relationship with the reader."

Removing the blog element from your site

If you don't want to have a blog on your site, first follow the steps in the preceding section, "Calling your blog by a different name," to put your blog on a specific page rather than on your home page. (It doesn't matter what you name the page, though you might want to give it a sensible title — or no title — in case anyone accidentally stumbles across it.)

Ensure that your blog page is *not* linked to in your navigation menu. If you haven't yet created a custom menu, follow the instructions in "Arranging your WordPress menu," earlier in this chapter, to make one.

Chapter 10

Crafting an Effective Sales Page for Your E-Book

A sales page is simply a web page that has the role of selling your e-book. Sometimes, you hear sales pages called *landing pages* or even *sales letters*. They act as brochures for your e-book — brochures that are available all over the world, at any time of the day or night.

If you've written a nonfiction e-book, your sales page is a crucial tool in persuading readers to buy it. A fiction e-book may not need a specific page devoted to selling it, but you can use similar elements on other pages of your website.

In this chapter, I explain the reasons that sales pages work to sell your e-book — and I debunk common myths and misunderstandings. I describe the critical elements that your sales page needs, and help you design and craft an effective sales page for your e-book.

How Sales Pages Help You Sell Your E-Book

A sales page has one goal: to get readers to click the Buy button. The sales page might be a page on your website or a one-page website. Sometimes, an author creates a stand-alone site to sell an e-book — without a blog, an About page, contact information, or other distractions. This strategy can be quite powerful if you have a niche nonfiction book to promote. If you plan to write a series of books or you're using your books as only one part of your business, you'll probably want to have a whole website in addition to your sales page.

Assuming that your sales page is part of a larger site, it helps the reader by collating all the information about your e-book in one place. Busy readers don't want to hunt on your website for a table of contents here, quotes from reviews there, and snippets of information in long-buried blog posts somewhere else.

Your sales page should be as positive as possible. It isn't the place to voice doubts or worries about your e-book. Obviously, you must not lie or exaggerate — but you can and should be enthusiastic about how your e-book can help (or entertain) the reader.

Overcoming Common Myths and Misunderstandings About Sales Pages

If you've been looking into marketing online, for e-books or for any sort of product, you've probably come across some advice about sales pages and some examples of sales pages. You may have mixed feelings about creating a sales page for your own e-book: Perhaps you don't like the format, or you're concerned that your page isn't as good as you want it to be.

Take a look at these myths — and see whether you need to rethink any of your assumptions about sales pages.

Myth 1: All sales pages are scams

The sales pages you may have seen give off a nasty stench. They have lots of flashy icons, they pressure you to buy *right now* in order to snag a great deal, and they even create pop-up boxes when you try to leave in order to encourage you to stay on the site.

Sadly, scammers are out there. People run dubious "businesses" online that exist only to sell overpriced, shoddy products. But plenty of legitimate businesses also use sales pages — including lots of reputable authors who have sales pages for their e-books.

Every online store has a sales page for each book (even if that page doesn't hold much information). Many publishing companies also have sales pages, especially if you can buy e-books directly from them. Figure 10-1 shows the *For Dummies* sales page for this book, *Publishing E-Books For Dummies* — note the use of bullet points to highlight key benefits of the book.

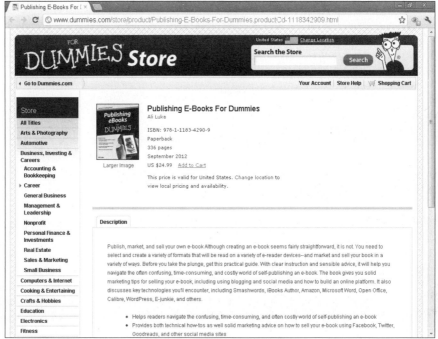

Figure 10-1:
Publishing E-Books For Dummies in the *For Dummies* store.

Myth 2: I need to be an expert copywriter to create a sales page

Some people (particularly copywriters) want you to believe that you absolutely need to hire a professional, at an eye-wateringly high rate of pay, to create a sales page for you. Of course, a professional copywriter can do an excellent job of selling your e-book — and if you have the budget for copywriting, then by all means go for it. But if money's tight, nothing is stopping you from creating your sales page yourself.

You're a writer, and a sales page is simply a form of writing. You might not be used to marketing yourself and your books — but the rest of this chapter will help you with that task.

Myth 3: A good sales page has to be long and give lots of details

It's true that some sales pages relate in-depth information — but yours probably doesn't need to do that. Unless you're selling an e-book with a high price tag (perhaps including a lot of bonuses), your sales page can be quite short and straightforward.

Your sales page needs only a few must-have elements, so don't feel that you need to include everything. For example, you don't necessarily need to include a whole chapter list — several bullet points explaining the scope of your e-book may be enough.

Myth 4: I don't need a sales page — I'm selling my book on Amazon (or B&N or a related site)

Potential readers won't necessarily stumble across your e-book in an online store, especially when it's first launched. Also, you have limited space for (and little control over the design of) your book's description in these stores.

A sales page gives you all the space you want in order to tell readers about your e-book. It might simply be a page on your website with a description, a couple of quotes from reviews, and a short excerpt from the e-book — but that page gives you one easy place to direct potential new readers.

Even if you choose not to have a website or a sales page, you can still use sales page techniques to help craft your description on Amazon (www.amazon.com) and on Smashwords (www.smashwords.com).

Including Crucial Elements on Your E-Book's Sales Page

Whatever type of e-book you've written — whether it's a specialist, in-depth nonfiction guide or a genre novel — you need to put in place on your sales page all the essential elements described in this section.

A clear explanation of your e-book

Readers need to know what they're buying. That means giving them more than simply your e-book's title and its cover image. It might seem obvious to *you* what your e-book's about, but don't make assumptions about what the reader is and isn't familiar with.

For example, if you've written a thriller novel, use the word *thriller* somewhere in your description. (You probably want to be more specific, too. Is it a psychological thriller? A supernatural thriller? A technothriller?) Offer readers a hook to entice them — in the way that the blurb on the back of a book does.

If your e-book is nonfiction, clearly explain its scope. Rather than say that it's "advanced" or "for beginners" (which are rather subjective measurements), try to indicate the level that the reader should already have reached. If you've written a guide to basic plumbing, for example, you might simply say, "I walk you through it step-by-step, and I don't expect you to have experience." If you've written an advanced e-book on website design, you might say, "I assume that you have a working knowledge of HTML and CSS."

Explain how the e-book will be provided. You might need to offer extra guidance if your readers may not be used to buying e-books, using wording such as the examples in this list:

✔ You can buy [e-book title] direct from Amazon, to read on your Kindle or on a free Kindle app (available for PCs, Macs, tablet computers, and smartphones).

✔ When you click the Buy Now button, an online PayPal form opens. As soon as you've paid, you see a link to download [e-book title] as a PDF file. (You're also sent a download link by e-mail.)

✔ [e-book title] is available from Amazon and other major e-book retailers. Click the links to go straight to the store of your choice, where you can complete your purchase.

A Buy button so that customers can buy your e-book

The Buy button (or link) is the most crucial element of your sales page — without it, you won't sell any e-books. Your potential customers need a way to complete their purchases, and this button should be clear and unambiguous.

The Buy button is a graphical element that readers can click to complete their purchases during checkout. The button can be labeled Buy, Add to Cart, Download Now, or Get Your Copy — you may even want to experiment with using different text on the button. You can see examples of Add to Cart buttons in Figure 10-2. Note their bold colors and clear text. In Chapter 12, I explain how to use E-junkie to create your Buy button.

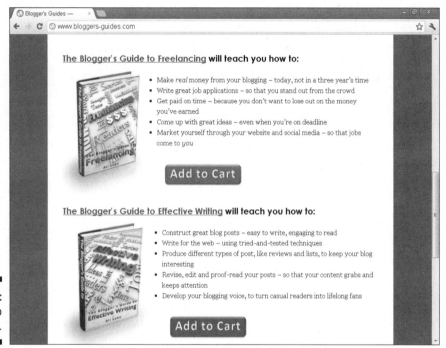

Figure 10-2:
The Add to Cart button.

Alternatively, you might simply link to the online store (or stores) where readers can buy your e-books. Make these links clear and unambiguous, perhaps by using a bold or larger font or by putting them on a separate line from the rest of your text, as shown in Figure 10-3.

Unless your sales page is quite short, have at least two Buy buttons and links — one near the top of the page and one near the bottom. If your page is long, you can even have three or four prompts to the reader to buy your e-book at different points in the text.

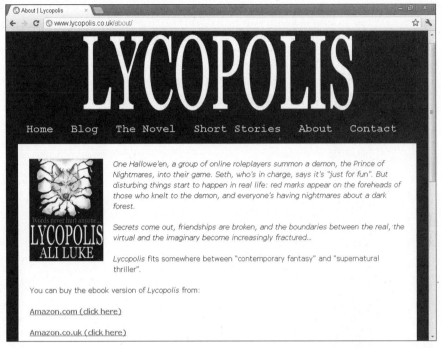

Figure 10-3:
Buy links.

Reviews or testimonials

Although readers may be drawn in by your enticing description of your
e-book and perhaps by the cover or other graphics on the page, these elements might not be enough to encourage them to buy. After all, unless they
know you already, they don't have much reason to trust you, and they may
wonder whether your e-book is truly as good as you say it is.

This is where reviews (or testimonials) become important — anything
positive that current readers have said about your e-book. Potential new
readers are more likely to buy your e-book when they see that others have
already purchased it and found it enjoyable or useful. You don't need to wait
until someone happens to e-mail you a few words of praise, either; you can
approach your existing audience (on Twitter, Facebook, or your blog) and
ask whether anyone wants a free copy of your e-book in return for a review.

If you have no reviews, or if you're crafting the sales page before your e-book
is even complete, you might use testimonials instead. They don't relate to

your e-book itself, but instead to your general expertise or skill in that area. For example, if you're a parenting coach and you've written an e-book about persuading your toddler to eat vegetables, you might have a testimonial from a grateful coaching client whose kids now happily clean their plates.

Whether you're using reviews or testimonials, make it easy for the reader to trust them. Sadly, certain unscrupulous authors invent positive reviews for their e-books, so make sure that yours are seen as authentic. A simple way to do it is to include a person's full name and a link to their website or Twitter account, if they have one. If you can get permission, you can also include a head shot of the person who provided the review or testimonial.

Don't forget that you can update your sales page at any time after you launch your e-book. If you get rave reviews on Amazon, you might want to quote them on your sales page. You can even take screen shots of tweets or Facebook postings about your e-book and include them, too: You can see in Figure 10-4 how I did this with a tweet.

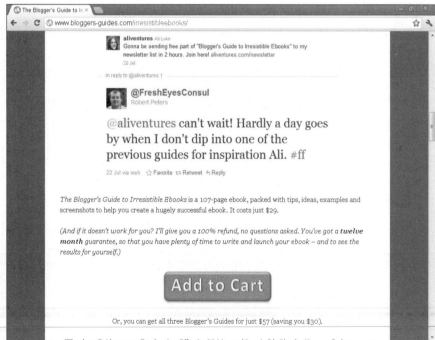

Figure 10-4:
Tweets
used as
social proof.

Designing and Creating Your Sales Page

You can start to design your sales page before you've finished your e-book. Give yourself plenty of time for this task because the sales page is one of the main ways in which you convert potential readers into paying customers — especially during the initial launch of your e-book.

In addition to the critical elements covered in the preceding section, you may want to include other pieces of content on your sales page, such as these examples:

- **Relevant biographical information about yourself:** If you have a PhD in psychology and you've written an e-book about ways to help a friend or relative with depression, your academic qualification is obviously relevant — information that readers will want to know about.

- **A short excerpt from the e-book:** This is more commonly included with fiction than with nonfiction, but nothing is stopping you from using the technique for any sort of book. With nonfiction, you might consider having several short quotes from your e-book at different points on the sales page.

- **Information about bonuses that you supply with the e-book:** For example, if you've written a nonfiction e-book, it might come with useful worksheets, recorded interviews with experts in the field, or other extras.

- **A downloadable sample of your e-book — perhaps the first few chapters:** This sample is a useful way to build readers' trust: They can get a real taste of what they'll be buying. If you've written a novel, those first few chapters should draw readers in — they'll want to know what happens next. With a nonfiction book, your sample might consist of the first chapters or one chapter from each part.

Drafting the copy for your sales page

Even if you're used to writing chapter after chapter of your e-book, writing a sales page can be a tough proposition. Most authors aren't natural marketers (in fact, the very thought of self-promotion might make you feel anxious) — I found it tough to write my first few sales pages.

At some point, though, you need to sit down and start writing. I suggest beginning with a clear description of your e-book. If you're not sure what to write, imagine what you'd say to a friend who asks, "So what's your book about?"

You might find that it's useful to study the sales copy for similar books. For example, if you've written a romance novel, take a look at several different blurbs to see what elements they have in common and what seems to work. If you've written a book about starting a small business, look around online for e-books on similar topics to see how other authors have put together their sales pages.

One piece of text that you'll want to pay close attention to is the *headline* — the title of your page. Though you can simply use the name of your e-book, the headline is, ideally, as compelling and attention-grabbing as possible. Focus on the key benefits to the reader — with nonfiction, that often means telling them what they'll learn, and with fiction, it means emphasizing the entertainment factor, as in these examples:

- ✔ Grow better, bigger tomatoes — in three simple steps.
- ✔ Learn everything you need to know about web design, from setting up your first site to starting a whole new career.
- ✔ Get my latest book, [title] — described as "a gripping read" and "an action-packed thriller that keeps you on the edge of your seat."

How much you need to write on your sales page is up to you. Generally, the more expensive the e-book, the more time you need to persuade potential customers that it's for them.

Explaining the benefits of your e-book

The benefits of reading a fiction e-book are usually implied — though you might want to write a sentence or two that hooks into the usual desires of readers in your genre. For example, literary readers will likely be looking for a different sort of experience from romance or crime fans.

With nonfiction, it's important to spell out what the reader will get from your e-book. A basic tenet of marketing says that it's important to focus on benefits, not simply on features. A feature, by the way, might read, "This e-book is 100 pages long." A benefit might read, "This fluff-free e-book for busy executives walks you through exactly what you need to know as quickly as possible."

Present benefits as bullet points whenever possible. Bullets make text easy to read and comprehend (and they look good on the screen). Between five and seven bullets is about right: Fewer bullets aren't enough to sway your potential customer toward buying; too many bullets make the customer start skipping to the next section.

When you're struggling to figure out how your e-book benefits readers, think about the answers to these questions:

- ✔ **How will your readers feel after they've finished the e-book?** Will they be more confident? Reassured? Entertained?

- ✔ **What will readers learn from your e-book?** Perhaps they'll gain a new skill, whether that's being able to put together a useful presentation or being able to take apart and repair a computer.

- ✔ **Who would find this e-book particularly useful?** Imagine who's likely to buy your e-book, and imagine which aspects of the book will be particularly relevant to them. For example, a book on starting a small business might be bought by people who are motivated by escaping from a day job, establishing a secondary income, or finally pursuing a dream. You can hit on all these benefits in your bullet points.

- ✔ **What might readers have tried and failed at in the past?** Perhaps your book on dieting is a straightforward guide, based on healthy principles — not a fad diet that doesn't even work. Be clear about how your book is different from (and better than) other books that readers may have come across.

Finding images and graphics for your sales page

Your sales page doesn't only need to be well-written — it also needs to look attractive. By including images and graphics, you add immediate visual interest for the reader.

Consider including these two important images:

- ✔ **Your e-book's cover:** This one isn't negotiable — there's no reason to omit it. You can simply put the cover on the page as a flat image. Some authors like to use software to turn their cover into a 3D graphic that looks like a little book, because they feel this helps give the e-book a more tangible form in readers' minds.

  If you've commissioned a cover from a designer, that person should be able to create a 3D graphic for you, so if you want this, let the designer know.

- ✔ **A photo of yourself:** A photo isn't absolutely essential, but a smiling picture of yourself helps establish an instant connection with potential readers. The photo can be a simple head-and-shoulders shot or a photo that relates to the content of your e-book. (I often use photos of me with various writing paraphernalia because most of my e-books are aimed at writers.) You can use the same photo that you have on your About page.

Lots of graphics packages are available to buy, usually quite cheaply. You can also purchase stock photography to use on your sales page, in the same way that you might have done for your e-book's cover. (See Chapter 5 for more on this topic.) Though you can find many freely available graphics on the web, make sure that they're truly free for anyone to use — you don't want to inadvertently infringe on someone's copyright. A better investment may be to purchase a cheap graphics package instead.

Visually, it's a good idea to try to use images from the same set to make an obvious stylistic connection between them. (It looks odd to have cutesy cartoon-style images mixed in with shiny, slick graphics.) If you have the budget, you can hire a professional designer to create your whole sales page, with unique graphics that all fit together well.

In addition to the Buy button, some graphics and images you might want to consider are described in this list:

- **Bullet-point graphics, such as a green check mark instead of the standard round dot:** Don't get too clever with these, though; they can become distracting.

- **Icons that help the reader to distinguish between different parts of what you're offering, especially if your e-book comes with bonuses:** For example, use a Microphone icon alongside a description of a recorded interview.

- **Screen shots of your e-book's contents, if it's nonfiction:** Screen shots can help readers gain a good sense of the book's purpose.

- **Photographs of reviewers or people who've written testimonials:** Be sure to get permission to use them. Try to format all photos in the same way — for example, have all of them as head shots measuring 150 x 150 pixels.

Using formatting to make your sales page look good

You can add graphics to your sales page, and you can use text formatting to add visual interest and to make it easy for the reader to comprehend it all. Even if you're not technically minded, these elements are easy to add using the visual editor in WordPress, shown in Figure 10-5. Note that to reveal the second row of buttons, you need to click the Show/Hide Kitchen Sink button, on the upper right. Hover your cursor over a button to see a brief explanation of that feature.

Show/Hide Kitchen Sink

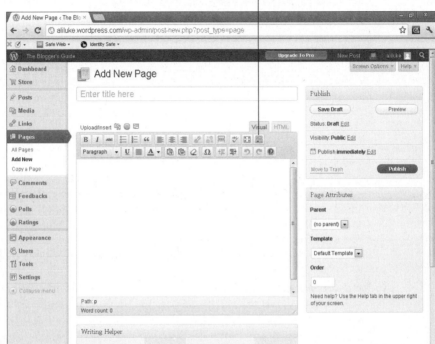

Figure 10-5:
The
WordPress
visual
editor.

Bold text

Bold text is a helpful way to make a phrase or sentence stand out. It's best used in a consistent manner (for the first sentence of each subsection or for the first phrase in each bullet point, for example). Avoid using bold text for individual words in the middle of sentences, because it can look choppy. If you need to emphasize a single word, try italics instead.

Subheadings

Readers often skim sales pages, looking for pieces of information that interest them. Subheadings not only help break the page into easily digestible parts, but also act as signposts to the reader. Phrases such as *About the Author* and *Contents List* are simple, functional ways to split your page into logical and useful sections.

White space

Reading text on a screen takes more physical effort than reading it on a printed page. Having plenty of white space helps make your page more attractive and easier to read — wide margins, space between individual lines of text, and short paragraphs. Bullet points are also an effective way to create white space.

Block quotes

If you're quoting from a testimonial or review, or even sharing a short excerpt from your book, try setting it off from the main text using the Block Quotes feature in WordPress. Quoted text is normally indented, and it's often presented in a different color or with a background. The exact styling depends on the blog theme you're using.

Colors

You can use fonts of different colors on your sales page, to draw attention. You might use red text, for example, to emphasize a special offer that's ending soon. Don't go overboard on different colors, though — pick one consistent color for subheadings rather than have a rainbow of different ones. Make sure that the colors you choose are easy to read against your background — which should usually be plain white or a light shade of a color.

Yellow highlighter pen

Some Internet marketers are fond of adding the "yellow highlighter pen" — putting a yellow background behind sentences or even whole paragraphs of text. Although this technique definitely helps draw the reader's eye, it has also become rather tacky and outdated, and it tends to carry an inevitable whiff of snake oil and used-car salesmen. Use at your own risk!

Considering Selling Your E-Book Only via Your Website

After you write a sales page, you might wonder whether you even need to sell your e-book from online stores. After all, readers can simply buy it directly from you — and you keep all the profits.

With some types of e-books, this route is a sensible one to take. If you've written a specialized e-book with a high price tag, you're unlikely to pick up impulse browsers in online stores (and you'll fall outside Amazon's royalty sweet spot between $2.99 and $9.99). You may also have access to an existing audience of likely buyers, whether it's via your blog or mailing list or contacts who have their own large online fan bases.

If you've written a low-priced book, though, it's worth putting it into online stores. After all, this is where book lovers naturally go to look for their next "fix." You're unlikely to have thousands of readers for your novel within your own audience — but your current audience might have enough members to get your book off to a great start in Amazon and other online stores that sell e-books.

If you decide to sell your e-book only via your own website, take the time to consider which formats you want to provide. Nothing is stopping you from creating MOBI and EPUB files to sell (as covered in Chapter 8) via your own site. Unless you have a good reason not to — such as your e-book involves lots of graphics, links, or interactive elements that work well only in PDF — it's worth the effort to supply your e-book in all three major formats.

Part IV
Selling Your E-Book

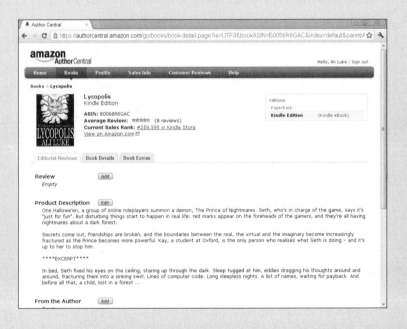

In this part . . .

Unless you're giving away your e-book, you need to put in place a system for selling it, and that system should be as automated as possible so that customers can buy your e-book without your direct involvement.

One tricky decision you face is how much to charge for your e-book. I devote Chapter 11 to this topic, by looking at nitty-gritty details such as how much of the cover price to keep and how best to price your e-book for maximum profit on Amazon. If you want to sell your e-book directly from your website, Chapter 12 covers a simple way to do it by using the E-junkie shopping cart software. In Chapter 13, I walk you through the steps to place your e-book on Amazon, and in Chapter 14, you can read how to distribute your e-book to other stores via Smashwords.

Chapter 11

Pricing Your E-Book Effectively

. . . .

In This Chapter

▶ Determining the best price for your e-book

▶ Understanding how e-book royalties work

▶ Knowing how best to set the price of your e-book on Amazon

. . . .

*O*ne tricky decision you face as an e-book self-publisher is determining how much to charge for your e-book. Unlike a print publisher, you have no manufacturing costs. After your e-book is written, delivering it to a new reader costs virtually nothing, so even if you charge only a few cents, you can still cover your costs.

Authors sometimes charge precisely $0.00 — they give away their work, to help build their reputations and their followings online. At other times, they choose to incorporate their e-books into fully featured digital packages with high price tags — perhaps as much as $100. The price of your e-book probably lies somewhere between these two points.

This chapter explains how e-book pricing works and how e-book retailers take a share of the price. It discusses fiction and nonfiction pricing, and offers clear recommendations so that you're well positioned to calculate the best price for your e-book. Finally, this chapter describes how Amazon complicates your pricing strategy.

Pricing Your E-Book As a Self-Publisher

Whenever an author signs a book contract with a traditional publisher, the publisher sets the price of the book. Examine a few book jackets in a nearby bricks-and-mortar store, and you can see a lack of pricing variety (except in some specialized cases, such as textbooks). You can expect a typical genre paperback, for example, to be priced around $14 to $16 — you won't find a thriller paperback priced at $3.99 or $29.99.

As a self-publisher, you have full control over every aspect of your e-book, including its price. Of course, selling your e-book only via specific stores is limiting (for example, the minimum price allowed at Amazon is 99 cents), but you can sell your e-book exclusively from your own site instead and at any price you want.

Charging what you want (or nothing at all)

No legal standard exists for setting the price of an e-book — you can let readers download your e-book for free or for hundreds or thousands of dollars (which likely isn't the best strategy for attracting sales).

Many authors, particularly of nonfiction, use free e-books to entice potential customers to join their e-mail lists. This strategy draws in customers and helps build strong relationships with them, especially when working on a specialized e-book that will command a high price when it's published.

You can list your e-book for free on sites such as Smashwords, which acts as a distributor for most major e-bookstores, with the exception of Amazon. (See Chapter 14 for more on Smashwords.)

If you're willing to make your e-book available exclusively to Amazon for 90 days, you can enroll it in the Kindle Direct Publishing (KDP) Select program and then offer it for free to Amazon users for five days within that period. Amazon Prime users (in Amazon's membership program) can borrow the book during the 90-day period for free. (See Chapter 13 for more on KDP.)

The price you charge (or don't charge) for your e-book is entirely up to you. Whatever its price, someone will almost always consider it too high, so don't be put off by any negative comments you see. If the price you've set is fair and reasonable for the value that readers receive — and if you're making sales — stick with it.

Changing the price of your e-book as frequently as you want

Because the recommended retail price (RRP) of a print book is usually listed on its back cover, a brand-new print run is required to raise the price — though special offers may be applied to lower it without having to replace the cover.

Your e-book's price is listed on its sales page on your website, if you have one, and on your e-book's page in online stores. Updating the price online is usually quick and easy, and you can do it as often as you like. If you've written a novel, for example, you might start off selling it at $2.99 to generate interest and raise the price to $4.99 later, after you've attracted reviews and social media chatter.

You can also change the price if you update or expand your e-book. Perhaps you've written a niche nonfiction e-book with a small but extremely interested target audience. You can sell the e-book initially for $29 and then bundle it with extra features, such as recorded interviews with experts in your field or video demonstrations to tie in with each chapter, and raise the price considerably.

If you suspect that you'll change the price of your e-book after its publication, maintain a list of sites that will need the updated price. Even if you're selling your e-book on only one page on your own site, you have to update two prices — the one that's listed (perhaps in more than one place) on the page and the one that's set in your shopping cart software. If you mention your e-book on several pages of your site and it's listed in online stores, you have to update the price in several locations.

Working Out How Much Money You'll Make

Though you may already have a price in mind to charge for your e-book — for example, $4.99 — this amount doesn't guarantee a $4.99 profit from every sale, even if you're selling your e-book only from your own website. Before you decide how much to charge, you have to know exactly how much of that $2.99, $4.99, or $9.99 will be paid to you.

Knowing how much per sale your retailer will keep

E-book retailers pay you *royalties,* or a percentage of the purchase price, for every copy of your e-book they sell. The percentage you get varies from store to store and, with Amazon in particular, also varies depending on the price of your e-book.

Amazon pays 35 percent royalties on e-books priced between $0.99 and $2.98 (inclusive) and $10 or higher. If you price your e-book between $2.99 and $9.99 (inclusive), you can receive 70 percent royalties instead — though, in this case, Amazon also charges for "delivery cost."

On a $4.99 e-book with the 70 percent royalty option, Amazon pays the author $3.47 per copy sold. (It deducts 3 cents for delivery costs.) You can see the royalty breakdown when you create a record for your e-book on Amazon, as shown in Figure 11-1, so don't worry about doing the math yourself. Chapter 13 describes the process of listing an e-book on Amazon.

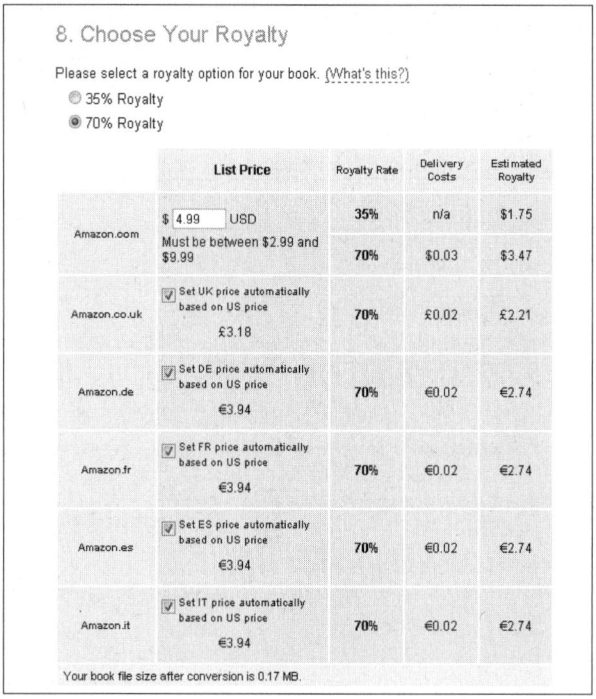

8. Choose Your Royalty

Please select a royalty option for your book. (What's this?)

35% Royalty

70% Royalty

	List Price	Royalty Rate	Delivery Costs	Estimated Royalty
Amazon.com	$ 4.99 USD	35%	n/a	$1.75
	Must be between $2.99 and $9.99	70%	$0.03	$3.47
Amazon.co.uk	Set UK price automatically based on US price £3.18	70%	£0.02	£2.21
Amazon.de	Set DE price automatically based on US price €3.94	70%	€0.02	€2.74
Amazon.fr	Set FR price automatically based on US price €3.94	70%	€0.02	€2.74
Amazon.es	Set ES price automatically based on US price €3.94	70%	€0.02	€2.74
Amazon.it	Set IT price automatically based on US price €3.94	70%	€0.02	€2.74

Your book file size after conversion is 0.17 MB.

Figure 11-1: The price breakdown of a $4.99 e-book at the Amazon site.

Other electronic bookstores have their own royalty rates. If you choose to publish your e-book via Smashwords, you can expect to receive these amounts:

- 85 percent of the net sale proceeds (the sales price minus the transaction fee) for direct sales at the Smashwords site
- 70.5 percent of the net sale proceeds for affiliate sales via the Smashwords site

An *affiliate* promotes your e-book via a special link, making money whenever a copy is sold to someone who bought the book after clicking the link.

✔ 60 percent of the retail price for e-books sold via most retailers, including Apple, Barnes & Noble, and Diesel in the United States

✔ 60 percent of the retail price for books distributed via Kobo and priced between $0.99 and $12.99

(Other sales at Kobo are at 38 percent of the list price.)

If these percentages sound confusing, don't worry: Like Amazon, Smashwords provides an explicit graphical breakdown, in the form of pie charts, when you enter a price. Figure 11-2 shows a pie chart for a $4.99 e-book sale directly from Smashwords, Figure 11-3 shows a pie chart for a sale via a Smashwords affiliate, and Figure 11-4 shows a chart for a sale via a third-party site.

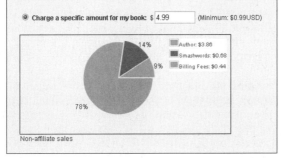

Figure 11-2: Pie chart for a Smashwords e-book sale.

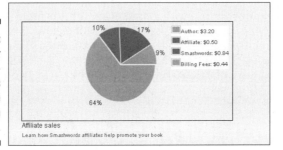

Figure 11-3: Pie chart for a Smashwords e-book sale through an affiliate.

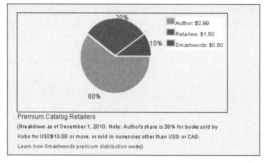

Figure 11-4:
Pie chart for
a third-party
Smash-
words
e-book sale.

Giving a portion to PayPal for payment processing

You might feel that Amazon and Smashwords are taking too large a portion of your e-book profits — but even if you sell your e-book via your own site, you incur costs. You have to pay for your shopping cart software. (E-junkie, recommended in Chapter 12, has a flat monthly fee of $5, regardless of how many e-books you sell.) If you use PayPal, the simplest and most popular option for payment processing, you also pay a fee for every e-book you sell.

The PayPal cut is 2.9 percent on every sale, plus a $0.30 transaction fee. For example, on a $5 e-book, PayPal gives you $4.56. If you have a large (more than $3,000) monthly sales volume, the percentage fee is slightly lower.

Paying taxes on your sales

The e-books you sell provide you with income — and it's taxable. Maintain accounts of your e-book income for tax purposes, and pay taxes as customary in your home country. Consider the potential tax burden when you create your pricing strategy, and after your e-book starts selling, set aside a percentage of the profit to cover your tax debt.

Pricing Your Nonfiction E-Book

If you've written a nonfiction e-book, you have a lot of flexibility over pricing, which can make nearly impossible the task of determining the best price to maximize revenue.

A higher price doesn't necessarily result in more income for you. E-book authors can profit considerably from a combination of a low e-book price and a high sales volume, or from a high price tag and the sale of only an e-book or two every month.

Looking at competing products

To start the process of pricing a nonfiction e-book, examine similar e-books on the market. If you've written a general interest book that you plan to sell on Amazon and in other stores, find the average price (and the lowest and highest price) of the top ten e-books in your book's main category (or categories).

If you've written a specialized nonfiction e-book, see what price other publishers in your niche are charging. For example, most of the e-books that are written for the blogging world (one of my areas of expertise) cost between $29 and $49 (though some cost as much as $99). I've priced all my Blogger's Guides at $29. Though the price seems steep, readers are quite willing to pay it because it's a good value within that market.

You don't necessarily have to follow standard pricing procedures, but if your e-book has a much higher price than readers would normally expect, you might harm sales. A much *lower* price can also cause problems. If I priced my blogging e-books at $2.90 instead of $29, for example, readers might wonder what was wrong with them, because these e-books would seem to be very low-priced compared with similar ones on the market — and most of us are unwilling to trust bargains that look too good to be true! (And even if sales doubled, I'd be making only one-fifth as much profit.)

Realizing that size doesn't matter (much)

The length of an e-book doesn't matter much in pricing it. What matters is *the value* of the e-book to readers. A 100-page e-book that's highly focused on a specific area of business might sell for $99.99 — as long as it's likely to help readers increase their own profits considerably.

Conversely, if you've written a 700-page e-book on a subject of personal interest (perhaps the story of your family over the past 100 years), it's unlikely to sell for a high price.

You can't completely omit size from the pricing equation, though. If your e-book is essentially a long article, of the type you might see in a magazine or newspaper, you're unlikely to be paid more than a few dollars for it. Specify the length of your e-book regardless of its price — you don't want angry, disappointed readers leaving 1-star reviews on Amazon after paying $9.99 for an e-book that's the equivalent of a few blog posts.

Asking potential customers for the amount they would be willing to pay

One simple and effective way to find out how much your e-book is worth to readers is to ask them. If you have an e-mail list, a blog, a Twitter account, a Facebook page, or any similar way to contact people who might be interested in buying your e-book, survey them.

Give your potential audience the basic details of your e-book (the same as you would on the e-book's sales page, described in Chapter 10). Let them know its scope and how it can benefit them, and then ask how much they would be willing to pay to purchase it. You can even ask this question in different ways:

- ✔ What price would make this e-book a true bargain?
- ✔ What price seems fair?
- ✔ What price seems too high?

Provide a range of prices to choose among — and be sure to include $0 as an option, or else you risk skewing your survey results, because readers who wouldn't pay anything at all will have to opt for the lowest price or ignore the question entirely.

Encourage survey respondents to supply their e-mail addresses so that you can alert them to the launch of your e-book. You can even offer a special discount code or another type of bonus as extra incentive.

Pricing Your Fiction E-Book

You can more quickly establish the appropriate price range of a fiction e-book than a nonfiction e-book — but you can also quite easily obsess over where exactly within that range to place your e-book. One dollar higher or lower than the perfect price can make a big difference.

Though almost all fiction e-books are priced between $0.99 and $12.99, most best-selling books priced toward or above the upper end of this range are from big-name authors with the backing of large publishing houses.

Looking at other books in your genre

Different genres have different pricing. Take a look at a dozen of the most popular e-books within your own genre, on Amazon and other sites. Figure 11-5 shows the four most popular e-books in the Thrillers section of the Amazon Kindle store.

If you spot lots of books in your genre that are written by big-name authors (or produced by big-name publishers), price your e-book slightly lower. Readers who haven't yet heard of you need extra incentive to buy yours.

In most genres, self-publishers agree that $2.99 to $4.99 is the right price point for a novel. (A novel is generally agreed to be a minimum of 40,000 words, and around 80,000 words is standard.) If you've written a shorter piece, price it below $2.99. Unless you're already a well-known author, you're unlikely to sell a 5,000-word short story for more than $0.99.

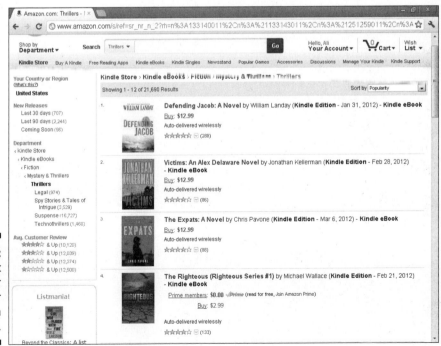

Figure 11-5: The most popular thrillers for the Amazon Kindle.

No magic formula exists for pricing your novel, and authors have different opinions about what works best. Consider these factors as you determine the price of your e-book:

- ✔ **Your personal price point for an impulse purchase:** For example, you might stock your Kindle with dozens of $0.99 books or happily pay $4.99 or more for books that sound intriguing.

- ✔ **The amount that your existing readership considers a good price for novels:** You can ask for their opinions on Twitter or Facebook, or encourage their comments on your blog.

- ✔ **The number of novels you plan to publish, such as a trilogy or a longer series:** If you plan to publish several related novels, consider making the first novel cheaper than the others to help draw readers into the series.

Pricing your e-book lower than a standard paperback

You may feel that $2.99, or even $4.99, is far too little to charge for your e-book — after all, you've spent the past year (or longer) writing your novel. If a bargain-basement price seems to devalue your hard work, you may be tempted to accept the standard $9.99 or $12.99 retail price. After all, some mainstream e-books are priced highly.

Many traditional publishers are still trying to get a handle on e-book pricing, and it's also a hot topic for readers and authors. Many readers feel (quite reasonably) that a digital version of a book should carry a lower price than its paperback version. After all, manufacturing and warehousing costs have decreased, and unsold copies are not an issue — a copy of an e-book is generated only when it's purchased.

To encourage sales of your e-book, be willing to price it lower than a standard paperback. Your readers are buying online, so consider also the discounts that major e-retailers (such as Amazon) offer. When a paperback with the standard price of $14.99 goes on sale for $8.99, you'll need to undercut the *discounted* price, not the RRP.

Ultimately, the unit price of your e-book is no measure of your worth as an author. The more significant figure is how much total profit you make. If you sell four times more books at $4.99 than at $9.99, for example, you're putting twice as much money in your pocket.

Pricing Your Book for Maximum Profit on Amazon

If you want to sell your e-book only from your own website, or via Smashwords (described in Chapter 14), simply consider what price point would maximize its sales and revenue. For example, if you average ten daily e-book sales at $9.99 ($99.90 per day) and nine daily sales at $11.99 ($107.91 per day), stick with the $11.99 price. On the other hand, if raising the price from $9.99 to $11.99 makes sales drop to seven copies per day ($83.30), you'll make more with the $9.99 price point.

If you want to sell your e-book on Amazon, though, keep these two crucial points in mind:

- ✔ **Amazon will lower the price of your e-book to match the lowest available online price.** You should maintain consistent pricing across all stores and sites that sell your e-book.

- ✔ **Amazon uses two royalty rates.** You receive 70 percent of the sale price on books priced between $2.99 and $9.99, and you receive only 35 percent on books priced outside this range.

Aiming for the $2.99—$9.99 sweet spot

Authors have differing views on how best to maximize their profits from selling e-books at Amazon. Some suggest focusing on the $0.99 price point because it obviously leads to more sales than the $2.99 price point — perhaps so many more that the 35 percent royalty rate still gives a great return on your time. Opting for a very low price can also be a good way to build the size of your initial audience: Many series authors, such as Amanda Hocking, price the first book in a series at $0.99 and price later books at $2.99, as you can see in the example shown in Figure 11-6. (The first book in Hocking's *My Blood Approves* trilogy carries the same low price as its much shorter tie-in title, *Letters to Elise.*)

If you have only one or two e-books for sale, price them in the range from $2.99 to $9.99, with fiction toward the lower end and nonfiction at the middle to high end. You would need to sell six times as many books at $0.99 to make the same profit as selling them at $2.99 — and if you're selling to an existing readership, they would probably pay the $2.99 rate.

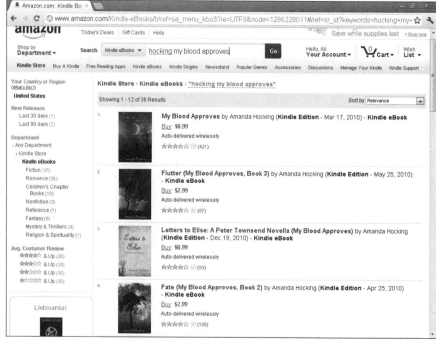

Figure 11-6:
Amanda
Hocking's
My Blood
Approves
series.

WARNING!

Do *not* price your e-book higher than $9.99. Your royalties will plunge to 35 percent — and you'll have to sell twice as many e-books (or the same number of e-books at twice the price) to earn the same profit. It's possible you could make more money on Amazon from selling an expensive e-book than one priced at $9.99, but in virtually every case, you're better off selling the expensive e-book from your own website.

Experimenting with the $0.99 "bargain" price point

Depending on your readership and marketing strategies and on your e-book's genre, the $0.99 price point can work well for you. If you plan to buy advertising, for example, you're more likely to sell your e-book for $0.99 than for $2.99, because readers who've never heard of you may need the incentive of a very attractive price to buy on impulse. For example, Kindle Nation Daily, a popular website for people who read e-books on the Amazon Kindle, has a prominent category for $0.99 e-books (and it offers a newsletter).

You can try the $0.99 price point when immediate revenue isn't important to you. For example, if your e-book is the first product in a *sales funnel* (designed to draw customers in and nudge them toward higher-priced products), you might be perfectly happy to sell it for $0.99 — even if you don't make much money from it. Your profit will come later.

You can lower (or raise) the price of your e-book at any time. An author might lower the price of an e-book until it ranks highly on the Amazon sales charts, for example, and then raise it again until the ranking starts to drop, and so on.

Ultimately, pricing requires trial and error. Whatever price you choose for your e-book, you'll make *some* money, so don't agonize over picking the perfect price point. Focus on a good price for your readership, in your genre or topic area, and be prepared to adjust it as necessary.

Chapter 12

Using E-junkie to Sell and Deliver Your E-Book

After you create an e-book, you need to be able to sell it to readers. If you plan to give away your e-book, you can skip this chapter. If you want to charge for your e-book, however, you should put a payment solution in place before continuing.

This chapter shows you how to take payments online, put your first e-book on E-junkie, and add the Buy Now button to your website. You can also check out other shopping cart solutions in case you need something more powerful than E-junkie.

Joining PayPal So That You Can Receive Payments

If you were printing paper books and selling them offline, you wouldn't need to put much thought into how to receive payment. You would accept cash and (maybe) checks, but prospective customers wouldn't necessarily expect you to accept credit cards. Because you're selling online, though, you can't ask customers to mail you a check via snail mail (postal mail) and then wait for you to cash it — they want to pay instantly and receive your e-book immediately.

You don't need to endure the hassle and expense of registering a merchant account so that you can accept credit card payments. Dozens of different services allow you to receive money online, and I give you instructions for the most popular — PayPal. I've chosen it because you may already have a PayPal account for shopping on eBay or on other sites, and your customers are likely to be familiar with it. Even if they have no account, PayPal lets them simply enter the details of their credit cards or debit cards when they purchase your e-book.

Signing up for a personal PayPal account

If you don't already have a PayPal account, registering for one is simple and straightforward:

1. **Go to** www.paypal.com.

2. **Click the Sign Up link (on the left side).**

   The Create Your PayPal Account page appears.

3. **Select your country or region and your language.**

4. **Choose a Premier account and then click the Get Started button.**

   The Premier account is under your own name, and the Business account allows you to use a company or group name. You don't need the PayPal Business account — both the Business account and the Premier account allow you to sell via your website. However, you may want the Business account if you're joining with other people to create a company selling e-books.

5. **On the next page, fill in your personal details.**

   To be able to withdraw your money from PayPal, you must use your real name, as it appears on your bank account. If you need to change the name on your PayPal account after registering, you have to contact the support team — you can't change it yourself.

6. **Review the PayPal terms-of-service agreement and then select the check box to indicate that you accept the terms of service.**

7. **Click the Agree and Create Account button.**

Adding a bank account so that you can withdraw money

To remove your money from PayPal as soon as you start selling e-books (unless you're planning on an eBay shopping spree), you have to register your bank account. Even if you already use PayPal for online shopping, you might not have added your bank account, so check it by logging in to PayPal and choosing the Profile⇨Add or Edit Bank Account command.

PayPal needs to ensure that you own the bank account you'll be withdrawing money to. After you add your bank account details to your PayPal profile, PayPal makes two small (less than a dollar) deposits to your account. After you receive these payments, you enter them in PayPal to verify the bank account.

PayPal deposits usually take only a few days to appear in a bank account, so don't wait around for your paper bank statement to arrive in the mail. You may be able to check your bank statement via online banking, telephone banking, or an ATM. Your bank should be able to advise you.

Signing Up for an E-junkie Account

To sell your e-book, you need to not only accept payment, but also deliver the e-book file to your customer. Some people do this and don't automate the process — they accept the payment directly into PayPal, check regularly for new orders, and manually e-mail every e-book. This time-consuming strategy assumes that your customers have inboxes large enough to receive your e-book file — or that you need to make the e-book file available on your website, where an unwitting or unscrupulous customer can easily share with friends the link to your e-book.

Thankfully, you have an easier way. Online *shopping cart* sites (which let customers select and buy items on a website), such as E-junkie, receive payments for you and automatically deliver the e-book to customers, at any time of the day or night. Because E-junkie hosts your e-book file *securely,* every customer receives an e-mail with a unique download link.

E-junkie is inexpensive ($5 per month, unless you're selling enormous e-book files) and simple to use. Plenty of shopping cart solutions are available, though, and you can read about three more at the end of this chapter.

It takes only a few minutes to set up your E-junkie account, and you get a free 1-week trial. Follow these steps:

1. **Go to** www.e-junkie.com.

2. **Click Register on the menu bar.**

3. **Fill in your e-mail address and password in the Register for Free Trial section.**

Your customers see your e-mail address when they buy your e-book. If you don't already have an e-mail account, you may want to create a new one (such as *yourname@yoursitedomain.com*) for business purposes.

4. **When you receive the activation code by e-mail, return to E-junkie and log in.**

   You're prompted to enter the code.

Next, you need to link your E-junkie account to your PayPal account so that customers can pay for your e-books. You must do this even if you're using the same e-mail address for both E-junkie and PayPal: E-junkie doesn't automatically fill in your PayPal address for you.

To add your PayPal address, follow these steps:

1. **Log in to E-junkie at** `www.e-junkie.com`**.**

2. **In the Manage Your Seller Account section, click the Edit Profile link.**

3. **In the Selling with PayPal section, enter your PayPal e-mail address.**

4. **Click the Submit button at the bottom of the page.**

Getting Your E-Book onto E-junkie

After your E-junkie account is ready to receive payments, it's time to add your e-book. Though E-junkie accepts files in almost any format, you can upload only one file for your e-book. If your e-book consists of several files (for example, if you're supplying EPUB, MOBI, and PDF versions), you zip them into a single folder to upload to E-junkie.

Adding a new product in E-junkie

To add your e-book to E-junkie, follow these steps:

1. **Click the Seller Admin link on the menu.**

2. **Click the Add Product link in the Manage Products section.**

   E-junkie opens a page for you to fill in details for adding a product, as shown in Figure 12-1.

3. **Complete the following information in the Product Configuration section on the left side of the screen:**

   • *Name:* Type the name of your e-book as you want it to appear in customers' shopping carts.

   • *Single File Download:* Leave this check box selected.

- *Let Buyers Edit Quantity in Cart:* (Optional) Deselect the check box. This step prevents customers from accidentally buying more than one copy of your e-book.

- *Price:* Enter an amount in the Price box, and select a currency.

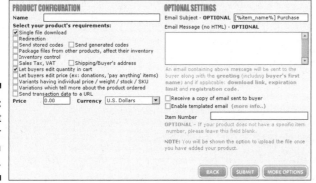

Figure 12-1:
The default options for adding a product.

You can ignore the optional settings on the right side of the screen. It's a nice touch, though, to add a short e-mail message thanking your customer for buying your e-book and asking him to e-mail you if he has trouble downloading the file.

4. **After you've entered all the details, click the Submit button.**

   Your product is created (you still need to upload your e-book file), and you see onscreen the code for the Add to Cart and View Cart buttons. You can click a tab to view the code for the Buy Now buttons. (And you can easily return to the code later.)

Click the More Options button on the E-junkie Add Product screen (before Step 4) to add these elements (you can also edit a product to add these at a later stage):

✔ **An expiration date for your e-book:** Add this date if you're offering your e-book for a limited period.

✔ **Download Link validity:** The default setting is 120 hours and 5 download attempts, to help prevent customers from sharing their link with other people. You can increase or decrease the time and the number of attempts, if you want.

✔ **Location of a Remote Product File URL:** This element is necessary only if your e-book file is so large that E-junkie cannot host it, such as when you package videos with your e-book.

Uploading your e-book file

After you click Submit to create your product (refer to Step 4 in the preceding section "Adding a new product in E-junkie"), you should see the Upload Product File button at the top of the page, where I've entered *My First e-Book* as the name of the e-book:

To add your e-book file, follow these steps:

1. **Click the Upload Product File button.**
2. **Click Choose File, and browse for the file on your computer.**
3. **Click Upload.**

    Keep the window open until the file has finished uploading.

Your e-book is added to E-junkie.

Adding the Buy Button to Your Sales Page

To buy your e-book, customers click the Buy Now button to open the E-junkie payment page for your e-book. The code may look daunting, so this section walks you through the steps.

Getting and using the Buy Now button code from E-junkie

When you create a new product on E-junkie, the last page you see after creating a new product presents the code for displaying the Buy Now button on your website. You can easily access the page again later by following these steps:

1. **Log in to E-junkie.**

2. **In the Manage Products section, click the View/Edit/Delete Products link.**

3. **Select your e-book from the drop-down list.**

    If you have only one e-book, it's automatically selected.

4. **Click the Get Button Code button.**

5. **Click the Buy Now Buttons tab.**

    You should see the screen shown in Figure 12-2, with the HTML code for the Buy Now button shown in the wide yellow box.

Figure 12-2:
HTML code
for the Buy
Now button.

You can copy and paste this Buy Now button code directly into the HTML view of your sales page in WordPress (described in Chapter 9), creating a button that customers can click to buy your e-book. To do so, follow these steps:

1. **Highlight the red HTML code in the wide yellow box, as shown in Figure 12-2.**

    Click and drag the mouse to highlight the code.

2. **Press Ctrl+C on the keyboard to copy the code.**

3. **Go to your sales page and open HTML view; decide where to place the Buy Now button, and position the cursor there; and press Ctrl+V to paste (insert) the Buy Now button code.**

4. **Click Preview to see your page (and the Buy Now button) as it will appear live.**

    When you click the button, you should be directed to a payment page for your e-book. The button looks like this:

Replacing the default Buy Now button graphic with your own

You may not like the default E-junkie Buy Now button. (I prefer one that's larger and more inviting, and, for variety, I often change its label.) If you search online for the phrase *free Buy Now button,* you can find plenty of sites offering different options. If you want a high-quality range of sales page buttons, you can purchase an inexpensive, downloadable pack of them. I use the Big Shiny Buttons pack, available from www.bigshinybuttons.com for $9.97.

If you have graphics software installed on your computer, such as Photoshop or Paint.NET (free to download from www.getpaint.net; see Chapter 5), you can even create your own Buy Now button. See *Creating Web Graphics For Dummies,* by Bud E. Smith and Peter Frazier (Wiley), for full instructions and guidance on designing buttons, banners, and other items.

After you have the Buy Now button, you can upload it to your sales page by using the WordPress media uploader. Follow these steps:

1. **Log in to WordPress, and choose the Pages➪All Pages menu command.**

2. **Find your sales page, and click the title to edit it.**

3. **Position the cursor wherever you want the Buy Now button to appear.**

4. **Click the Add Media icon above the posting box, as shown in Figure 12-3.**

   The icon, which is the first of the three Upload/Insert buttons, looks like a camera lying on a musical note.

   After you click the Add Media icon, you can upload your image on the screen that appears.

Figure 12-3: The editing box in WordPress.com.

5. **Drag and drop the Buy Now button file into the box, or browse for the file on your computer.**

   After the button is uploaded, you see the Add Media dialog box, which shows the details of an image, as shown in Figure 12-4.

In the Link URL text box, which defaults to the URL of the image itself, you enter the URL for the E-junkie Buy Now button, as described next.

Figure 12-4: The Add Media dialog box, where you enter the web address of the E-junkie button.

To turn the button graphic into a clickable button that readers can use to buy your e-book, follow the steps in the earlier section "Getting and using the Buy Now button code from E-junkie." This time, though, you need only part of the code — the first hyperlink, which is in the `<a href>` tag.

To copy the hyperlink shown in Figure 12-5, highlight the hyperlink and press Ctrl+C.

Don't enter the hyperlink shown in Figure 12-5 on your sales page for use in your e-book — it represents one of *my* products.

Figure 12-5: The E-junkie button code for the Buy Now button.

6. **To add the link to your button, enter it in the Link URL text box, as shown in Figure 12-6.**

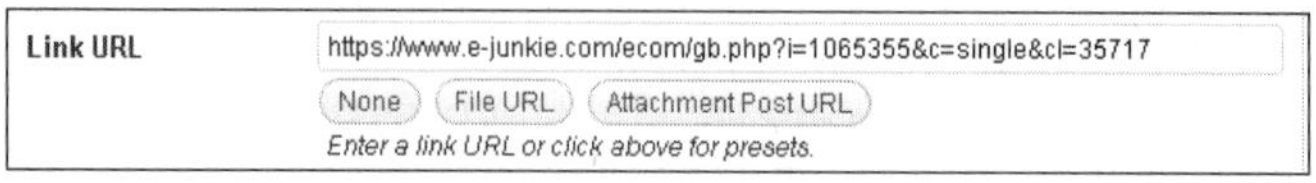

Figure 12-6:
Adding the
E-junkie link
to an image.

7. **Click the Insert into Post button, toward the bottom of the Add Media dialog box.**

The Buy Now button appears in your post.

Letting the shopping cart handle multiple items

If you have several e-books available for sale, your customers don't want to have to pay for each one separately. A shopping cart is useful because it holds multiple items before the customer completes the virtual checkout.

E-junkie provides code for a simple shopping cart, and you can access it from the E-junkie Shopping Cart Buttons tab, shown in Figure 12-7. One section of code creates the Add to Cart button (on the left), and the other section creates the View Cart button (on the right).

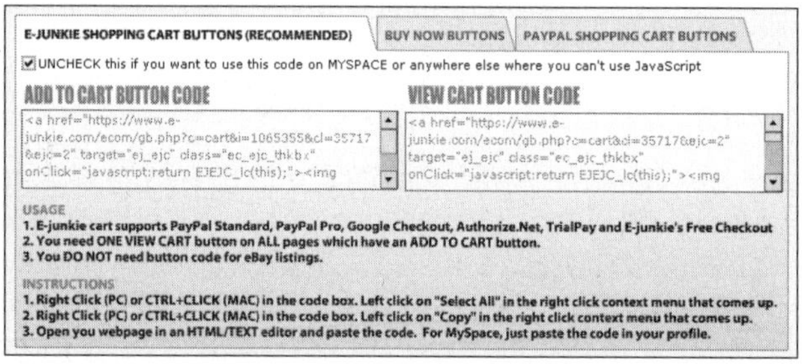

Figure 12-7:
The E-junkie
shopping
cart buttons.

These buttons, which can be "stacked" one above the other, work similarly to the Buy Now button, and you can copy and paste their code in HTML view on your sales page. E-junkie recommends adding at least one View Cart button on every sales page, though the Add to Cart buttons still work if you don't do it.

The default Add to Cart and View Cart buttons look like this:

ADD TO CART

VIEW CART

As with the Buy Now buttons, you can use your own images for Add to Cart and View Cart. In both cases, you need the first hyperlink, shown in Figure 12-7 as

```
https://www.e-junkie.com/ecom/gb.php?c=cart&i=1065355&cl=
        35717&ejc=2
```

```
https://www.e-junkie.com/ecom/gb.php?c=cart&cl=35717&ecj=2
```

 Request your own URLs from E-junkie. The URLs shown in Figure 12-7 work only for my e-book, not yours.

 The Add to Cart and View Cart buttons use JavaScript to open a new window during checkout (which doesn't happen if you create your own button and use only the hyperlink). If you prefer, you can copy and paste the code instead, and then replace these URLs with your own image URLs:

```
http://www.e-junkie.com/ej/ej_add_to_cart.gif
```

```
http://www.e-junkie.com/ej/ej_view_cart.gif
```

Considering Other Shopping Cart Options

E-junkie isn't your only option for selling e-books. Dozens of other good shopping carts are available. If you're planning to operate an e-book empire, or if you want to sell more complex digital products, look into the three popular options described in this section (from lowest to highest price).

WP e-Commerce

```
http://getshopped.org
```

If you're using self-hosted WordPress, you can install the free WP e-Commerce plug-in on your website. If your site runs on WordPress.com (described in Chapter 9), however, you can't use WP e-Commerce.

WP e-Commerce works with PayPal and other common payment processors, such as Google Checkout. It has all the features you need in order to sell e-books and more — in fact, some people find it too technical and overwhelming to use.

If you don't know how to install a plug-in or if you're unsure how they work, you can find out all about them at `http://codex.wordpress.org/Managing_Plugins`.

1ShoppingCart

`http://1shoppingcart.com`

As with E-junkie, you can use 1ShoppingCart on any website. You can test-drive it for $3.95, but the Starter package costs $34 per month (billed every four weeks, if you're on a monthly plan). A popular shopping cart system for small businesses, it offers more features than E-junkie. To gain access to all of them, you have to pay for a more expensive package.

You might choose to use 1ShoppingCart if you want extra features, such as recurring billing, that E-junkie doesn't support. (You wouldn't use recurring billing for a single e-book, but you might do so if you were producing a short e-book every month or two for your customers.)

1ShoppingCart also has an integrated *autoresponder,* which lets you easily send customers automatic e-mail. For example, you can choose to send an e-mail to every customer two weeks after they purchase an e-book, asking whether they want to provide a brief testimonial.

Infusionsoft

`www.infusionsoft.com`

If you're running a full-fledged online business, consider using Infusionsoft. It integrates sales, marketing, and customer relationship management (CRM). The monthly package price ranges from $199 to $999.

Though Infusionsoft has a powerful set of tools and is widely used in the online business community, some people see it as too expensive and packed with features unnecessary for small businesses.

Chapter 13

Listing Your E-Book on Amazon's Kindle Direct Publishing

Amazon is *the* largest e-book retailer (in profit and e-book sales), selling 60 percent of all e-books globally in the first quarter of 2012. Although Smashwords (described in Chapter 14) has agreements with other sites, it has yet to begin distributing via Amazon, so if you want to sell your e-book from the Amazon site, you need to put it there yourself.

The good news is that Amazon has a relatively straightforward system for filling out information about your e-book and for uploading it — plus plenty of documentation and friendly community forums, where you can find help and support.

This chapter tells you how to set up a Kindle Direct Publishing (KDP) account and explains how to add your e-book to your account, by filling in the correct information and uploading the file. You can see how to create an about-the-author page on Amazon to help boost the sale of your e-book.

Deciding Whether to Sell Your E-Book at Amazon

The books that Amazon sells on its site are formatted as AZW files, a proprietary format that's based on MOBI and used on the Kindle. You cannot sell an AZW file from your own site or any site other than Amazon. To cater to

Kindle users and bypass Amazon, you can create a MOBI file using Calibre and sell it on your own website. (See Chapter 8 for instructions for using Calibre, and see Chapter 12 for help with selling from your site.) Kindle users can send MOBI files to their devices by e-mail or by plugging the Kindle into their computer and transferring the file via USB cable.

The main benefit of having your e-book available on Amazon, however, isn't simply to provide Kindle readers with a file format that works for them — it's to benefit from having the biggest book-buying audience in the world. When readers browse the web for a new e-book to read, they're likely to head straight to Amazon (rather than search at Google). Unless your e-book is available on Amazon, they won't be able to find it.

Of course, for a few reasons, you might not want to make your e-book available on Amazon. Perhaps it costs more than $9.99, and you'll therefore receive only 35 percent royalties — and a few disgruntled readers. Or perhaps you have personal or political reasons for choosing not to join forces with Amazon.

If your main objection concerns the 70 percent royalty rate (you may feel that Smashwords offers a better deal, or you may want to sell the e-book yourself and retain as much of the profit as possible), consider Amazon's share as payment for providing you shelf space and a platform. After all, a bricks-and-mortar bookstore also takes a hefty cut of the profit.

Creating Your Kindle Direct Publishing (KDP) Account

Setting up an account at Amazon KDP is quick and free. Follow these steps:

1. **Go to** `https://kdp.amazon.com`.

2. **If you have an existing Amazon account, click the Sign In button and then sign in; if you don't have an Amazon account, click the Sign Up button and then follow the steps to create one.**

3. **Read and accept the KDP terms of service (TOS) that open onscreen.**

   You should see the KDP Bookshelf, shown in Figure 13-1, where all your published e-books are listed.

4. **In the upper-right corner of the screen is a warning that your account information is incomplete; click the Update Now link.**

5. **Complete the form for your account, as shown in Figure 13-2.**

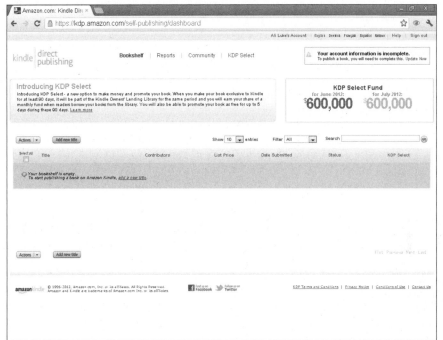

Figure 13-1:
The KDP
Bookshelf,
awaiting
titles.

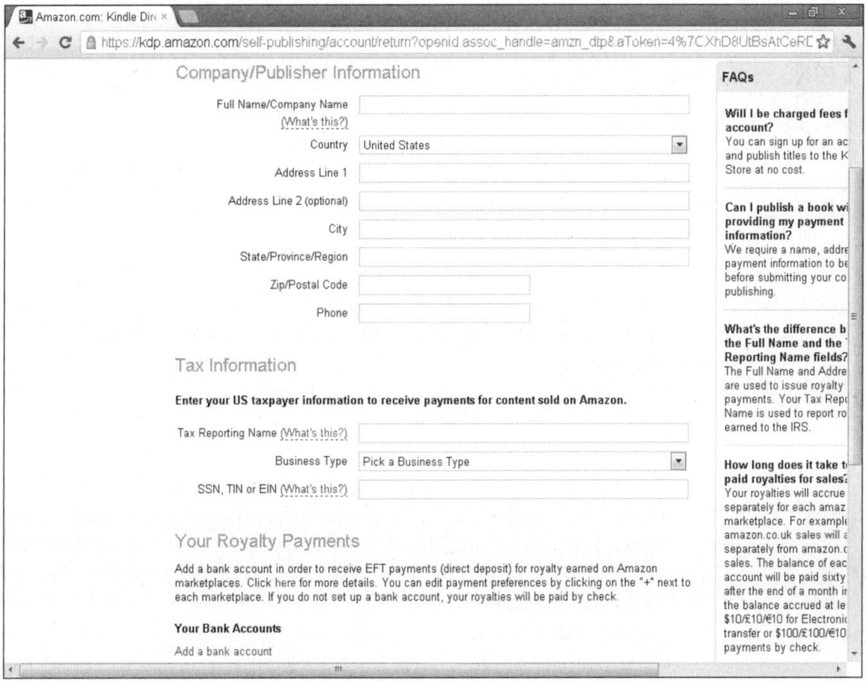

Figure 13-2:
Filling out
the Your
Account
form.

Enter information in these three sections:

- *Company/Publisher Information:* If your publishing business has a company name, enter it here. Otherwise, use your full name.

- *Tax Information:* Your tax reporting name is your full legal name.

  If you aren't a U.S. citizen, but you live in a country with a tax treaty with the United States, obtain an individual tax identification number (ITIN), and file a W8-BEN form. If you don't do this, your royalties are subject to withholding tax.

  Read these instructions from Amazon:

  ```
  https://kdp.amazon.com/self-publishing/
  help?topicId=A1VDYJ32T5D3U4
  ```

- *Your Royalty Payments:* You can be paid by check or by direct deposit in an electronic funds transfer, or EFT. If you choose EFT, you need to have a bank account in the correct currency.

  You enter payment information before you can publish a book, though you can change the information later.

Skim the explanatory text on the right side as you fill in details.

6. **After you enter all the details, click the yellow Save button at the bottom of the page.**

Congratulations — your KDP publisher account is set up. Now you can move on to adding and publishing your first e-book.

Filling In Your E-Book's Information Correctly

To add your first e-book to the Amazon site, follow these steps:

1. **Click the yellow Add New Title button on the KDP Bookshelf (refer to Figure 13-1).**

   You can add a new title before entering your account information (as described in the preceding section), but you can't publish your e-book and have it available on Amazon until your account information is complete.

When you start to add a new book, a prominent section above the Your Book form asks whether you want to enroll your e-book in the KDP Select program, which debuted in December 2011. The later sidebar "The advantages and disadvantages of using KDP Select" can help you decide whether KDP Select is for you.

The first part of the form for adding your book to Amazon — Your Book — is shown in Figure 13-3.

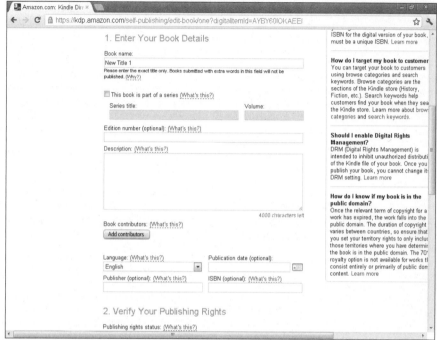

Figure 13-3:
The Your
Book form.

2. **Fill in these options in the Enter Your Book Details section:**

   - *Book Name:* Enter the title of your book, including a colon and the subtitle, if appropriate.

   - *This Book Is Part of a Series:* Select this check box, and add the series title and volume number if you're publishing a series of books. You can update this information later, if you create a sequel.

   - *Edition Number:* The first time you publish an e-book, you're publishing its first edition. You can leave this check box alone.

   - *Description:* The book description appears whenever readers view your e-book's page on Amazon, which is where they find information about your e-book (and purchase it, you hope). The description acts as the blurb, to promote your e-book to potential customers.

   When readers browse e-book titles on their Kindle devices, they see only the first few words of the description unless they click the Read More link. Try to make these first words compelling.

   You can't add formatting to the e-book description while entering it in the Description box. To use HTML code in the description — for bold or italic text, for example — register at Author Central and edit the description there. (For information about Author Central, see the section "Using Amazon's Author Central to Increase Sales," later in this chapter.)

- *Book Contributors:* When you click the Add Contributors button, the Add or Change Contributors dialog box opens, as shown in Figure 13-4. Enter your first name and surname (or your pen name), and select Author from the Title drop-down list.

  If you're publishing an e-book that several people have contributed to, you can list them all in this dialog box. For example, if you're working with a co-author, you can list two authors. If your anthology includes work from several authors and has been edited by a separate individual, you can list all the authors and the editor.

- *Language:* The default setting is English. If your book is written in a different language, select it from the drop-down list.

- *Publication Date:* You can choose only the current date or a day in the past; you can't upload your book to be published on a future date. If you don't select a date, Amazon specifies the date of publication.

- *Publisher:* Though a publisher name isn't required, consider using your own name or the name of your company, if it has one.

- *ISBN:* An International Standard Book Number, or ISBN, isn't required in order to publish an e-book, but if you want to use an ISBN, enter it in this text box. Don't use the ISBN from the print edition of your e-book — every edition must have a separate ISBN.

3. **In the Verify Your Publishing Rights section, indicate whether this e-book is in the public domain.**

   Unless you're publishing your work in the public domain (usually, books that are out of copyright), select the This Is Not a Public Domain Work radio button.

4. **In the Target Your Book to Customers section, fill in the following information:**

   - *Categories:* Click the Add Categories button and then choose a category or two for your e-book from the dialog box that opens, as shown in Figure 13-5. Then click Save.

     Note that you can click a plus-sign (+) icon to expand a category. Try to find the best possible fit — categorizing an e-book inappropriately only causes confusion and frustration for readers.

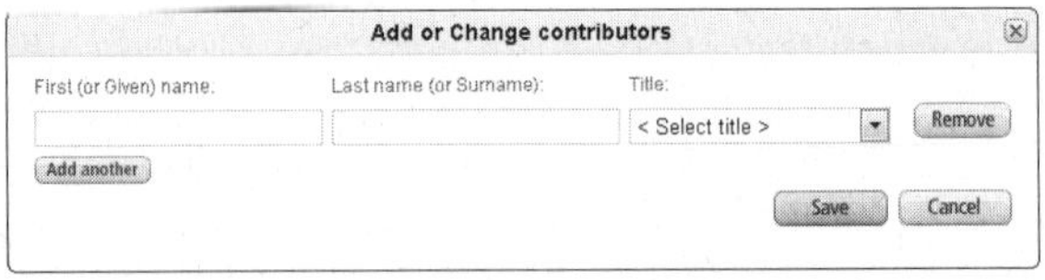

Figure 13-4: Adding your e-book's contributors.

Add or Change contributors

First (or Given) name:

Last name (or Surname):

Title:

< Select title > Remove

Add another

Save   Cancel

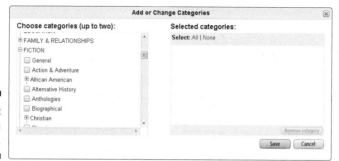

Figure 13-5:
Selecting a
category.

- *Search Keywords:* Choose words and phrases that are relevant to your e-book's content, and separate them with commas. Think about the terms that readers might search for when browsing titles on Amazon. For example, if you've written a romance novel set in Italy, your keywords might be words and phrases such as *Italy, romance,* and *vacation romance.*

   These words and phrases become *tags* (descriptive labels) for your e-book, and readers can add more tags. Examine similar books in your niche or genre to see what tags are being used.

5. **In the Upload Your Book Cover section, click the Browse for Image button, and select from your computer the image file that will become the cover of your e-book on Amazon.**

   (See Chapter 5 for more on creating an e-book cover.)

   The cover file must be in either JPEG/JPG or TIFF/TIF format. Amazon recommends that a cover image measure 2,500 pixels on its longest side, for maximum quality, with an ideal height:width ratio of 1:6. Amazon doesn't accept any cover image that isn't at least 1,000 pixels on its longest side.

6. **In the Upload Your Book File section, fill in the following information:**

   - *Select a Digital Rights Management (DRM) Option:* You can enable *digital rights management,* or *DRM,* which is a form of file protection intended to stop the unauthorized sharing of e-books. You decide whether to enable DRM. Some authors feel that DRM is an important protection, and others feel that it unnecessarily annoys readers.

   - *Book Content File:* Click the Browse for Book button. In the Open dialog box, navigate to your e-book's content file, and click Open. Finally, click the Upload Book button.

   Though you can upload a Word document or an EPUB file, a PDF file, or even a TXT file, for the best result, your e-book should be formatted in the HTM/HTML or MOBI file format. I prefer MOBI because you can easily preview the file on your own Kindle before uploading it.

If you're in a hurry and your e-book was created in Microsoft Word, you can save the file using the Web Page, Filtered format and then upload it to Amazon. If aspects of the text didn't convert correctly, follow the instructions in Chapter 8 to create a MOBI file with Calibre.

After you click Upload Book, the Preview Your Book section appears.

7. **In the Preview Your Book section, you can preview your book two ways:**

   • *Simpler Previewer:* Click the Preview Book button to see a preview of the e-book. The Amazon onscreen preview isn't perfect, so preview your e-book after uploading its content file. (The preview doesn't show margins, for example. Your text doesn't appear as close to the edges of the screen on an e-reader device.)

   In the example shown in Figure 13-6, notice that the *Chapter 1* text is in a header font and starts a new page. Check at least the first few pages of your e-book, and its last few pages, to ensure that all the text is formatted correctly. Look out for problems such as missing special characters (quotation marks and dashes, for example) and bold or italic text that doesn't end correctly.

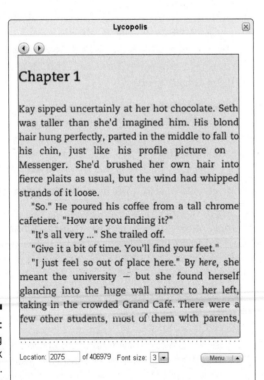

Figure 13-6: Previewing your e-book onscreen.

The advantages and disadvantages of using KDP Select

Authors using the Amazon Kindle Direct Publishing (KDP) Select program can make their e-books available for Amazon Prime members to borrow, for a minimum of 90 days, from the Kindle Owners' Lending Library. (The Amazon Prime membership program offers various perks, such as free shipping.) Because authors using KDP Select can also offer their e-books for free for 50 days, any Amazon user can obtain a free copy during that period.

KDP Select — which is the only way to list your e-book on Amazon for free — can be an excellent way to publicize your e-book. Under its lending scheme, you're paid, depending on how many copies of your e-book are borrowed, a share of the month's total amount available for KDP Select. Choosing to use the free days can result in attracting much more attention to your e-book than would otherwise be possible.

Using KDP Select has drawbacks, however — primarily that you must remove your e-book from sale on all other websites, including your own. You must make your e-book available exclusively from Amazon for the entire 90-day period. Also, because a high ranking on Amazon's list of free books no longer translates to a high ranking on its list of paid books, you may not see significantly increased sales after using KDP Select.

Self-publishing authors have mixed views of KDP Select. Some are enthusiastic advocates, and others believe that its benefits aren't significant enough to withdraw their e-books from sale elsewhere. If you want to give KDP Select a try, do so before *selling* your e-book via other websites.

- *Enhanced Previewer:* Download your e-book file (using the Enhanced Previewer option), even if you have used none of the Kindle Format 8 features. The file is downloaded in MOBI format. You can also download the Previewer software, though you may prefer to view the file on your Kindle device or Kindle app.

8. **When you're happy with the way your e-book looks, click Save and Continue at the bottom of the page.**

   The rights and pricing information page appears; see the next section for details on filling out this information.

Setting the Rights and Pricing of Your E-Book

The second page of the form for adding a book — Rights & Pricing — is where you set your Publishing Territories and your price. Follow these steps to fill in the information on this page:

1. **In the Verify Your Publishing Territories section, select the territories for which you hold rights.**

   Authors normally have worldwide rights to publish their e-books. If you've sold the rights to your material in one country, however, you need to select your rights by individual territories.

2. **In the Choose Your Royalty section, select the royalty option for your e-book.**

   Select the 70 percent option if your e-book is priced between $2.99 and $9.99. In the List Price section, the first row of the table represents Amazon.com, and you enter the price of your e-book (in dollars). You can either set the other prices individually or let Amazon set them based on the Amazon.com price.

   When you specify a price for your e-book, Amazon shows you the royalty amounts you'll receive, as listed in the rightmost column of Figure 13-7.

   You can read important information about pricing underneath the pricing table to see how Amazon sets its non-U.S. rates.

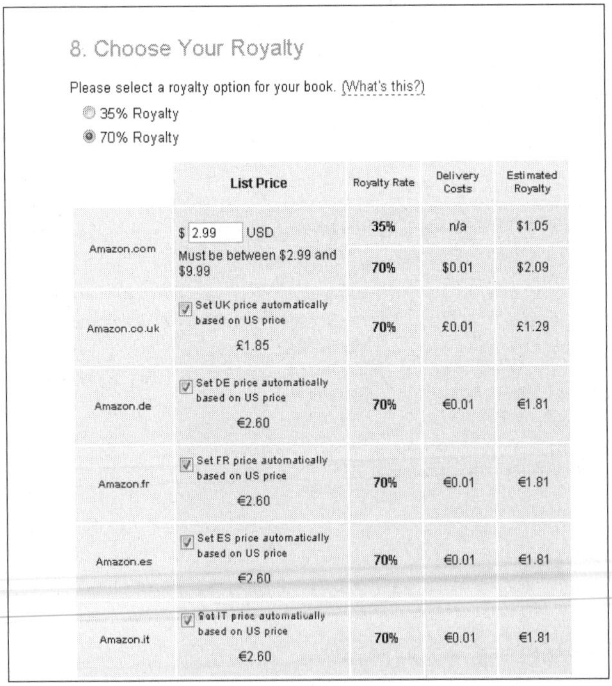

Figure 13-7: This pricing table shows the royalties offered by different Amazon stores.

8. Choose Your Royalty

Please select a royalty option for your book. (What's this?)
- ○ 35% Royalty
- ◉ 70% Royalty

	List Price	Royalty Rate	Delivery Costs	Estimated Royalty
Amazon.com	$ 2.99 USD Must be between $2.99 and $9.99	35% 70%	n/a $0.01	$1.05 $2.09
Amazon.co.uk	☑ Set UK price automatically based on US price £1.85	70%	£0.01	£1.29
Amazon.de	☑ Set DE price automatically based on US price €2.60	70%	€0.01	€1.81
Amazon.fr	☑ Set FR price automatically based on US price €2.60	70%	€0.01	€1.81
Amazon.es	☑ Set ES price automatically based on US price €2.60	70%	€0.01	€1.81
Amazon.it	☑ Set IT price automatically based on US price €2.60	70%	€0.01	€1.81

3. **In the Kindle Book Lending section, specify whether you want to allow lending in the Kindle Book Lending program.**

   This option, which is different from the KDP Select program, lets individual readers lend their e-book titles. A reader can loan your e-book to a friend for as long as two weeks. (Readers who enjoy a borrowed e-book may well buy their own copies — the more readers you can attract, the better.)

4. **After you fill in the form on this page and you're ready to publish, select the By Clicking Save and Publish Below check box, and then click Save and Publish.**

   If you want to publish later, you can select the Save for Later option instead.

Reviewing Your E-Book After Publication

When your e-book shows up live on your KDP Bookshelf (`https://kdp.amazon.com/self-publishing/dashboard`), it's available for purchase. You can check by searching Amazon.com for your e-book title. You should see your e-book in the search results. Though seeing your e-book on the virtual bookshelves can be thrilling, take the time to review it carefully before spreading the word to all your friends and family.

Checking your e-book sample for errors

After you publish your e-book, download the sample to ensure that all the text is correctly formatted. Assuming that you've checked the file for obvious errors (such as italicized text or an abnormally large font) during the publication process, you should see no nasty surprises. View the sample on your Kindle, if you have one. If you don't, you can use the free Kindle app on your computer, tablet, or phone.

If you find formatting errors, you can re-create the MOBI file and upload it again in the KDP dashboard. No one who has already purchased your e-book receives the new version automatically (though they can contact the Amazon Customer Service department to request it), so be sure that all the text in your e-book looks good *before* telling the world about it.

Reviewing your e-book's page

Open your e-book's page on Amazon. Examine these three areas of the page to ensure that all elements of your e-book display correctly:

- ✔ **Cover:** Examine the cover image on your e-book's page to ensure that it looks good. If the e-book title or your name is illegible, for example, you might need to create and upload a new version. If the image is missing, you may have forgotten to upload it when you published your e-book.

- ✔ **Book Description:** Review the description of your e-book carefully for typos and formatting errors. An element that looked fine in the KDP dashboard might not seem quite right now, especially if you copied the book description from a Word document. A blank line should appear between paragraphs, and you should see no odd characters and no remaining HTML code.

- ✔ **Product Details:** Check to ensure that the publisher's name and date of publication appear the way you intended.

To edit your e-book, click its title in your KDP Bookshelf. After you make changes, you can alter nothing else until those changes take effect — usually, in less than a day. The previous version of your e-book's page remains in the meantime.

Viewing your e-book's page in other Kindle Stores

If you want to view your e-book's page on other countries' versions of Amazon, simply follow these steps:

1. **Log in to your KDP account, and go to your Bookshelf.**

2. **Select the check box to the left of your e-book.**

3. **From the Actions drop-down list, select the store in which you want to view your e-book.**

   The store page automatically opens on a new tab.

In stores outside the United States, the price of your e-book may not be what you expect. In countries in the European Union, the 3 percent value added tax (VAT) is applied. If your British pound price is set to £2.99, for example, the price of your book at www.amazon.co.uk is £3.08. If necessary, adjust your prices slightly to allow for this system.

Viewing your e-book's page from a Kindle

After you view your e-book's page on your computer, try to see also how it appears on a Kindle. Many readers will want to sample it or buy it using their Kindle devices rather than the Amazon website on their computers.

Grab your Kindle (or borrow one from a friend), and choose the Menu➪Shop in Kindle Store menu command. Search for your e-book, and click its title to open your e-book's page on the Kindle.

On a standard-size Kindle, only the first few words of the book description appear, accompanied by the Read More link. You should tweak this text to make it as compelling as possible, or else readers may not bother to click the link.

If your e-book's cover is heavy on color, it may display well in black-and-white. The text may be almost invisible. If that's the case, consider making changes — although some readers will use the Kindle Fire (a color tablet), many others will see only the black-and-white version of the cover.

Using Amazon's Author Central to Increase Sales

Readers who are interested in buying your e-book might look to see what else you've published or to find out more about you. By creating an author page through Author Central, you can reserve a tiny corner of Amazon where you can add everything from a biography to videos. This page can help cement readers' interest by encouraging them to buy your e-book. If you have several books for sale, the author page can help readers find them too.

You can use Author Central to add extra information to your e-book's page on Amazon (the page that readers visit to find out about, and buy, your e-book). Using Author Central, you can (for example) add extra formatting to your e-book's blurb.

Signing up for Author Central

You need to have at least one e-book (or print book) published on Amazon in order to join Author Central. After your e-book is available, follow these steps:

1. **Go to** `https://authorcentral.amazon.com`.

2. **Click the Join Now button on the right side of the page.**

3. **Sign in with your Amazon account.**

4. **Read and accept the terms and conditions, and then click Accept.**

   Amazon automatically searches for books listing you as the author.

5. **Click the Yes, This Is Me link for every book that belongs to you; click No, I Am Someone Else for every book that isn't yours.**

   You can add other books to your profile later.

   Selecting a book creates your Author Central account, and Amazon sends you a confirmation e-mail labeled *Author Central Registration Confirmation.*

6. **Click the link in the e-mail message to activate your account.**

You may not see your author page appear on the Amazon site for as long as a week, while your identity is verified, but you can fill out your profile in the meantime, as described in the next section. (The verification process prevents authors from claiming another person's book as their own.)

Filling out your Author Central profile

After you set up an Author Central account, click the Profile tab to see a Profile page similar to the one shown in Figure 13-8. Click the Add link in a section to add related information. When you click the link, you see instructions in a pop-up window and a box for entering the appropriate information.

The sections in the Author Central profile are described in this list:

- ✔ **Biography:** Enter your biographical details in plain text — no bold, italics, or HTML code. Your bio appears on your author page, which you can visit using the link near the top of the screen, next to the Author Pages icon. (For me, that link is Visit Amazon's Ali Luke page. Your link will obviously be slightly different, as it will include your own name.)

  Any relevant qualifications are useful in your biography, as are your years of experience in a particular job, and you may want to share a little of your personal life, such as your spouse, kids, or pets. Biographies are commonly written in the third person, such as "Ali Luke lives in the UK" instead of "I live in the UK."

  Write at least 100 characters, or about 20 words. If you're writing more than a few sentences, remember to press the Enter key to create paragraphs.

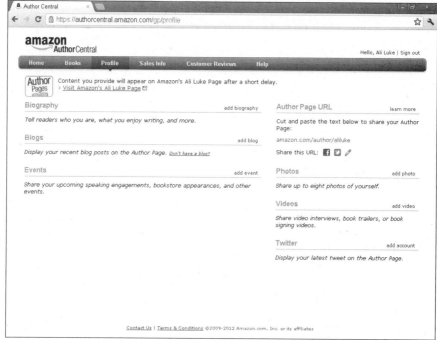

✔ **Blogs:** If you have a blog, you can automatically publish your blog posts on your Amazon page. You need to add the URL of your RSS feed. For a WordPress.com blog, it's usually your blog's URL with */feed* at the end. Mine, for example, is `http://aliluke.wordpress.com/feed`.

✔ **Events:** If you're attending a book launch or book signing, or if you're speaking at a conference, you can add this information to your author page. Though the fields are self-explanatory, you need to select a book from the Book drop-down list (even if you have only one).

✔ **Author Page URL:** By default, the URL of your author page looks like this: `www.amazon.com/-/e/B006RIWB5G`, which doesn't look good on business cards (and is a nightmare to relay by phone). To spruce up the custom author page URL, you can create a customized (and more attractive) author page URL, such as `www.amazon.com/aliluke`.

✔ **Photos:** The photos you add to your author page must be in JPG format and must meet the Amazon requirements (which are shown when you click the Add Photo link). You can use photos of yourself or photos that in some way represent you as an author. (For example, you might have a photo that relates to the topic of your books.) You *must* have permission to use the photo if someone else took it or if it includes other people.

✔ **Videos:** You can add videos in most major formats, though they can be no longer than ten minutes and no larger than 500MB. You might like to make a video specifically for your author page, to talk about your e-book, read from it, or even create a screencast or instruction video if it's nonfiction.

✔ **Twitter:** If you have a Twitter account, you can display your tweets on your Amazon page. It can be a good way to encourage readers to find you on Twitter, but if you use your Twitter account mainly for personal chat, or if you rarely tweet about topics that relate to your e-book, you may prefer not to add it to your Amazon page.

You can edit your Amazon profile at any point if you decide to add, change, or remove information. Changes may take 30 minutes or so to appear live on your Amazon page.

When you edit your profile, you may want to edit the information that Amazon lists for your book, to have a way to include formatting in the book description. (When you set up an e-book on Kindle Direct Publishing, you can use only plain text in the book description.) To edit your e-book's description, follow these steps:

1. **Click the Books tab and then the title of your book.**

   Figure 13-9 shows an e-book with its KDP description, ready for editing.

2. **Click the Editorial Reviews tab below the image of your e-book, and click the Edit button in the Product Description section.**

3. **Add bold or italics or whatever other type of formatting you want to help enhance your book's description.**

4. **Click Preview to see how the new book description will look and then click Save Changes if you like it, or click Go Back to make alterations.**

You can also use this page to include sections such as About the Author, to give readers more details about you and your qualifications for this particular book. If your e-book has been reviewed by newspapers, magazines, journals, or blogs, for example, you can copy these reviews into the Editorial Reviews section.

If you have multiple versions of your book (perhaps a paperback and hardback as well as your e-book), edit the product description for each one separately. Editing a single description has no effect on the pages for other versions of your e-book. You can switch between versions by clicking the Editions links on the right side of your book's page within Author Central.

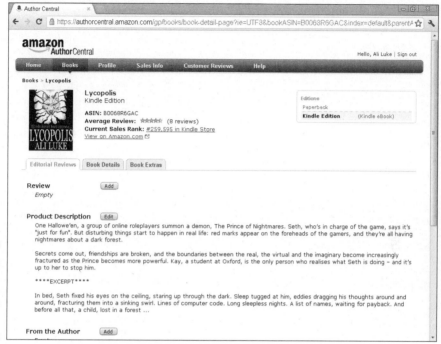

Figure 13-9:
Editing a
book in
Author
Central.

Chapter 14

Using Smashwords to Distribute Your E-Book to Other Retailers

Although Amazon has a straightforward, author-friendly system for adding your e-book to its site, other online stores aren't as obliging — Barnes & Noble, Kobo, Sony, and Apple all have different requirements. (After attempting to wade Although all the different documentation, I needed a restorative cup of tea.)

Thankfully, you can easily distribute your e-book to multiple stores by using Smashwords. Though Smashwords doesn't yet have an arrangement to distribute to Amazon, the site has agreements with most other major online bookstores. It also sorts out the conversion of your Word document into EPUB and MOBI files (and other versions) for you.

This chapter leads you through the Smashwords process, from creating your account to distributing your e-book to various stores.

Getting an ISBN for Your E-Book

Consider obtaining an International Standard Book Number, or ISBN, for your e-book. Every edition of a print book has one of these unique identifying numbers. (For example, a hardback title has one ISBN, and its paperback version has another.) As a self-publishing author, you can either buy your own ISBN, by registering as a publisher with your country's ISBN agency, or use a free

ISBN provided by Smashwords. If you prefer to buy your own ISBN, remember to allow time for it to be issued. (Ask your country's issuing agency for a delivery estimate.)

You can add an ISBN after publishing your e-book on Smashwords (as described later in this chapter), so you don't need to decide now. After you've assigned an ISBN to an e-book, you can never transfer it to another book. Neither can you change it after Smashwords has sent it to retailers.

Purchasing your own ISBN

An ISBN for your e-book isn't a necessity, though some sites (including Apple, Kobo, and Sony) don't accept e-books without ISBNs.

If you're planning to publish multiple e-books, you may want to register as a publisher and purchase your own set of ISBNs. (Purchasing ten ISBNs is usually more economical than purchasing only one, and some countries require you to purchase at least ten.) ISBN pricing varies among countries, but it is always cheaper per ISBN to make a bulk purchase of 10, or even 100, ISBNs.

In the United States, you can purchase ISBNs from R.R. Bowker at

    www.myidentifiers.com

In the United Kingdom, you can purchase ISBNs from Nielsen:

    www.isbn.nielsenbook.co.uk

In Australia, you can purchase ISBNs from Thorpe-Bowker:

    https://compay.com.au/ThorpeBowker/ISBN/Default.aspx

Your allocation of ISBNs normally arrives in a couple of weeks, though you can pay extra for expedited service.

Opting to use a Smashwords ISBN

If you don't want to pay for an ISBN, you can get one from Smashwords for free. To get this seemingly fantastic deal, however, Smashwords — not you — is shown as the publisher of your e-book. As Smashwords notes, though, this arrangement doesn't make the site your legal publisher in any way. Alternatively, you can pay $9.95 for a premium ISBN from Smashwords, which will list you as the publisher and list Smashwords as the distributor in Bowker's Books in Print database. This distinction generally isn't reflected in online stores, though, which will show Smashwords as the publisher. You can't get a premium ISBN if you live outside the United States, but you can get the free one.

Creating Your Smashwords Account

Before you can add your e-book to Smashwords, you have to open an account. To create yours, follow these steps:

1. **Go to** www.smashwords.com/signup.

   You should see the Smashwords sign-up form, shown in Figure 14-1.

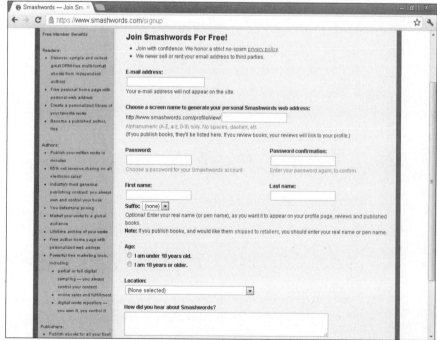

Figure 14-1:
The Smashwords sign-up form.

2. **Fill in these areas of the form:**

   - *E-Mail Address:* Enter an address that you have access to. Double-check to ensure that you've typed it correctly —Smashwords sends an e-mail to this address so that you can activate your account.

   - *Choose a Screen Name:* Supply your real name, your pen name, or your publisher name.

   - *Password and Password Confirmation*: Choose a strong password that someone can't easily guess.

   - *First Name, Last Name:* The names you enter for these options appear on your profile page and the individual pages for your e-book(s) on the Smashwords site. You can use a pen name, if you want.

   - *Age:* Select the correct radio button for your age.

   - *Location:* Select your country from the drop-down list.

   - (Optional) Mention how you heard about Smashwords.

3. **After the form is complete, click the Sign Up! button.**

   You see a page labeled Important Final Registration Step with instructions for confirming your account. (You also receive an e-mail with a link to click.) If you've typed your e-mail address incorrectly, contact Smashwords to ask them to change it.

4. **Follow the instructions in the e-mail to confirm your account.**

5. **Log in to Smashwords by going to** www.smashwords.com **and entering your e-mail address and password.**

Adding Your E-Book to Smashwords

Before you publish your e-book at Smashwords, you'll likely need to make changes to your Word manuscript. Smashwords works by running your manuscript through its proprietary (and unpleasant-sounding) Meatgrinder feature. It creates published versions of your e-book in multiple formats, to give readers as much choice as possible — without creating extra work for you.

The following sections explain how to fine-tune your manuscript formatting and then upload the final version to Smashwords.

Following the Smashwords guidelines

You can download the Smashwords Style Guide for free at www.smashwords. com/books/view/52.

The Smashwords Style Guide has quite a bit of information to review, but Mark Coker, the founder of Smashwords, wrote the guide in a beginner-friendly way — you definitely don't need to be a technical expert to use it. Read the guide before starting to format your e-book.

If you follow the instructions in Chapter 4 for formatting a Word manuscript, you shouldn't have much work to do. Follow this crucial advice:

- ✔ **The manuscript must contain no more than four consecutive line breaks anywhere.** If you insert lots of line breaks in the front matter of your e-book or between sections or to end chapters, for example, you have to take them out.

- ✔ **Your e-book must have a copyright page.** It likely already has one, but at Smashwords, the page must include *Smashwords edition* (or similar) wording.

- ✔ **Do not use fonts larger than 18 points.** Don't even use them on the cover page or in the front matter.

The simpler the formatting of your manuscript, the more likely Smashwords is to accept it — and the more likely it is to reproduce well in various forms.

If you have trouble formatting your manuscript correctly, you can pay someone to do it for you, starting around $35. Smashwords will supply a list of people to contact for this task — e-mail list@smashwords.com to receive an instant, automated response.

Creating or amending your copyright page

Although most manuscript errors don't completely prevent the publication of your e-book by Smashwords, a copyright page that's missing or incorrect does. The copyright page in your e-book must include these elements:

✔ The title of the e-book

✔ Your name

✔ The word *Copyright* followed by your name and the year of publication

✔ The phrase *Smashwords Edition* or *Published at Smashwords* (or, if you prefer, *Published by XYZ Publishing at Smashwords*)

Of course, you can also include other details on the copyright page, this list shows only the minimum required elements. You can view examples of acceptable copyright pages at www.smashwords.com/about/supportfaq#copyright.

After your e-book manuscript is ready, you can add it to Smashwords, as described in the next section, "Filling out the details of your e-book and uploading your manuscript."

Don't worry if your manuscript isn't in perfect condition. Smashwords displays AutoVettor errors if it discovers potential formatting problems. Immediately after uploading your file, you see a message about these errors and a link to review recommended modifications. You can view recommended modifications from the dashboard. (Click the Dashboard tab at the top of any Smashwords page.) The Premium Status column displays the words *Needs Modification* and provides a Details link for you to view recommended changes.

Filling out the details of your e-book and uploading your manuscript

To add your e-book's details and upload your manuscript to Smashwords, follow these steps:

1. **Log in to Smashwords, and click the Publish tab.**

   You should see the publishing form, shown in Figure 14-2.

2. **Complete these areas on the form:**

   • *Title:* Supply the full title (and subtitle, if you want) of your e-book.

   • *Short Description:* Add as many as 400 characters (about 80 words) to describe your e-book briefly. Readers see this description while browsing Smashwords and viewing your e-book or a list of search results. Some retailers also use it.

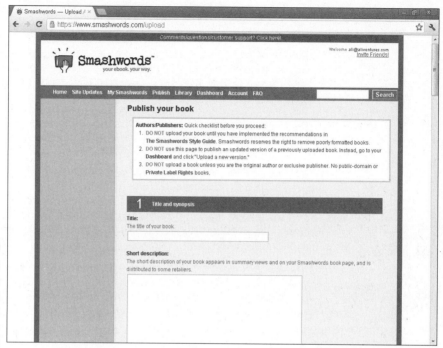

- *Long Description:* Write as many as 4,000 characters (about 800 words) to add detail about your e-book. This description appears on your e-book's page at Amazon, and most retailers use it, too.

- *Language of Book:* Select from the drop-down list the main language that your e-book is written in.

- *Adult Content:* If your e-book is unsuitable for readers under 18, select My Book Contains Adult Content.

- *Price:* You have three options: Offer your e-book for free, let readers choose how much to pay for it, or charge a specific amount. If your e-book is available on Amazon, you must charge at least as much as its price at Amazon. If you don't, Amazon discounts your e-book.

- *Sampling:* Make at least 15 percent of your e-book available for free so that readers have a chance to get hooked. A free sample is also required for some mobile app catalogs. If you prefer not to make a portion of your e-book available, deselect the Enable Sampling check box.

- *Primary Category:* Start by selecting a broad area that fits your e-book, such as fiction or nonfiction. A second box appears, with a list of sub-categories — select the best fit. In many cases, a third box appears, and you select another subcategory. Categorizing is necessary because it helps readers find your e-book. Avoid choosing an ill-fitting category simply because you believe that it might be popular — you'll run the risk of having to endure negative reviews from disappointed readers who expected something different from your e-book.

- *Secondary Category:* If you want, you can give your e-book a second category. Again, make sure it's relevant.

- *Tags:* Tags help readers find your e-book by topic, theme, or type. For example, if you're written a collection of humorous short stories about cats, you might choose the tags *cats, kittens, humor,* and *short stories.* After you start typing tags, Smashwords automatically offers a list of suggestions based on tags that other authors and readers have used.

- *E-Book Formats:* By default, all formats are made available. If your e-book has lots of images, disable the Plain Text option. You should have no reason to disable any other formats — the more you allow, the more readers you can cater to.

- *Cover Image:* Click Choose File and select a cover image. Your e-book can't appear in the Premium Catalog (for distribution to e-book retailers) if it has no cover image. The cover file can be in GIF, JPG, or PNG format.

- *Select File of Book to Publish:* Click Choose File, and select the `.doc` file that contains the Smashwords version of your manuscript. Note that the file *must* be a `.doc` file — you can't upload a `.txt` (plain text) or `.rtf` (rich text) file here. If you don't own Microsoft Office, you can download the free Open Office word processor and create the file in that program.

3. **Read the publishing agreement and then click Publish to start the publishing process.**

   You should see the screen shown in Figure 14-3 — the number of books in the queue in front of yours depends on the time and day.

An e-book normally takes just a few minutes to be published; the site e-mails you when the e-book is ready. The e-mail also notifies you about any potential problems that the AutoVetter has found in your manuscript.

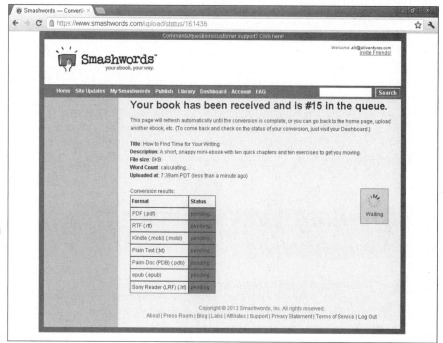

Figure 14-3:
An e-book being processed by Smashwords.

Previewing your EPUB file

After your e-book is published, you should ensure that the major formats are displayed correctly. Smashwords lets you download all versions of your own e-book for free by following these steps:

1. **Click the Dashboard tab near the top of the page.**

   Your dashboard opens.

2. **Click the title of your e-book to see its page on the Smashwords site.**

3. **Scroll down to the Available E-Book Reading Formats option to download your book.**

The EPUB version of your e-book is the one that will be distributed to major retailers, so download it and view it in an e-reading app on your computer or on your e-reader (unless you have a Kindle, which doesn't read EPUB files). You can use Calibre to view EPUB files and for file conversion (See Chapter 8 for more information about Calibre.) If you have an iPad, you can use the iBooks app to view EPUB files.

If you notice any glaring errors (such as incorrect characters, a lack of paragraph indents or spacing, or sudden font changes), return to the original manuscript to correct the problem. You can upload the manuscript again from the dashboard by clicking the Upload New Version link in the Operations section.

Distributing Your E-Book via Smashwords

You may choose to simply have your e-book for sale on the Smashwords site. However, in most cases, you can take advantage of Smashwords' links with big-name online stores. By adding your book to the Smashwords premium catalog, you can reach a wider audience.

Joining the Smashwords premium catalog

After your book is published on Smashwords, it's available via Smashwords itself. Although some readers like to buy e-books from Smashwords (for its multiple e-book formats), others prefer to use a retailer's site, especially if they have that retailer's e-reader device.

To distribute your e-book to major retailers (including Apple, Barnes & Noble, Kobo, and Sony), go to your dashboard. The rightmost column, labeled Premium Status, should show you a link to enroll your e-book in the premium catalog.

If the status is Needs Modification, you should see a note indicating why your e-book can't yet be added to the premium catalog (such as *needs cover image*) or a link you can click to open a page with more details. Read the Current Status section carefully to find out what changes you need to make.

Opting in and out of different channels

Smashwords now distributes to Sony, Barnes & Noble, Kobo, Apple, and Diesel. It's also seeking to arrange distribution to Amazon and Baker-Taylor. By default, when you submit your e-book to the premium catalog, it's listed for distribution to all these stores. (It will be sent to Amazon and Baker-Taylor only if Smashwords finalizes an agreement with these stores in the future.)

You can omit some of these stores, described as *channels*, from your distribution list by logging in to Smashwords and following these steps:

1. **Click the Dashboard tab at the top of the page.**

2. **Click the Channel Manager link on the left side.**

   This step should open a page of information. Scroll to the bottom of this page to see the channel manager, as shown in Figure 14-4.

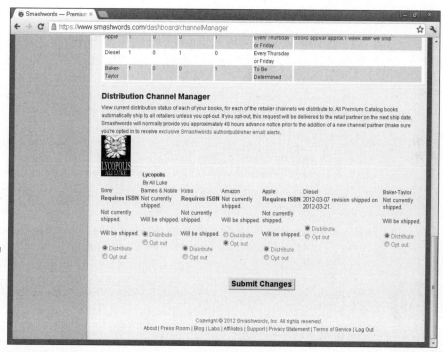

Figure 14-4:
The Smashwords channel manager.

3. **Omit a channel by selecting the appropriate option button.**

Unless your book is already in one of the stores via a separate arrangement, you probably shouldn't omit any channels. I choose to opt out of the Amazon channel because I already publish my e-books there directly — and I don't want to create confusion if Smashwords suddenly starts distributing to Amazon.

4. **Click Submit Changes to save your selection.**

Assigning an ISBN after publication

Opting in to distribute to a particular store doesn't necessarily mean that your e-book is being distributed to that store. If your e-book doesn't have an ISBN, Apple, Kobo, and Sony won't accept it into their stores.

To add an ISBN after publication, log in to Smashwords, and follow these steps:

1. **Click the Dashboard tab at the top of the page.**

2. **Click the ISBN Manager link in the left column.**

3. **Scroll down to the bottom of the page, and click the Assign an ISBN link for your book.**

   You should see the ISBN assignment form, shown in Figure 14-5, with three options to choose among.

4. **Select one of these options:**

   - *I Already Have a New, Unused ISBN:* Enter the ISBN itself and then enter your publisher contact details at the bottom of the page.

   - *Free ISBN:* Click Review Order at the bottom of the page without filling in further details.

   - *Premium ISBN*: This option (which costs $9.95) is available only for e-books that have been accepted into the Smashwords premium catalog.

   Use either your own ISBN or the free Smashwords ISBN. (You gain no particular advantage by using the premium ISBN, and you can do so only if you live in the United States.)

5. **Click Review Order.**

   After you've assigned an ISBN to your e-book, it make take a couple of weeks for your e-book to appear in the Apple, Kobo, and Sony stores.

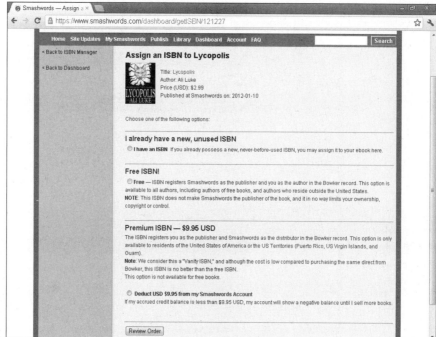

Figure 14-5:
Assigning
an ISBN.

Getting Paid by Smashwords

You don't need to enter your payment information in order to publish books on Smashwords — but unless you're giving away your e-book, add it as soon as you start making sales.

Follow these steps to add your payment information:

1. **Click the Account tab at the top of the page.**

2. **Click the Edit/Update Payee Information link.**

   You see a page of information, including the payee form, shown in Figure 14-6.

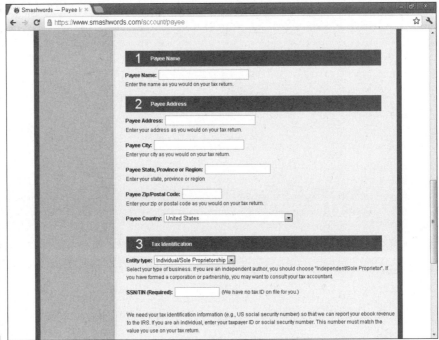

Figure 14-6:
The Smashwords payee form.

3. **Read the information carefully and then fill in these options on the form:**

   • *Payee Name:* Supply your legal name, as it appears on your tax return.

   • *Payee Address:* Add your address, as it appears on your tax return.

   • *Tax Identification:* Select your business type. It's probably the default Individual/Sole Proprietorship, unless you have set up a company for your publishing activities.

   Enter your Social Security Number (SSN) or Taxpayer Identification Number (TIN). If you have no SNN or TIN in the United States, you must obtain an ITIN (Individual Taxpayer Identification Number) and send Smashwords a completed W8-BEN form. Read the notes at the top of the page for assistance.

   • *Payment Method:* You can choose to be paid only by check or PayPal. Unlike Amazon, Smashwords doesn't offer an electronic funds transfer to your bank account.

   PayPal charges you a small fee for receiving payments.

4. **When you finish entering your information, click Save Payee Settings at the bottom of the page.**

Part V
Marketing Your E-Book

In this part . . .

After you publish your e-book, you need readers. You may not be aiming for the bestseller charts — many niche e-books earn extremely high profits with sales of only a few hundred copies. But whatever sort of book you write, you need to do some marketing.

Part V covers optimizing your book's page on Amazon to encourage sales (see Chapter 15), engaging with readers using the popular social media sites Facebook and Twitter (see Chapter 16), and promoting your e-book using Goodreads, the social networking site for readers (see Chapter 17). In these chapters, I list specific tips to help you use these social sites effectively and avoid common pitfalls. In Chapter 18, you find out how to build an audience and promote your e-book effectively using a blog or an e-mail list.

Chapter 15

Marketing Your E-Book via Amazon and Other Online Stores

Many authors, after writing e-books and successfully publishing them online, believe that the hard work is done. They may even crack open the champagne, sit back, and wait for their e-books to rocket up the best-seller charts.

Sadly, these authors are doomed to disappointment. Millions of e-books are available from big-name stores, such as Amazon, and thousands more arrive every day. A brand-new e-book, with a basic description and no reviews, is unlikely to attract much attention.

This chapter sets you up for marketing success by showing you how to optimize your e-book's page at Amazon.com. Readers use this page to find out about your e-book before buying it — you can see an excellent example at www.amazon.com/Pentecost-An-ARKANE-Thriller-ebook/dp/ B004JHYA6A. (Though similar tips apply to other stores, I use Amazon as an example because it has, by far, the largest share of the market.) This chapter describes how to craft your e-book's blurb, collect reviews, categorize your e-book correctly, model the success of other authors in your genre or niche, and use price pulsing to boost the sales of your e-book.

Even if your e-book is available only from your website (and not from established e-stores), glance through this chapter. You may find new tips to try, particularly for writing, or rewriting, the blurb.

Crafting a Compelling Blurb That Helps Sell Your E-Book

The blurb is a vital marketing tool. Amazon calls it the *product description,* but you can consider the *blurb* to be the enticing text you find on the back of a paperback or on the dust jacket of a hardback.

Most authors find blurb writing incredibly difficult, so give yourself plenty of time to craft and edit the blurb. (Mine required a fair bit of pencil chewing and tea drinking, along with lots of crossing out and starting again.) If you typed a few hasty sentences while listing your e-book on Amazon, you definitely need to revisit that description.

Study the blurbs of bestselling books in your genre or category. For example, if you've written a nonfiction book about running a restaurant, head to the category Hospitality, Travel & Tourism (under Business & Investing and then Industries & Professions). Or, if you've written a love story about vampires, take a look at the Fantasy, Futuristic & Ghost category in the Romance section.

Print several blurbs from other authors' e-books (or copy them to your computer). Review the blurbs, and note which ones make you want to read their books. Underline sentences or phrases that seem especially effective, and see whether you can use similar wording for your e-book.

For a fiction e-book, the blurb should

- ✔ **Briefly introduce the main characters:** A newspaper report might describe a character as "19-year-old intern Rachel Harris."

- ✔ **Describe the key conflict or problem:** An example is "John Thomas, a professor at Harvard, is wanted by the police."

- ✔ **Give the reader a sense of the style and tone of the e-book:** You might describe a "fast-paced" or "lyrical" or "warm and heartfelt" story.

The blurb you write should *not*

- ✔ **Contain spoilers:** If Chapter 10 reveals that John Thomas murdered a student, don't spill the news in the blurb. You can hint at mystery, though: "John can no longer run from the secret that he's been hiding for ten years."

- ✔ **Include every member of the cast:** Even if your story has several key characters, you may be able to identify only one or two by name. Use phrases such as *her three best friends* or *a group of bikers* or *four cousins* to hint at additional characters without wasting words naming them.

If you're writing nonfiction, your blurb should

- ✔ **Clearly introduce the topic of your e-book:** Though this advice might sound obvious, authors sometimes have difficulty taking a step back to explain their key message or theme in a few words. Ask a few friends or fellow writers to review the blurb to ensure that it's clear.

- ✔ **Include the reader:** Use the word *you* to make a connection, as in the phrases *You'll learn how to* or *You'll find out.* Make a clear promise to readers: Let them know what they'll be able to understand or do, or how they might feel, after reading your e-book.

- ✔ **Apply formatting (perhaps via Amazon's Author Central) to help readers easily absorb the most important points.** For example, add boldface to key sentences or selling points.

Your blurb should *not*

- ✔ **Be too short:** A short blurb about a work of fiction can be quite effective. For nonfiction, which tends to cost more than fiction, readers may want to see the full details before sampling or buying your e-book. If the first few sentences sum up the book, the remainder of the blurb can serve as a sales page.

- ✔ **Make false claims or give readers undue expectations:** Be upbeat and enthusiastic about your e-book, but don't try to represent it as something it isn't. Although you may make some initial sales, they'll be followed by poor reviews (from readers who will be unlikely to buy from you again).

If you belong to a writers' workshop or a group of writing-oriented friends online, ask them to review your blurb. Persuade them to point out confusing text and suggest clarifications. Enduring round after round of edits on your blurb may seem frustrating, but the stronger it is, the more books you'll sell.

Letting Great Reviews Encourage New Readers to Buy

Before you start to promote your e-book widely — and certainly before you consider paying for advertisement space — you need to gather at least a few online reviews.

When readers looking for a book on Amazon go to investigate it in more detail, they see only three pieces of information about the book: the cover image, the title, and the star ranking. (The number of reviews is listed in parentheses.) You can see for yourself by browsing any category on Amazon or by using the Search box to find books on a particular topic.

If your e-book has no reviews and thus no star rating, many readers may simply ignore it. Even if your book has garnered a review or two, most readers will prefer an e-book with at least a dozen or so reviews.

A curious reader who selects your e-book's title sees reviews displayed prominently, including a breakdown of the number of reviews and their star ratings. In Figure 15-1, you can see reviews of my novel, *Lycopolis*. Note how much space Amazon allows for these elements. (The blurb, in contrast, appears farther up the page but is truncated until the reader clicks the Show More link.)

How can you attract those crucial first few online reviews? Sometimes, a casual reader enjoys your e-book enough to take the time to leave a review — but there's no guarantee that this will happen, especially when you've just launched your e-book and its sales figures are low. This section discusses how to strategically seek out reviews.

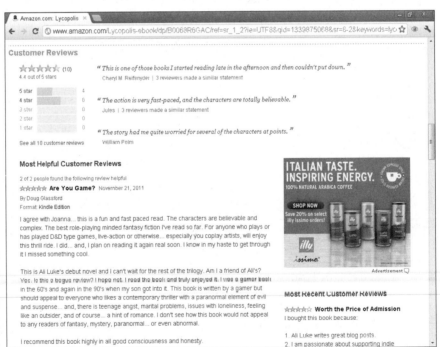

Figure 15-1:
Customer reviews on Amazon.com.

Finding readers to review your e-book

To start the ball rolling on gathering reviews, follow these suggestions for finding readers:

- ✔ **If you've asked beta-readers to review drafts of your e-book, let them know that you'd appreciate a few minutes of their time to post a review on Amazon (or, if you prefer, on another online store's website).** Giving these folks copies of your finished e-book isn't simply a goodwill gesture — it lets them base their reviews on the finished product rather than on the earlier work-in-progress.

- ✔ **If you belong to an online forum related to the topic of your e-book, offer review copies of your e-book there, too.** If you do this with your mailing list or blog, avoid giving away too many copies to your core fan base — and negatively affecting sales.

- ✔ **Ask family members or friends who might be interested in your e-book to review it.** Be careful, though: Readers are skeptical of glowing, 5-star reviews that appear to be written by people associated with the author.

Whenever you approach people to post reviews of your book online, simplify the process by supplying this vital information:

- ✔ **The blurb:** It helps them decide whether to review your e-book.

- ✔ **Your author bio:** Provide this information if it's appropriate to do so.

- ✔ **Available formats:** It can be MOBI (Kindle-compatible), EPUB (most other e-readers), or PDF (mainly for computers but also viewable on e-reading devices).

Send reviewers your e-book in the correct format, and supply the URL of the site where you want their reviews posted, such as your e-book's page at Amazon or another store.

Anyone who wants to post a review on Amazon.com is required to have already bought at least one product (not necessarily yours) from the site.

Many book bloggers, who copy all or part of the reviews from their own blogs to Amazon and other book sites, have long waiting lists for reviews, so don't rely on them for immediate help. (Chapter 18 offers guidance on approaching book bloggers to review your e-book.)

Don't be disappointed if a friend or contact awards your e-book 4 stars instead of 5, because ratings are subjective and some writers feel that only truly outstanding books are worthy of 5 stars. In fact, a mix of reviews can work in your favor: A mix of two 4-star reviews and two 5-star reviews looks more authentic than four 5-star reviews. (Reviews of your e-book at Amazon.com will likely be a mix of 3, 4, and 5 stars.)

Dealing with negative reviews

At some point, every book receives negative reviews, because you simply can't please all the people all the time. Don't ignore negative reviews — sometimes, the feedback they contain can be genuinely valuable. If a negative review is valid (it points out that your e-book is riddled with typos or factual errors, for example), you might produce a revised edition, as explained in Chapter 21. If the review is related to the price (for example, the content was good, but $9.99 is too much to pay), consider lowering the cost. For more on pricing, see Chapter 11.

Though authors sometimes reply to negative reviews with explanations of why the reviewers are wrong, you should avoid engaging directly with people who have posted negative reviews. You're highly unlikely to change anyone's mind — and starting a heated argument in the Customer Reviews section of your e-book's Amazon page makes you look bad.

If a negative review seems truly unwarranted (for example, if the reviewer clearly hasn't even read your e-book), you can contact Amazon and ask them to remove it. Sadly, some unscrupulous authors rate competing titles negatively and occasionally even explicitly recommend their own e-books instead. If your e-book receives a suspicious-looking review, see whether you can spot a pattern in other, unrelated reviews written by the same person.

Categorizing Your E-Book Correctly at Amazon.com

Readers use the Amazon.com site (www.amazon.com) in different ways: Some people simply search for book titles that are familiar to them; others want bestsellers. Many shrewd readers, though, head straight to their favorite virtual shelf — the category that represents a favorite genre or niche.

When you categorize your e-book, focus on its visibility. Because certain categories are more popular and contain more e-books, your e-book may not rank highly (though a wider pool of readers browses these categories). In less popular categories, your e-book can more easily reach the top ten, which increases sales (and gives you a claim to fame).

Ideally, you'll choose a larger category and a smaller, more specialized category. Don't choose them over a sensible, well-targeted category, though. If your thriller is an action-packed, plot-driven story, the psychological-thriller category isn't a good fit. Figure 15-2 shows how the number of e-books within a category can vary widely, even within a single grouping, such as *thriller*.

Though you can list your e-book in only two categories via Kindle Direct Publishing (KDP), you can add categories by using tags. A *tag* serves as a label for your e-book that can relate to the content (vampires or online marketing, for example), the style (first-person or fast-paced), or any other aspect of the text. You can tag your e-book yourself via KDP, but readers can also tag e-books. If enough readers tag your e-book with a particular key word, you may find that your book is placed in a third, or even fourth, category, giving you greater visibility on Amazon. (For more on KDP, check out Chapter 13.)

Figure 15-2:
Thriller sub-
categories
on Amazon.

Modeling the Success of Other Authors in Your Genre or Niche

The e-book world is still in its infancy, with e-books only starting to achieve mass popularity in 2007 with the release of the Amazon Kindle e-reader. Now is an exciting time for independent authors — but figuring out what works and what doesn't can be difficult, especially in marketing an e-book. By learning from successful authors in your genre or niche, you can improve your chance of success.

Look at the top five or ten books in your categories, and study their pages on Amazon.com and their authors' pages at Author Central (if applicable). See whether your e-book is missing any elements or whether you can do something more effectively. For example, you might find that other e-books' Amazon pages include an About the Author section with a couple of lines of biographical information. You can add this information by way of your Author Central account. (See Chapter 13 for more details on Author Central.)

Do what you can to find out how certain authors have marketed their e-books outside Amazon, too. Search for the author's name and the e-book title at Google to see what results are returned. For example, you might find that a popular author has a lot of reviews on book bloggers' sites or has a website of her own that seems to have a large audience.

Find out whether any best-selling e-book authors in your genre have written blog posts about their experiences. Or look for them on social networking sites. Though many of these authors are extremely busy, they might be willing to answer a quick question or two via Facebook or Twitter.

Using Price Pulsing to Boost Sales

Price pulsing your e-book changes its price in order to elevate your work on the sales chart. The regular price of your e-book might be $3.99, but you can drop the price to 99 cents to help your e-book sell more copies and gain visibility. After your e-book has gained a more prominent position, you can raise its price again — and if it drops too far, you can lower the price again, and so on.

However, some authors believe that Amazon's algorithms now promote e-books priced $2.99 or higher in favor of those priced between 99 cents and $2.98. (The Amazon *algorithm* is the behind-the-scenes math that gives e-books prominence on the site — not only in the charts, but also in other locations, such as in the recommendations shown to readers on their home pages.) For this reason, you may want to set the standard price of your e-book at $2.99 or more and only occasionally lower it as part of a marketing push.

When Amazon first brought out KDP Select (a program described in Chapter 13), authors found that by enrolling in this program and making their books free for five days, they could rapidly rise up the ranks — and maintain a high ranking even when their book wasn't free. Now Amazon has changed this algorithm so that a high ranking on the free chart isn't maintained on the paid chart.

Price pulsing is an especially useful technique if you have published several e-books. If the sales of one are lackluster, you can drop the price and gain new readers. (This technique may well result in extra sales for your other e-books.) With your first e-book, you may prefer to stick with only one price, or you can launch the e-book at a lower price to encourage an initial surge of demand and then increase it to your regular selling price.

Chapter 16

Promoting Your E-Book on Facebook and Twitter

After you craft your Amazon page to encourage readers to buy your e-book (as described in Chapter 13) or set up a sales page on your website (as explained in Chapter 10), you need to bring potential readers to that page. If no one knows that your e-book exists, they can't consider buying it.

Even if you're no technowhiz, you've probably heard of Facebook and Twitter. They're *social networking* websites, where people gather online and make new connections. Facebook now has nearly a *billion* active users (as of the summer of 2012), and Twitter has over 150 million. Both are useful sites for building your network. The Facebook Pages feature works well to engage with readers and potential readers; Twitter can be an excellent place to interact with readers too, but it's also a brilliant way to start and build on your relationships with other writers.

This chapter walks you through the process of creating and using a Facebook page to engage with your e-book's readers (and potential new readers). It describes the best practices for making connections with writers and readers on Twitter — and lists the Twitter names of 20 outstanding self-publishing writers to follow.

Setting Up a Facebook Page for Your E-Books

If you already use Facebook, you've probably already seen Facebook *Pages*. This feature is separate from a personal account — with different features and a different focus. Huge companies and brands have pages. The *For Dummies* page, for example, has more than 60,000 "Likes," as shown in Figure 16-1. Many individual authors have pages, too — you don't need to be a big business to set one up.

Creating a page for yourself, your e-books, or your business on Facebook is easy and free. After you set up that page, your readers can click the Like button to not only see updates from you in their Facebook feeds, but also show their friends that they've Liked the page. Those friends can then check out your e-books. The Facebook *News Feed* is the list of updates (newest at the top) that you see when you log in to your personal Facebook account.

Figure 16-1:
The *For Dummies* page on Facebook.

Don't name your Facebook page after an individual e-book unless you plan to write only one book. Instead, gain fans for a series of e-books, for you as an author, or for your business: That way, you can also promote your next few e-books or other products from that page. If you set up a separate page for every e-book you write, you have to repeat the process of persuading your readers to Like it all over again.

After you decide on the type of Facebook page you want to create, follow these steps to set it up:

1. **Go to** www.facebook.com/pages/create.php.

   The Create a Page page appears.

2. **Choose among the options shown in Figure 16-2.**

   I'm assuming that you're setting up an author page. Other pages work similarly.

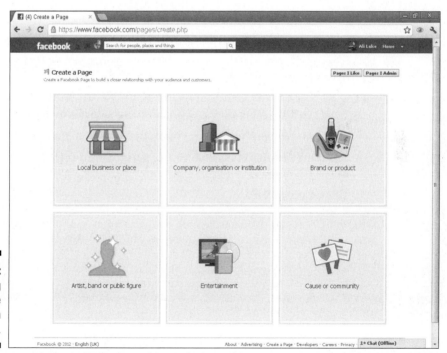

Figure 16-2:
Selecting page options on Facebook.

3. **Select Artist, Band, or Public Figure.**

   The options shown in Figure 16-3 appear.

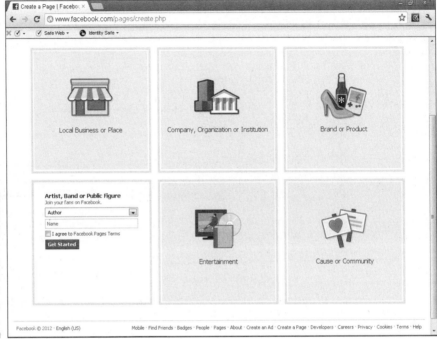

Figure 16-3:
Selecting
Author
from the
Artist, Band
or Public
Figure page
option.

4. **Select Author from the Choose a Category drop-down list.**

5. **In the Name text box, enter your name or pen name.**

6. **Read the Facebook Pages terms of service, and select the check box to agree to them.**

7. **Click Get Started.**

After you've created your page, you can populate it with text and images to give readers more information about you and your e-book.

If you already have a personal Facebook account, setting up a Facebook page for your e-book may seem unnecessary. You might want to promote your e-book to all your friends and family members who are already friends on your personal profile. Before you encourage your readers to add you as a Facebook friend on your personal profile, consider these major disadvantages:

✔ **You have to manually accept every single friend request.** If your e-book sales take off, and you receive a large number of friend requests, this task can be a pain. When you have a page, you don't have to seek Likes — they happen on their own.

> ✔ **You may want to be able to share personal updates with only friends and family.** You won't necessarily want complete strangers to know about every update, even if they have read your e-book.

Encouraging People to Like Your Facebook Page

After your e-book's Facebook page is set up, try to acquire its first few Likes quickly so that potential new readers aren't put off by seeing that only a few people in the world like your page (or by seeing the vision of tumbleweeds blowing across the page).

The best way for your e-book to score its first few Likes is for you to call on family and friends. Asking them to click the Like button isn't asking much — even if they aren't especially interested in your e-book or your business. Post a link in your Facebook profile to your Facebook page, and encourage people to click the Like button — and don't forget to Like your own page.

After a few people (perhaps a dozen or two) Like your e-book's page, you can share your Facebook page more widely. If you have a website, add a Like button there, too. To do so on a WordPress site, go to `http://developers.facebook.com/docs/reference/plugins/like`, and fill in the form to create, view and copy the code for your Like button. (See Chapter 9 for more on WordPress.)

After you accumulate 50 Likes, you can get a smarter-looking URL (web address) for your Facebook page. When I set up a Facebook page for my business, Aliventures, its URL was `www.facebook.com/pages/Aliventures/178553938852399`, an unattractive collection of characters that certainly doesn't fit easily on business cards. After I surpassed 50 Likes, I acquired the much nicer-looking URL `www.facebook.com/aliventures`. As soon as you have 50 Likes, you can do the same. Go to your page, click the Edit Page link, and then click Update Info. When you click the Create a Username for This Page link and enter your chosen name, you receive it immediately (unless it's already taken).

Authors and businesses sometimes offer incentives to readers who Like their pages. For example, you can sponsor occasional competitions on your Facebook page and give away copies of your e-book or offer a free nonfiction report or short story to people who Like your page. Regardless of whether you offer an incentive, you may find that you attract plenty of Likes without the extra commitment of organizing one.

Using Your Facebook Page to Engage with Your Readers

Enticing people to like your page is only the first step in engaging readers. After they're on board, either encourage them to buy your first e-book, or (if they've already bought it) keep them engaged and interested so that they're more likely to buy from you again.

If weeks go by and you don't update your page, readers will forget about your e-book. If you update only with promotional messages (or with chatty messages that seem irrelevant to your readers), they'll hide your updates from their Facebook News Feed (and they may Unlike your page, too).

Ideally, you should add new material to your Facebook page at least three times a week or even every day. Updating needn't take long — and Facebook has plenty of ways for you to add interesting items, such as updates about your current e-book in progress or photos.

You can easily post a link to a new blog post, which Facebook automatically formats to include the first few words of your post, plus an image from it. (If your post has several images, you get to select one.) You can see one of my blog post links in Figure 16-4, complete with a thumbnail version of my photo from New York City.

Figure 16-4: Posting a link on Facebook.

Asking questions to start a conversation

One simple way to engage your readers is to ask questions. If people rarely comment on your page updates, asking questions is a helpful way to make your page more active and attractive to new readers. (Even if lots of people have clicked the Like button on the page, a lack of comments may make it look deserted.) Ask open-ended questions that require more than a simple yes or no answer.

You don't need to do anything special to ask a question. Simply type it into the Update Status box on your page.

Ask readers questions such as these:

- **What did they learn from reading your e-book, or what did they enjoy most about it?** Encouraging readers to think about the benefit of reading your e-book increases the likelihood that they'll buy from you again. It also offers proof to potential readers that your e-book is useful or entertaining.

- **What was their biggest struggle with a certain topic?** If you write non-fiction, it's a useful way to form ideas for new blog posts, freebies, or even your next e-book.

- **What is their favorite blog about a certain topic?** Establish a good starting point on which bloggers you might want to write guest posts for and perhaps build a mutual working relationship. Encourage people to tell you why they like that blog so that you can see which elements to incorporate into your own blog or your next e-book.

This can give you a good starting point on which bloggers you might want to write guest posts for and/or build a relationship with.

After you've asked a question, check back regularly for responses. Reply to the responses, or at least acknowledge them with a quick "Thank you!" You can also click the Like button on a response to your question to indicate that you liked the answer.

Creating polls for quick feedback

Though open-ended questions are useful for engagement, they aren't always the perfect tools for the job. If you want a yes/no answer (or for the reader to choose a response from a list), a poll works well. You can use these responses to gather useful data or simply to encourage engagement.

To create a poll, click the Ask Question link in the updates area. (If you can't see the option, click the item to the right. You should see the plus-sign [+] symbol next to it — and Questions will appear.) You can then type your poll question and enter the options for your readers to choose among. Figure 16-5 shows this process in action. As you can see, on my own Facebook page, I had to click the Event, Milestone + button to see the Questions option.

Figure 16-5:
Creating
a poll on
Facebook.

On your poll page, explain that you're starting to write your next e-book, and ask questions such as these:

- ✔ Which interests you more — growing prize-winning vegetables or reading money-saving gardening tips?

- ✔ What free bonus would you prefer?

- ✔ Who is your favorite character? (List your characters' names.) Note that this question applies only if your e-book is a sequel to one that readers have already read.

- ✔ Which type of chocolate do you like best — milk, dark, or white?

Avoid having too many off-topic polls. An occasional fun or quirky question is fine, but ask too many, and your Facebook page can quickly become a place for general chatter rather than discussions related to your e-books or your business.

Sharing news, updates, and interesting links

One key way to use Facebook is to share information with your audience. You can share news ("My latest e-book is out!") or updates ("I'm writing Chapter 16 now — not far to go!") as simple text or upload a photo or an image. The visual interest may be more likely to grab your readers' attention.

When you share a piece of news, such as a new e-book release, encourage readers to let their friends know by adding "Please share!" to the end of your post, for example. Don't do it too often, though, or it loses its impact.

Updates can be a useful way to let people know how a new project is going, but don't overwhelm your audience with notes about your current word count. Phrase your updates carefully, too; you don't want to give the impression that you dislike writing your e-book (even if, on some days, you tire of it). If your readers feel that you're careless or indifferent, they may have concerns about the quality of the finished e-book.

Sharing interesting links with your Facebook audience is a helpful way to show that your knowledge of your genre or niche is current. For example, if you write fiction, you might share a link to the Amazon.com page for a novel that you're reading — ideally, one that relates to your own work. If you write nonfiction, you might link to a blog post that covers ground similar to a chapter in your e-book.

Of course, you can also share links to your own e-book's page (on your site or on Amazon) or to blog posts or other material you've written. Aim for a balance: Don't promote only your own work, but equally, don't be shy about linking to your own blog posts and e-books. Not every Facebook fan will necessarily realize that you have a blog or even an e-book, so remind them from time to time.

Connecting with Fellow Writers on Twitter

Twitter is a slightly newer social network than Facebook, so you may not already have an account. Twitter is quite popular with writers (especially e-book writers), so it's a useful place to interact with other authors and acquire tips and ideas — as well as emotional and practical support.

If you're used to Facebook, you'll find Twitter simple in comparison — even a bit minimalist. On Twitter, the only way to interact is to write a short post. (Twitter is a *microblogging* service.) Your post is limited to 140 characters. Figure 16-6 shows how to write a post on Twitter. (You can see that five characters remain.)

Figure 16-6: Writing a post on Twitter.

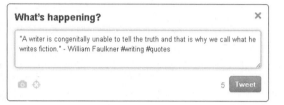

> **What's happening?** ✕
>
> "A writer is congenitally unable to tell the truth and that is why we call what he writes fiction." - William Faulkner #writing #quotes
>
> 📷 ⊕   5 [Tweet]

Twitter uses a system of *followers* rather than Likes or friends. People can follow you without your following them in return. When someone follows you, they see your updates. If you choose to follow the person in return, you see their updates.

Unless you choose to protect your account, anyone who visits your Twitter profile (at www.twitter.com/xyourtwittername) can see all your updates. To protect your account, go to www.twitter.com/settings/account and select the Protect My Tweets check box in the Tweet Privacy section. Click Save Changes at the bottom of your page. Note that if you protect your account in this way, it will be harder to gain followers, as potential new followers won't be able to see any of your tweets before choosing whether to follow you. You also need to approve new followers before they can see your tweets.

Many authors with large Twitter followings switch off their notifications of new followers, so they probably won't follow you back simply because you follow them. The best way to get someone's attention is to send a reply using the @ symbol followed by the person's name. For example, if you want to contact me on Twitter, you can write

@aliventures I'm on Chapter 16 of Publishing E-Books For Dummies. Hi!

Everyone who's following both you and me sees that tweet in their Twitter feeds. Anyone who views your Twitter page (at www.twitter.com/yourtwittername) sees the tweet too. If you want the message to appear in the feed of all your Twitter followers, add text other than @name at the start. For example:

I'm reading Publishing E-Books For Dummies by @aliventures.

Twenty writers to follow on Twitter

The writers in the following list are all e-book self-publishers who tweet regularly about topics related to writing and self-publishing. Follow them on Twitter to learn useful information — and to see how they interact with their followers.

To reach a writer's page directly on Twitter, go to `www.twitter.com/`*thetwittername*`—`without the at-sign (@). For example, Nina's page is `www.twitter.com/NinaAmir`.

Twitter names are conventionally written using the @ symbol — it's how you include a person in a tweet. If you hang around with technical types, you may even see people with business cards or contact information on their websites that use only the @ symbol and their Twitter name — with no explanation.

Capital letters are allowed within Twitter names — you can type a name with or without capitalizing, and it still works. I've capitalized the names in the following list according to the preference indicated on each person's Twitter page.

Nina Amir: @NinaAmir

Wally Bock: @wallybock

Lindsay Buroker: @GoblinWriter

Scott Bury: @ScottTheWriter

Mark Coker: @markcoker

Tony Eldridge: @tonyeldridge

Joel Friedlander: @JFbookman

Jonathan Gunson: @JonathanGunson

Rob Guthrie: @rsguthrie

Patricia de Hemricourt: @epublishabook

Rob Kroese: @robkroese

D'vorah Lansky: @marketingwizard

Steven Lewis: @Rule17

John Locke: @DonovanCreed

Gary McLaren: @PYOEbooks

Jason A. Paul: @JA_Paul

Joanna Penn: @TheCreativePenn

Sean Platt: @SeanPlatt

Dana Lynn Smith: @bookmarketer

K.M. Weiland: @KMWeiland

Many writers — even the big names — are happy to answer quick questions on Twitter. If you feel shy about contacting someone directly, *favorite* (click the Star button) or *retweet* (share with your followers) some of their tweets instead. It's a helpful way to support them and to begin building a connection. In Figure 16-7, you can see how one of my writing friends, Lorna Fergusson, has retweeted one of my messages. Though the tweet appears on Lorna's page, it still has my name and face attached.

Figure 16-7:
A retweeted tweet.

Ali Luke @aliventures   14 Jun
Even if you didn't listen to my #digipub session live, you can get the replay (for 3 hrs) here: bookmarketingalliance.com/schedule/
↻ Retweeted by Lorna Fergusson
Expand

Don't contact writers and ask them to tweet about your e-book, though. That's usually a fine strategy if you already have a strong relationship with someone, but it comes across as demanding, and even spamlike, if you begin a new connection with that type of request.

Spreading the Word to Readers on Twitter

As well as being a great place to network with fellow writers, Twitter is an easy way to stay in touch with your readers — and to gain new ones. It's encouraging — and sometimes illuminating! — to engage with your readers on Twitter. They might tell you how much they enjoyed your first e-book and that they're waiting eagerly for the next, or they may have questions about a topic that you hadn't fully considered or ideas for a topic they want you to write about.

Encouraging your readers to follow you

As on Facebook, let your readers know about your Twitter account, and encourage them to follow you there. You can even add the Follow Me button to your website, using `https://twitter.com/about/resources/buttons`. Figure 16-8 shows the options you can choose among when creating this button.

You can also list your Twitter name in the back of your e-book, on the contact page of your website, and on your business cards. Unless your readers know where to find you, they can't follow you.

Engaging with your readers on Twitter

After a bunch of readers are following you on Twitter, make sure that you stay visible. In the fast-moving environment of Twitter, not all your readers will see all your updates. In fact, there's a good chance that many of them will log in only once or twice a day or even once or twice a week — so you should repeat any important messages.

Be aware of different time zones, too. A message posted at noon Eastern time won't be seen by many Australians, for example. You may want to use a service such as the one at `http://twuffer.com` or `http://futuretweets.com`, or schedule tweets ahead of time so that you can send out tweets while you're asleep.

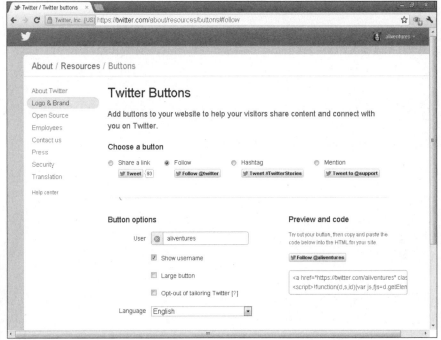

Figure 16-8:
Creating the
Follow Me
button.

What you tweet about is up to you, but I suggest centering your activity around your e-book's genre or topic. For example, if you've written a paranormal romance, you might tweet about other novels you're reading in that genre. If you've written a nonfiction e-book about healthy eating, you can link to related news items and blog posts.

One helpful way to build buzz around your e-book is to throw a *Twitter party,* an event held online where a group of people gather on Twitter to talk. Authors sometimes hold Twitter parties in conjunction with conference calls, encouraging their readers to tweet about the topic being discussed. You can come up with a *hashtag* — the pound symbol (#) followed by a word, acronym or phrase — for partygoers to use.

A *hashtag* is label that's attached a tweet. At online gatherings such as Twitter parties, and at offline gatherings such as conferences, organizers often create specific hashtags. Clicking one initiates a Twitter search for that hashtag so that users can easily find other tweets related to the party or conference. Twitter users also use hashtags for more general purposes: Many writers, for example, use the hashtag #amwriting to connect with other people who are also writing during the day.

Chapter 17

Promoting Your E-Book on Goodreads

*O*n the Goodreads book-centered social network, readers (and authors) can list and rate the books they're reading, send messages to other members, and engage in group discussions. Founded in 2007, the site now has more than 9 million members.

If you've ever had good intentions about keeping a *book journal,* or a list of all the books you've read and the books you plan to read, you'll enjoy Goodreads. It's an easy way to keep track of the books that you've read or that you're planning to read — and to inspire ideas about what to buy next.

As an author, though, you can benefit from Goodreads in other ways. You can see which members have rated and reviewed your e-book, and you can even see who has added it to the To Read list (known as a *shelf* on Goodreads). If you want, you can befriend those people. You can also join groups on Goodreads where you can promote your e-book.

This chapter first explains how to set up your Goodreads account. (You need to apply for a special author account.) It then walks you through the process of adding an e-book to Goodreads, finding readers who might enjoy your e-book (by making friends and by joining groups), and getting the word out about your e-book without causing annoyance to other Goodreads users.

Setting Up a Goodreads Account

Goodreads, like other social networks, is quick and free to join. Simply go to www.goodreads.com, enter your name and e-mail address, and choose a password. When you click Sign Up, your new account is created.

This process gives you only a reader account, however. You can interact with the site as other readers do — rating and reviewing books and joining groups, for example — but you can't yet edit the details for your book.

Before you publish your e-book, you may want to set up your Goodreads account so that you can start adding books that you've read and ones that you plan to read. As on other social networks, you get much more out of Goodreads if you're an active, engaged member rather than someone who uses it only for self-promotion.

To join the Goodreads author program, which gives you access to extra tools, you need to have at least one book already published or in the process of being published, and it must be listed on Goodreads.

Adding your own e-books to Goodreads

If your e-book doesn't yet appear on Goodreads, you have to list it there before you can set up an author account. You have two options:

✔ Apply for librarian status, and add your e-book yourself.

✔ Ask a Goodreads user with librarian status to add your e-book for you.

If you choose the first option, follow these steps:

1. **Ensure that you have at least 50 books listed on Goodreads.**

   To see how many books you have, log in, and go to your Goodreads home page at www.goodreads.com. To see the total number of books you have, look for the My Profile area on the right side of your home page.

2. **If you don't have 50 books listed, add books to your Goodreads account.**

   You can list books that you're reading now, books that you're planning to read, and books that you've already read.

3. **Apply for librarian status at** www.goodreads.com/about/apply_librarian.

   You have to explain briefly your reason for wanting librarian status.

4. **Go to** www.goodreads.com/book/new, **and complete the Add a New Book form, shown in Figure 17-1.**

   Only the Title, Sort by Title, and Author fields are mandatory, but fill in as much information as you can — curious readers who visit your e-book's page may be more likely to purchase your e-book.

If you prefer not to become a Goodreads librarian and add your book yourself, find a librarian who can help you by listing your e-book:

✔ **Ask writers in your social network, such as Twitter or Facebook, for help.** One of them is likely to be a Goodreads librarian (or to know someone who is).

✔ **Go to** www.goodreads.com/group/show/220-goodreads-librarians, **and join the group; then post a request in the Adding New Books section.** For more on Goodreads groups, see the later section "Joining Goodreads groups."

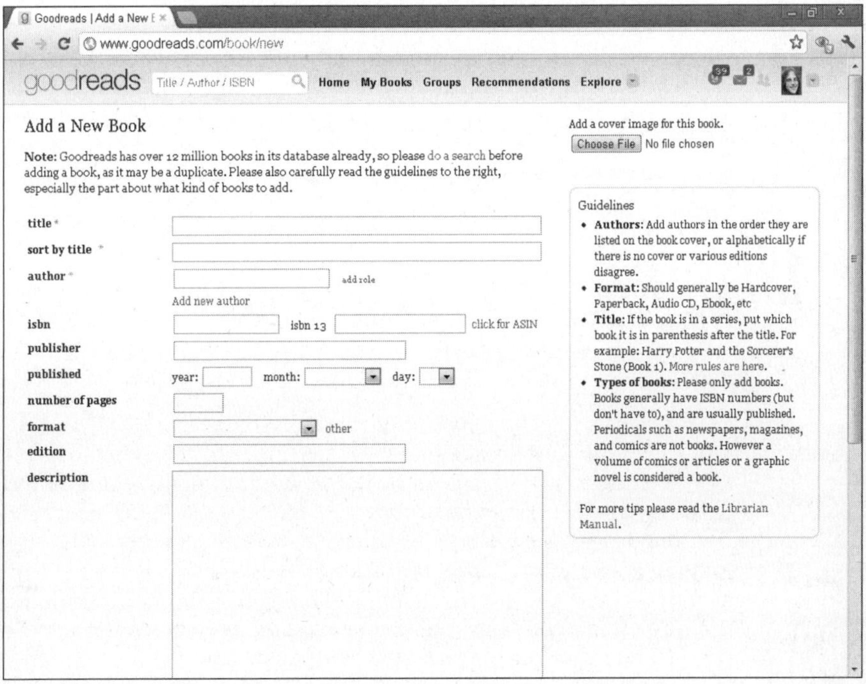

Figure 17-1:
Adding a
new book.

Joining the author program

After your book is listed on Goodreads, follow these steps to create a full author account:

1. **Go to your e-book's page, and click your name.**

   This step directs you to a basic author-profile page.

2. **On the author profile, scroll to the bottom of the page, and click the Is This You? link.**

   You can then send Goodreads a message, and it will create your full author account within a few days.

After you have your author account, you can update your e-book's page on Goodreads. You may need to add the cover image and the blurb, if these items haven't already been included.

The Shelfari (`www.shelfari.com`) site, owned by and linked to Amazon, has similar features and functionality to Goodreads. You might want to create an account there, too. Shelfari hasn't found such widespread adoption as Goodreads, but you can use it to add extra information about your e-book that Kindle readers can access, including details about the characters or people mentioned in your e-book, any locations or themes, and more. You can see the applicable categories listed in your Author Central account.

Finding Readers Who Might Enjoy Your E-Book

Goodreads is a *social* network of readers, so compared with users of Twitter and Facebook, Goodreads members are more likely to be interested in your e-book. Unless you engage with the network, though, your e-book isn't easily visible.

As time goes by, you'll find that friends of friends — and friends of friends of friends — start buying your e-book. To begin with, though, you need to get the ball rolling yourself.

You can interact on Goodreads in two key ways:

- **Make friends.** They can see your recent activity on their home pages.
- **Join groups.** You can take part in discussions about book-related topics.

Goodreads wants to make life easy for authors — but it also wants readers to have a great experience at the site. Read the Goodreads recommendations (and take note of what they dislike) at www.goodreads.com/author/guidelines.

Making friends on Goodreads

When you start out on Goodreads, you have no friends listed on your account — making it difficult to interact with anybody.

To build your friend network, you can

- ✔ **Start with your current contacts.** Goodreads lets you send out friend requests to your Facebook, Twitter, and e-mail contacts. Although you already have a way to engage in conversation with these people, making a connection on Goodreads means that it's easier for you to talk about your e-book.

- ✔ **Write a post on your blog, or send an e-mail to your mailing list.** You're announcing your new Goodreads presence — and encouraging your readers to add you as a friend. You may have blog readers or mailing list contacts who aren't on Twitter or Facebook.

- ✔ **Join groups on Goodreads, engage in discussions with other readers, and then send them friend requests.** Groups are based around all sorts of different topics — you might want to join one for your genre, or one for your local area or a particular interest. You can join as many groups as you want, though you may find it difficult to keep up with more than a handful. The next section goes into more detail about groups.

Readers may choose to keep their friendship group deliberately small. Don't get upset or angry if someone declines your friend request. Goodreads recommends that you make friends by first meeting people on the discussion boards, and it discourages you from sending a friend request to every single person who has read your book or related books. This behavior can get you flagged as a spammer.

Joining Goodreads groups

Goodreads *groups* resemble Facebook groups or online forums. After you join a group, you can take part in discussions there — and many groups have special areas for authors to promote their books and areas where readers can gather and discuss books that they've read.

To browse the available groups, click the Groups link on the Goodreads navigation bar, or go directly to `www.goodreads.com/group`.

Find a group you like — you can choose among the ones displayed by category or search for a group by entering a keyword such as *romance* or *fantasy* on the Search bar. You can also browse groups by tag (on the right side of the screen). In Figure 17-2, you can see that I'm a member of four groups and that my home page shows a variety: Featured Groups, Recently Active Groups, and Groups in the United Kingdom (where I live).

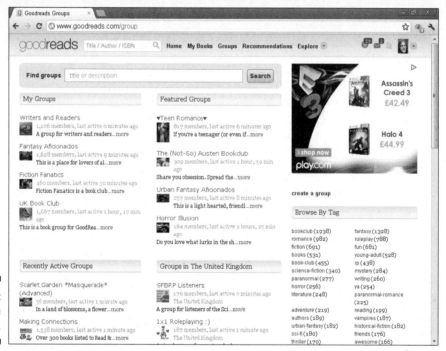

Figure 17-2:
Groups on
Goodreads.

After you join a Goodreads group, you can almost certainly find an Introductions thread, where you can post a message introducing yourself to the group. Keep your introduction short — and remember that (unless you've joined a writing-focused group), Goodreads is primarily a community of readers rather than authors. Focus on your reading tastes rather than on promoting your e-book heavily — though it's fine to mention what you've written.

In Figure 17-3, you can see the introduction I wrote in the UK Book Club group. Unlike other social networks, Goodreads displays only your first name on your posts — and many people introduce themselves by first name only.

> **message 3371:** by Ali   Jun 14, 2012 03:39pm
>
> I'm Ali, keen reader, keen writer. I live in Oxford. :-) I love reading anything with strong characters and a fairly fast pace, and I'm particularly partial to fantasy/supernatural elements … but not so into swords-and-sorcery type fantasy. I published my first novel *Lycopolis* a few months ago.
>
> As well as reading and writing fiction, I blog all over the place (mostly about writing), and I'm currently working on *Publishing e-Books For Dummies* with Wiley.
>
> I'm really enjoying getting to grips with Goodreads -- will finally be able to achieve childhood ambition of keeping track of all the books I read … and all the ones I mean to read!

Figure 17-3:
The author's
introduction.

Getting the Word Out About Your E-Book Without Stepping on Toes

Obviously, you shouldn't spam all your new friends with constant promotional messages about your e-book — but you do need to be able to let people know that you have an e-book available.

To encourage a Goodreads friend to check out your e-book, you can send a direct message to let the friend know about your e-book. You may want to take a look at a friend's bookshelves first, to see whether that person has read any similar titles. That way, you can mention that you noticed they enjoyed a certain book or books and that you think they'll like your e-book, too.

To send a direct message to a Goodreads friend, follow these steps:

1. **On your profile page, click the name of your friend in your Friends list.**

   Your friend's profile page opens.

2. **Click the Send Message link near the top of the page, on the left side.**

   The Compose New Message page appears.

3. **Fill in a subject, type a message, and click Send.**

You can't use the Goodreads Recommendation feature to recommend your own book — though you can use it to recommend other books. It's a nice way to offer value to your reader friends and to help promote authors whose work you've enjoyed. Good karma never goes amiss!

Crafting your message to a group

One simple way to spread the word about your e-book is to join a relevant group and write a message there.

Many Goodreads groups have specific areas for promotional content, so make sure to put your message in the right place — and do *not* repeat a message in several areas within the same group. It's a surefire way to have your posts deleted and to annoy other members.

There's no perfect way to write your message, but as you craft it, you'll want to follow these suggestions:

- ✔ **Spend time on your discussion title.** It's the only thing that group members see before deciding whether to click and read the message you've created. Titles such as *Free Book* and *Reviews Wanted* and *My Book* lack information.

- ✔ **Include a blurb about your e-book.** Goodreads gives you little in the way of formatting tools for your message, so keep it short.

- ✔ **Quote from complimentary reviews you've received.** Again, keep these quotes short.

- ✔ **Tell readers explicitly how to find your e-book.** Include a link to its page on Amazon (or the sales page on your website).

- ✔ **Offer review copies of your e-book.** Offer them review copies as well as (or instead of) encouraging people to buy it.

Read at least a few messages from other authors within your group. Look for messages that have received a good number of views and replies — they're probably doing a good job of attracting and engaging group members. You may also look at messages that haven't received much attention, to see what you can learn from other authors' mistakes.

Encouraging readers to review your e-book

As well as encouraging your writing friends or beta-readers to join Goodreads and write reviews of your e-book, you should reach out beyond your current circle to your Goodreads friends and fellow group members.

One quick and simple way to encourage reviews is to start with the people who've rated your e-book. If you notice that someone has rated your e-book favorably but has left no review, drop that person a line to ask for a few spare minutes and a short review. Make your request friendly and polite, and don't pressure the person.

You can offer free review copies of your e-book in a discussion forum or run a Goodreads giveaway. Yes, you might miss out on a potential sale or two — but you'll also put your e-book into the hands of eager readers who are likely to review it on the site.

Responding to Reviews of Your E-Book on Goodreads

Some authors like to respond to reviews and say thanks, either to build up a stronger connection with a reader or to simply be polite. For some readers, though, this behavior can come across as overbearing — as though you, as the author, are monitoring the reviews. (You may well be, but it's often a good idea to stay quiet and let readers have their space!) Plus, after your sales start increasing, you may receive too many reviews to easily respond to.

If you want to say thanks to someone for a thoughtful review, you can use the Goodreads messaging feature to contact the person privately: Click the person's name and then click the Send Message link. In Figure 17-4, you can see a message that I sent to Elizabeth (who knows me from my blog) to thank her for her review.

When you see negative reviews, don't respond. Walk away from your computer, if you have to. If you feel that you simply must reply and defend your e-book, promise yourself that you'll at least sleep on it. If you get into a heated discussion with a reviewer, you're extremely unlikely to change the person's mind about your e-book — and it will put off other potential readers who see the discussion. In rare cases when you think that a reply is warranted (for example, if someone clearly hasn't read your e-book or has mistaken someone else's e-book for yours), contact the reviewer privately.

> you said to Elizabeth: Jun 14, 2012
> Hi Elizabeth,   03:52pm
>   view | delete
>
> Just wanted to say thank you so much for your lovely review of Lycopolis --
> hugely appreciated! :-) And big thanks for posting it on Amazon too. I'm really
> glad you enjoyed it (and that the online gaming angle didn't put you off
> giving it a try!)
>
> Thanks again,
>
> Ali x

Figure 17-4:
A thank-you
message.

Chapter 18

Using Blogs and E-Mail Lists to Promote Your E-Book

Social media sites — such as Facebook, Twitter, and Goodreads — provide you with helpful ways to interact with your current readers and to attract new ones. But every site has obvious limitations. On Twitter, for example, you can post only short messages, and you can't be sure that your followers will see them.

On your own blog or mailing list (or with access to someone else's), you can quickly and easily reach your audience in whatever format you want. Sending out an e-mail to promote your latest e-book, for example, is more likely to reach people than only tweeting about it.

This chapter describes different ways to promote your e-book via blogs and mailing lists. You don't even need to have a website of your own. You can take advantage of other people's sites and lists.

Selling Your E-Book via Your Own Blog or E-Mail List

Whether or not your e-book is available directly from your website or a web page (see Chapters 9 and 10), you can use your blog or e-mail list to promote it. You simply include a link to your e-book's page at Amazon.com or on other major e-retailers' sites.

When you launch your e-book, let your existing audience know about it. If you've been blogging for a few months, or if you've started an e-mail list where readers can opt in to receive updates about your e-book (and your other projects), get in touch with your audience, and point them toward your new e-book.

If your e-book isn't yet finished, you can still start a blog or an e-mail list. In fact, you produce better results by building the readership of your blog or e-mail list *before* your e-book is ready — that way, you have plenty of people to contact on launch day.

Comparing blogs and e-mail lists

Blogs and e-mail lists are different beasts, and readers engage with them differently. This list can help sort them out:

- ✔ **Blog:** A chronological list of commentary on a website. Readers can dip in and out, reading only a couple of posts or several, and they can easily share links to your blog and its posts with their friends via Facebook or Twitter or other social media sites.

- ✔ **E-mail list:** A list of people who share a common interest and subscribe in order to exchange information. Their messages generally don't appear publicly on the web (though it's an option). Readers receive all mailings — unless they opt out of the list — and can easily forward mailings to their friends.

In practice, many readers will choose to *subscribe* to your blog via e-mail so that they receive your new blog posts straight to their e-mail accounts. Others will use an *RSS* (Really Simple Syndication) reader, like Google Reader, to receive new blog posts. Even so, a mailing list gives you slightly more control — and many online marketers emphasize the importance of building an e-mail list so that you have direct access to your readers' inboxes.

If you're just starting out, you may find a blog easier to handle than an e-mail list. Enable e-mail subscriptions on your blog — e-mail is a familiar, and favored, technology for many people. If you choose to create an e-mail list as well as (or instead of) a blog, look into Aweber (www.aweber.com) and MailChimp (http://mailchimp.com). These reputable providers ensure that your e-mail is delivered successfully to readers, and they offer insight into vital statistics, such as how many people open an e-mail and how many click a link.

Using your blog or e-mail list — or both

The ways in which you use your blog and mailing list may differ slightly. Here are my suggestions:

- ✓ **Use your blog to write about subjects that will be of interest to readers of your e-book.** If you've written (or you're writing) a nonfiction book, it's a relatively easy task. You can create content that ties in with specific chapters, you can take a topic further, or you can give readers a beginner's guide to the area.

  If you're working on fiction, you may need to be a little more creative in coming up with topics. For example, if your novel is a romance set on a Mediterranean cruise, you might choose to write about your own experience on cruises or about interesting areas of the Mediterranean that your characters visit. Alternatively, you can use your blog to publish short stories that relate to the world of your novel. This strategy can be quite effective if you're working on a series of books.

- ✓ **Use your mailing list to send out occasional, short updates.** Most readers don't read in-depth articles from an e-mail list, so you may simply want to use your list to let them know when your book is out, or to occasionally advertise a special sale. However, try not to let so much time pass between mailings that your audience forgets who you are! You can even commit to sending a short update every month or two to let your readers know how the book is progressing.

  Some writers, particularly of nonfiction, provide incentives to encourage readers to join their e-mail lists. It might be a miniature e-book on a related topic, an audio recording, or even a series of videos. If you have the time and resources to create a valuable piece of free content, an incentive will definitely help grow your e-mail list. You can see in Figure 18-1 how my list membership has increased. After months of seeing slow list growth, I introduced my first incentive, a free e-book, in June 2011. I added several others "goodies" during the next 12 months, and by June 2012, I had more than 2,000 subscribers.

When you craft a sales message on your blog or for your e-mail list, make sure that you

- ✓ **Remain positive and enthusiastic.** Don't apologize for sending a "promotional" e-mail, and don't slip in a line about your new e-book at the end of a long blog post or a chatty e-mail update: Make it the focus of at least one post or mailing.

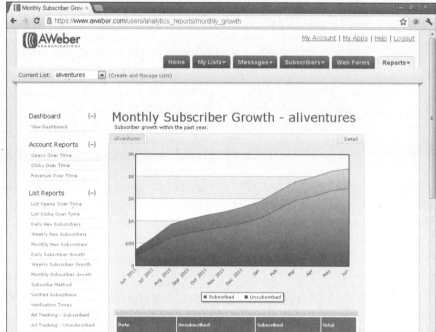

Figure 18-1:
The growth
of an e-mail
list over 12
months.

✔ **State explicitly how to buy your e-book.** Explain that it's available only in digital, downloadable format (unless you've created a paperback version). Emphasize the advantages: Your readers can buy your e-book at any time, from anywhere in the world. Let readers know that they can view e-books on their computers, tablets, or phones; they don't need to have dedicated e-reading devices.

✔ **Avoid cluttering your message with options.** It's tempting to give readers lots of links — to your e-book's page in every online store and to your presence on Twitter, Goodreads, and Facebook, for example. Rather than confuse your readers with different choices, suggest one or two links — perhaps to Amazon.com and any other major store that you know will be popular with your audience. Then simply add a note telling them that they can search for your book by title in other online stores, too.

Approaching Book Bloggers for a Review of Your E-Book

Your own blog might not have many readers yet — and even if you have a large readership, you'll still want to reach out beyond your blog to other audiences.

One of the best ways to do this is by getting your e-book featured on book-related sites. This technique is particularly useful for fiction, where many individuals run review sites. (The later section "Writing Guest Posts for Relevant Blogs" guides you through a similar process for a nonfiction e-book.)

The book-blogging world is full of dedicated readers who love writing about the books they've been enjoying. Many of these people are enthusiastic about *indie* authors — people who have published books on their own, without the backing of a major publishing house. Some book bloggers have small, quirky websites that they run in their spare time, and others have created a major online presence, often with teams of reviewers.

 A busy book blogger may not be able to read and review your e-book for many months, and some bloggers are inundated with requests and might not even reply to your e-mail. Target as many book bloggers as you can (rather than rely on only one or two), and work as far ahead as possible if you're planning for a launch or major promotional effort.

Creating an e-book information sheet

Many book bloggers, especially established ones with larger audiences, receive far more review requests than they can handle. To boost the possibility of your e-book being accepted for review, show that you're serious and professional about your writing — and make the fulfillment of your request as easy as possible.

One effective way to do this is by creating an *information sheet* for your e-book: This one- or two-page PDF document captures crucial information about you and the book so that reviewers have it all in hand. In Figure 18-2, you can see an example, in my own information sheet for my novel, *Lycopolis*.

Include these items on your information sheet:

- ✔ **A blurb (a short description of your e-book):** You generally don't need to give a whole synopsis. The blurb you wrote for Amazon or other stores works fine.

- ✔ **The cover image:** It makes sense to put this image alongside or above the blurb. Be sure that you have several versions of your cover image, in different sizes, saved on your computer. Then you can easily send them out to book bloggers when your review requests are accepted.

- ✔ **Excerpts from reviews about your e-book:** Ideally, you'll have at least a couple of reviews on Amazon before approaching book bloggers to request a review on their sites. (Yes, it sounds like a Catch-22 — your first reviews might come from writer friends who've helped you with the editing phase of your e-book.)

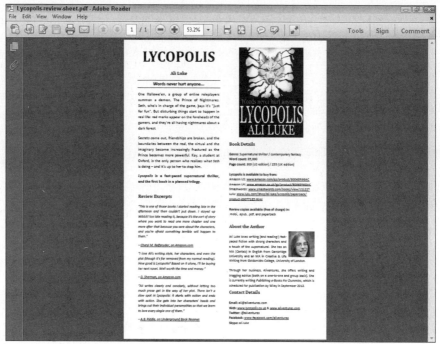

Figure 18-2:
The PDF
information
sheet for
Lycopolis.

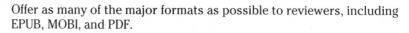

✔ **Information about you, including relevant qualifications or experience:** If you've published other e-books, or if you've written for magazines or large blogs, you may want to mention them here, to help reassure book bloggers that your writing is of high quality.

✔ **A photograph of you:** A photo isn't essential, but it helps create visual interest and a personal connection.

✔ **Details of where your e-book is available online:** A book blogger who writes a review will almost certainly want to link to your e-book at Amazon and, potentially, in other stores.

✔ **A note on formats available for review:** Book bloggers will want to know whether you provide their favorite formats.

Offer as many of the major formats as possible to reviewers, including EPUB, MOBI, and PDF.

Finding book bloggers who cover your genre or niche

Some book bloggers cover a wide range of material, including almost any genre of fiction, plus some nonfiction. Many, though, specialize in certain genres, and others have lists of genres that they never review.

Don't waste your time — and a book blogger's time — by sending out review requests to someone who doesn't deal with your type of book. Do some research yourself, and create a list of book bloggers who will be a good fit for you.

In Figure 18-3, you can see how I researched this topic: I created a spreadsheet for myself, based on an existing list of book bloggers. (Thanks to Rachel Abbott and Greg Scowen.) You can see the list at `http://rachel abbottwriter.wordpress.com/2012/03/13/reviews-the-good-the-bad-and-the-scams`. I looked at every blog, read their review guidelines, determined the sorts of books they dealt with, and marked up the spreadsheet accordingly by color-coding the lines with these colors:

- ✔ **Red:** These blogs no longer existed, were closed to submissions, didn't accept e-books, declined books from independent authors, or definitely didn't deal with my genre.

- ✔ **Yellow:** These blogs accepted books in my genre but didn't specialize in it.

- ✔ **Green:** These blogs specialized in my genre or were good targets in other ways, such as having large readerships.

You're free to come up with a different system. For example, you can choose a color for blogs that would be a good fit but are closed for submissions. That way, you can return to them several months later.

If you find a blog that seems to be a good fit (I've labeled some in green on the spreadsheet shown in Figure 18-3), check out the sites that they link to in their sidebars, often in the Blogroll section.

Some book bloggers cover nonfiction, memoir, or biography — but check their guidelines carefully. You may find that instead of being featured on book-related blogs, it's easier to get your nonfiction e-book mentioned on subject-specific blogs, as covered in the next section.

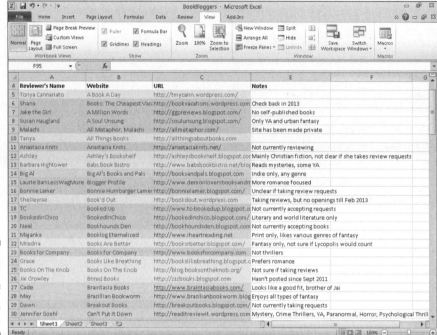

Figure 18-3:
Spread-
sheet of
book
bloggers.

Writing Guest Posts for Relevant Blogs

One technique I use for promoting my specialized nonfiction e-books, such as my *Blogger's Guides* series, is writing guest posts for large, related blogs. A *guest post* is free content that a writer adds to someone else's website. If you write a guest post, you might add your name to your bio, describe your e-book, and add a link to your Amazon page or your own website.

You don't have to wait until your e-book is published to start guest posting, though. Writing guest posts is quite an effective way to build the readership of your blog or e-mail newsletter — before you launch your e-book. Writing guest posts can also boost your credibility and reputation, especially if your field is one with a strong online presence.

Authors sometimes worry that they need large online followings in order to secure guest-post slots. The truth is that most blog editors don't care how many readers you have — they're interested in the quality of your content.

In fact, when I started out guest posting to promote the first e-book in my *Blogger's Guide* series, I had no active blog or mailing list of my own. I had only a website with a sales page for the e-book. (I had stepped back from the two blogs I had run in the past, to focus on my freelancing work on larger blog sites.) But despite not having a blog of my own, I was able to promote the first *Blogger's Guide* effectively by guest posting.

Crafting your guest post carefully

When writing a guest post, follow all the usual guidelines for writing outstanding online material. (You can use many of the tips for sales pages in Chapter 10, such as having short paragraphs and lots of subheadings and using bold text to highlight key points.) Keep these tips in mind, too:

- ✔ **Choose a target blog before writing your guest post.** Don't write an article and then look for a blog that would be a good fit — you're more likely to succeed with a piece that you've specifically planned and written for a particular site. You can usually tell whether a blog accepts guest posts by looking for lots of different authors' names. (Good clues are sentences that begin with the words *This is a guest post from. . . .*)

- ✔ **Read any guest-post guidelines that are provided.** Many large blogs have pages known as *guest post guidelines* or *guest postings.* These pages often include details on the preferred word count and format, and on how to submit your post. If you can't find guidelines, read several recent posts, and work out the standard length and any common features in the writing style.

- ✔ **Consider several topics for your post before settling on one.** Ideally, your topic should fall within the domain of your target blog — but it should also be one that the blog hasn't yet covered (or at least not recently). The topic you choose should also relate to your e-book or to your own blog's subject. Otherwise, readers won't have much incentive to check out your material.

- ✔ **Allow plenty of time for writing your guest post.** Even if you're already an experienced blogger, guest posts can be tough to get right. You want to show off the best work you can do, and you may also need to alter your usual style slightly to fit well with the target blog. Edit carefully — not only for typos and spelling mistakes, but also for overall flow and structure.

Using your bio effectively

Include a link to your e-book or a specific resource in your bio. Don't link only to your website — it isn't enough of an incentive to encourage people to check it out. Your bio is a mini sales pitch, so make it good!

You might choose to promote an in-depth post on your website or a free resource you've created for your readers. I've had great success in promoting my free e-books (available only to my newsletter subscribers) and linking to the opt-in page on my newsletter.

If you want to promote your e-book directly, include a couple of phrases from reviews, especially if you're guest-posting to promote your fiction work, where a short book description alone might not be enough to sell readers on your e-book. I wrote the following bio to promote my novel, *Lycopolis:*

Ali Luke is currently on a virtual book tour for her novel Lycopolis, *a fast-paced supernatural thriller centered on a group of online role players who summon a demon into their game … and into the world. Described by readers as "a fast and furious, addictive piece of escapism" and "absolutely gripping", Lycopolis is available in print and e-Book form. Find out more at www.lycopolis.co.uk.*

You can do the same with nonfiction, though a description of your e-book's content should let readers know that it's a good fit for them:

Ali Luke is a writer and writing coach. Her e-book The Blogger's Guide to Effective Writing *helps with every stage of the blogging process, from idea-generation to editing and polishing. It also includes templates to help you build solid posts, step by step. Click here to find out all about it.*

A well-established blog that links to your site can help your site appear higher on a list of search engine results. For maximum effect, you may want to use *keywords* — phrases that members of your target audience are likely to search for — for the link that you put in your bio. This suggestion applies more to nonfiction writers than to novelists, though if you write fiction, try keywords such as *cheap paranormal romance* or *technothriller*. Keep in mind, though, that overoptimizing is frowned on by Google, so vary your links, perhaps sometimes using the name of your e-book or your blog instead. You may also draw more responses when you use a phrase such as *Click here* as the link.

Responding to comments on your guest post

Even if your own blog receives few comments, your guest posts will almost certainly receive a few more — perhaps even a few dozen. Some of these comments will be simple ("Great post!"), but others may include questions or discussion points you've raised.

Your host blog will probably expect you to respond to comments. Its hosts may even set up your post so that you receive an e-mail every time a reader leaves a comment, which helps you reply in a timely fashion. Whether or not you receive e-mails about comments, you should try to check in on your post a couple of times on the day of publication and during the next day. Respond to any questions, and thank readers for adding to the conversation.

The only time you might *not* want to reply is if a reader posts a negative comment. Perhaps the person disagrees with your post. Your subject matter, your writing style, and even the formatting of your post can all come under attack. Even if you feel upset and angry at this type of comment, never write a reply in the heat of the moment. If you're unsure how to respond, or if the comment is addressed to the host blogger, contact your host, alert that person to the comment, and ask what you should do.

The vast majority of the comments you receive will be positive, though. You can be confident that a blog editor who has accepted and published your post will consider it of high quality. Any nasty, unkind comments you receive say more about the person writing them than they say about you.

Some bloggers like to reply to every single comment, even if that reply is a simple "Thanks!" Others prefer to respond only when their replies are meaningful. Unless you've had specific instructions or guidance from your host blog, it's up to you how you choose to respond.

Being Interviewed on a Blog

Sometimes, instead of guest posting, bloggers invite you to be interviewed on their sites. Usually, the interview takes the form of a text interview. (For information about audio interviews, see the later section "Being Interviewed on a Podcast.") The bloggers send you a list of questions, and you provide answers.

You normally have the option to veto or edit questions that don't fit perfectly, and the host bloggers may even ask you to suggest questions or areas you want to cover. You may want to provide them with standard information about you in advance, perhaps sending your book information sheet or basic biographical facts. Offer a free copy of your e-book — the host bloggers may have neither the time nor the inclination to read it, but if they do, it can make for a great interview.

Book bloggers sometimes interview authors, and they may even be willing to review your book *and* interview you. If so, jump at the chance! Yes, granting an interview is extra work, but by placing yourself and your book in front of the blog's readers twice, you increase the possibility that they'll remember you and buy your book.

Large blogs are less likely to interview up-and-coming authors, preferring to focus on established writers. To follow best practices, avoid asking for an interview unless the blog hosts have specified that they're looking for people to feature in this way. You may find that most interview opportunities are on smaller, newer blogs. Don't be put off by this situation, because these blogs can have loyal and dedicated followings.

Being Interviewed on a Podcast

Many podcasts are actively looking for people to interview. A *podcast* is a sort of radio show, published on the Internet, that listeners can subscribe to in order to have new episodes sent to their iTunes accounts, for example, or to simply download individual episodes to their computers.

Often, podcasts feature a new person (or new people) during an episode, which can easily be weekly. Unless you already have name recognition within your genre or industry, you probably need to take the first step yourself and initiate contact with a podcast host. Look for podcasts that deal with fiction or with writing (if you're a novelist) or podcasts related to your subject (if you write nonfiction).

After you've lined up an interview, or even when you're looking at potential podcasts to approach, listen to at least one recent show to get a sense of the site's usual style and know what to expect. For many writers (me included), being interviewed and recorded can seem daunting. The good news is that most podcast hosts are experienced, confident interviewers who do their best to put you at ease.

Before the recording takes place, a podcast host might send you questions in advance. The questions only roughly outline the topics that the host expects to cover during the interview, so the host may well abandon questions or throw in others, depending on how the conversation goes. Sometimes, podcasters don't supply questions in advance because they want to allow maximum freedom in the interview. If you have a particular no-go area, let the host know.

Most, though not all, podcasts are edited before production. Double-check with the host to see whether this is the case (if you haven't already been told). Usually, if a podcast will be edited, the host is happy for you to restart an answer or repeat a sentence if you feel that you didn't say it properly the first time.

Advertising on Blogs and E-Mail Lists

If you're short on time, a quick(ish) way to promote your e-book is to pay for advertising. Rather than spend hours writing guest posts and being interviewed, you can simply hand over money and the details about your e-book — and reach a large audience.

Along with the rapid growth of e-books has been a surge in websites and e-mail lists aimed at readers of those e-books. A site or mailing list may have an audience that runs to the tens of thousands, or hundreds of thousands, of people — a helpful way to get your e-book noticed and bought. Two popular advertising sites for e-books are Kindle Nation Daily (www.kindlenation daily.com) and The Kindle Book Review (www.thekindlebookreview. blogspot.com). As is obvious from their names, your e-book needs to be available on the Kindle in order for you to advertise it on those sites. Goodreads (described in Chapter 17) also offers paid advertising.

Preparing your e-book before buying advertising

If early readers have pointed out problems with your e-book, such as a formatting error or a few typos, you'll want to correct them before buying advertising. Your first few readers likely already knew you, so they'll have been happy to overlook any minor flaws in your e-book. The hordes of strangers who (you hope!) buy your e-book after reading an ad won't be as forgiving.

In addition to ensuring that your e-book itself is properly formatted and carefully proofread, you should make sure that the Amazon page (or the sales page on your website) is doing a great job of promoting it. Follow these tips:

- **Ensure that your e-book has at least five reviews.** You may even want to aim for ten. The review is a critical success factor. If you have no reviews, or only one or two, new readers aren't likely to buy.

- **Read the blurb again, and consider whether you want to make changes.** Ask fellow writers for feedback, if you haven't done so already.

- **Join Author Central.** Then you can format the blurb and add sections labeled About the Author, for example, to your e-book's page.

- **Ensure that the cover design looks great.** Ask a writing colleague, or an interested reader, for an honest opinion.

Planning ahead with advertising campaigns

Many large sites offering advertising are booked up months ahead of time. If you want sales to come in quickly after your e-book launch, book your slot before you release your e-book. (Make sure you've allowed enough time in your plan for those inevitable moments when a task takes much longer than you thought it would.)

You have the option to run several ads at a time or to spread ads over a period of weeks or months. The benefit of running them all at one time is that readers may see your e-book featured on several large e-mail lists or websites — and be more likely to pay attention and buy it. However, if you have several ads running at a time, you won't have a chance to make changes in light of what you learn.

Consider your budget for advertising, too. If you have little to spend up front, look at smaller websites. (Try to contact previous advertisers there, to see whether they saw good returns on their investments.) As you sell more copies of your e-book, set aside some of the profit to pay for future ad campaigns.

No website or e-mail list can guarantee results based on advertising, so don't spend money that you can't afford to lose. However, if your e-book is good, and if your sales page is well optimized with a compelling blurb, a great-looking cover image, and several excellent reviews, you have a good chance of at least making back the money you spend.

Part VI
The Part of Tens

The 5th Wave   By Rich Tennant

"Someone want to look at this manuscript
I received on e-mail called 'The Embedded
Virus That Destroyed the Publisher's Servers
When the Manuscript was Rejected?'"

In this part . . .

In The Part of Tens, I share more tips and tricks for
troubleshooting, polishing, and even furthering your
career by publishing an e-book — and for using it as a
springboard to larger-scale projects.

If you've hit a roadblock, head to Chapter 19, where I give
you solutions to ten common e-book problems. If you've
finished the first draft of your e-book, turn to Chapter 20
for tips on how to edit and proofread effectively. After
your e-book is out on the web and selling, try some of the
ideas in Chapter 21 to expand your publishing vision —
which might even mean writing a sequel or starting a
brand-new career.

Chapter 19

Ten Common E-Book Problems — and How to Fix Them

*W*riting an e-book can be an exhilarating ride. You'll experience plenty of joy along the way — and you may find that you enjoy being in full control of the writing and publishing process. Most e-book authors come across at least one or two roadblocks, though, on the journey from original idea to published book.

This chapter lists the most common problems you're likely to face and suggests tips and tricks for overcoming them and moving on. Whatever stage you're working on, you can find help here.

I Have So Many E-Book Ideas That I Don't Know Where to Start

Writers who have dozens of great ideas for book-length works are fortunate. Perhaps you want to produce nonfiction e-books to sell — and you can reasonably specialize in several topics. Maybe you've mapped out a fantasy trilogy — along with a couple of thrillers, a cozy crime novel, and a few romances. Perhaps you enjoy (as I do) writing both fiction and nonfiction, and you're unsure which genre to tackle first.

This problem sometimes presents itself as "I have nothing to write about." If you have lots of ideas bubbling away in your mind, pulling one to the surface to focus on can be difficult. Try these tips to help narrow your list of possible topics:

1. **To start, write down *all* your ideas.**

   Create a list of titles and topics — ideally, adding a few notes about the general scope of each one.

   Don't judge your ideas now. Some might seem silly or unworkable, but you never know what they might lead to.

2. **After you create a list, consider where best to start:**

   - *For your first e-book, choose an idea that's easily implemented.* If your book requires a ton of research or if it's likely to take five years to write, you might get stuck partway. (If you do, see the next problem and solution.)

   - *If you're writing nonfiction, make sure that an audience for that e-book exists.* Don't pick an idea only because you love it. (Ask your existing readers to help you choose among three or four options.)

   - *If you're writing fiction, though, choose a topic that you genuinely love rather than one that you believe will be easy to market.* Remember that with fiction, you're selling entertainment value rather than informative content.

I'm Only Partway Finished, and Now I Have Writer's Block

A few chapters into writing your e-book, you've stalled. It tends to happen in the early stages of writing an e-book. (Many authors find that their resistance slackens later in the process and that they can more easily push toward the end.) You may feel that you have a *very* long way to go, and you may well have already been working on your e-book for months or even years.

"Stuckness" takes on different forms. Even when a writer believes that her creativity is blocked, in most cases, the situation isn't that serious. The problem isn't that the writer *can't* write — she has simply come across a problem within her e-book, or within her life, that's making writing difficult.

If you're stuck on what to write in your e-book, try these steps:

1. **Review your initial plan, such as character outlines or scene ideas for a work of fiction.**

2. **Review the material you've already written to determine whether you need to revise or reshape your plan:**

   - *If you realize that drastic changes are necessary earlier in your e-book, write down a few brief notes now, and continue writing as though you've already made those changes.* Your notes could simply be "Change the introduction and Chapters 1–3 to focus on allotments, not on home gardens" or "John should be 16, not 11." You don't want to go back and make those changes yet, though. By continuing to write, you'll reach the end of the first draft much sooner — and you might also find that you come up with more changes along the way, making rewriting more efficient.

   - *If your e-book plan is solid, reassess your personal goals and priorities.* Being stuck might be an external issue — perhaps you've simply lost motivation, or your life has become much busier than you expected. You may need to put aside your e-book for a while, or you may need to create a clearly defined schedule with intermediate deadlines, such as "Finish Part I before vacation begins." Chapter 3 has more solutions for you to try if you face this sort of problem.

I'm Struggling to Edit My E-Book

The editing process can be grueling, especially if you're creating your first book-length work. The techniques you might have used on articles or short stories in the past may not seem to work as well. Perhaps you know that your e-book needs fairly major revisions (not just typo corrections), but you aren't sure where to begin. If you're struggling to edit your book, try these suggestions:

1. **Request feedback from readers about the structure of your book.**

   If you have a few willing friends — or, better, a writers' circle — ask them to read your e-book and give you "big picture" constructive criticism. At this stage, you're looking for feedback about the overall shape and structure of the e-book and for comments about any areas that aren't quite working. (Perhaps your nonfiction e-book is too detailed, or your readers detest a certain character in your novel.)

If your blog or e-mail newsletter has an established readership, ask for volunteers to read your upcoming e-book. Pick four to eight people for a good range of opinions. Fewer than four, and one person's strong opinion can unduly skew your feedback; more than eight, and you might feel overwhelmed by the number of different suggestions. Give guidance on what you're looking for: You might ask specific questions such as "Does Chapter 11 work?" or "Did you find the ending believable?"

2. **After all major elements of your e-book are in the right places, start editing on a more detailed level.**

   Pay attention to spelling, grammar, and punctuation and to more subjective aspects of your writing, such as the tone and style. Some authors enjoy polishing their e-books to perfection; others find it difficult or simply unpleasant. Don't forget that you can hire a freelance editor to help out, if necessary.

If your budget is tight, you might pay for help with only a small section of your e-book — review all your editor's corrections and suggestions carefully to see how you can apply them to the rest of your manuscript.

1 Have No Design Skills and No Money to Pay a Designer

The cover is a crucial factor in the success (or failure) of your e-book. A great-looking cover gives readers confidence in the quality of your work, and a shoddy, amateurish cover waves a red flag that warns them to stay away. Even a decent-looking cover that doesn't fit your genre or topic well can turn off readers — most crime fans won't pick up a novel that looks like a romance. Color and typography play a big role in cover design.

Regardless of the size of your e-book publishing budget, spend it on cover design to get the most impact for your money. If you're truly cash-strapped, follow these tips:

- ✔ **Design your own cover (by following the advice in Chapter 5).** If you lack visual-design skills, make several covers, and ask your readers to vote on which one they prefer. (This strategy helps generate excitement about your upcoming book.)

- ✔ **Call in a favor from a friend.** Someone with an artistic bent might be willing to design your cover inexpensively or as a gift or in return for a favor. For example, you could help the friend write his résumé.

> ✔ **Ask your writer contacts to recommend a student designer or a gradu-ate who's starting out as a freelancer.** This person may be willing to design your cover for a reasonable rate, especially if you're happy to provide a testimonial.

> ✔ **Launch your e-book with a basic cover you've created.** Use the first $200 of revenue to pay a designer. You should be able to easily update the cover image on Amazon, Smashwords, and your own site.

The Formatting of My E-Book Has Gone Wrong

Software packages have their own, special quirks — as do different e-readers and e-retailers. If your e-book turns out looking quite different from what you wanted, you might need to do some troubleshooting.

Always allow plenty of time for formatting your manuscript correctly, espe-cially for your first e-book. Preview the text on at least one physical e-reader device (such as a Kindle or NOOK), and look at it using e-reader software on your computer. If it doesn't look quite right, do your best to fix it.

Keep these points in mind to handle formatting gone awry:

> ✔ **One common cause of formatting problems is the special character.** After I created my first e-book in the MOBI and EPUB formats in Calibre, I found that all the quotation marks had been stripped out. They were present in my HTML file, but in the form of smart quotes (known as "curly" quotes). The solution was easy: I used the Find and Replace feature in Word to change all smart quotes to straight quotes, and then I repeated the conversion process in Calibre with the Smarten Punctuation option selected. It doesn't sound logical — but it worked. (See Chapter 8 for more on converting files in Calibre.)

> ✔ **Characters such as en-dashes, bullet points, or copyright symbols may not display incorrectly in your MOBI or EPUB e-book file.** If this is the case, replace these characters in the HTML version with their cor-responding ASCII codes. Don't worry if that term doesn't mean much to you — plenty of lists of ASCII codes are available online.

> ✔ **A particular type of formatting simply may not translate well into MOBI or EPUB format.** The Kindle, for example, has only two font faces — a standard serif font and a monospaced code font — so if your manuscript involves several different fonts, you can't replicate that on the Kindle. You may have to rethink how to display text. In my novel, the print version has sans serif text in certain sections, and the digital versions use bold text instead.

If you've spent hours struggling with the conversion process (or if you simply want to avoid it), you can outsource this task for a small fee. Bear in mind that lowball conversion offers are usually too good to be true — you may find that your manuscript still has errors and problems. Ask around for recommendations, and ask to see examples of manuscripts that the company has formatted for other clients.

No One Is Buying My E-Book

You've finished your manuscript, converted it into the proper formats, and displayed it in e-bookstores. Perhaps you've even purchased an International Standard Book Number (ISBN) — a unique identifier for your book — so that your e-book can be distributed as widely as possible. The problem: No one seems to be buying it.

If you experienced a rush of sales to begin with, selling 20 or 30 or even 100 copies on the day you launched your e-book, but you've sold only a handful of copies since then, chances are good that the initial buyers were people who already knew you — family and friends or your blog or e-newsletter subscribers. You were able to easily reach them with your launch message, but now you've exhausted your initial pool of readers.

The main reason your book isn't selling is that no one knows about it. Hundreds of thousands of e-books are sold on Amazon, with more being published every day, so there's a relatively small chance of someone stumbling across yours while browsing. Be proactive about marketing your e-book. You can read ways to do this in Part V.

If you're doing lots of marketing with no upswing in sales, take a long, hard look at your e-book's cover, description, and reviews. Does the cover look professional and eye-catching? Does the book's description do a good job of selling the book? Do you have several 4- and 5-star reviews? Though your core fan base might well buy regardless, readers who don't know you will judge your book based on what they can easily find out from the book's page on retail sites.

No One Is Reviewing My E-Book

A new, potential reader who comes across your e-book will want to take a look at its reviews. For some readers, simply noting the star rating will suffice; others will be eager to read at least one or two reviews, and will take note of the total number of reviews. All else being equal, the more reviews you have (and the better they are), the more books you'll sell.

You can't simply wait around, therefore, and hope that readers will review your e-book. You may well have plenty of more-than-satisfied customers — but they won't necessarily take the initiative to write reviews without a little prompting.

During the launch of your e-book (or even beforehand), ask friends or online contacts if they'd like a review copy of your e-book. Explain that you'll give them free copies, and in return, you'd be grateful if they'd write short reviews. Many, many indie authors do this — and traditional publishers send out review copies to newspapers, related magazines and journals, and bloggers.

After you do that, encourage readers to leave reviews by occasionally prompting them via social media. For example, you could write a blog post highlighting some early reviews, asking anyone else who has read the book but not yet reviewed it to add their opinion, too. If you receive e-mails or read tweets (on Twitter) from happy readers, ask them to take the time to write quick reviews on Amazon or Goodreads. (These two sites are the most likely places for potential readers to look for reviews, so focus on them at first.)

Reviews of My E-Book Are Critical

In a situation that's more soul-destroying than stony silence about your e-book, you see reviews, but they're critical — one or two stars, with nasty comments about your e-book or even about you as a person.

Follow these suggestions for handling negative reviews:

✔ **The first step is to consider whether the reviews contain the truth, even if it's hard to take.** Perhaps three people have rated your e-book at two stars, saying that though the content was helpful, it's riddled with typos and factual errors. You might want to pull it off the shelves temporarily while you update it and find editors or advance readers.

✔ **If the reviews seem to indicate that readers had unrealistic expectations of your e-book, check whether you've inadvertently caused confusion with the category or description you chose.** If you've written a vicious religious satire, for example, you might have created problems by categorizing it as religious fiction. Even though it's about religion, it probably isn't what most of the readers browsing that virtual shelf are expecting.

✔ **If a review seems completely unwarranted — such as a personal attack on you — contact the site in question, and ask for the review to be removed.** If the reviewer clearly hasn't even read the e-book (the reviewer believes that your topic or title is silly, for example, or has a vendetta against you), you have a good case for removing the review.

Avoid being drawn into an argument. You may be tempted to leave a response to a review that explains why the reviewer is wrong — but this strategy can all too quickly descend into a furious quarrel, and it won't benefit your author brand in any way. All writers, however good, receive negative feedback. Find any book that you love on Amazon or Goodreads, and look at its one- and two-star reviews. The best thing to do is to hold your head high and continue writing.

No One Is Reading My Blog

If your e-book is part of a broader online presence, you probably have a related blog (see Chapter 9). A blog is a fantastic way to build a loyal readership: It's easy to add to and update, it lets readers get new posts delivered automatically to their inboxes, and it's a great way to have a dialogue. When you start your blog, though, it can feel as though you're sending your words into a huge vacuum. You might receive no comments, and you may have only a few visitors a day.

It takes time, patience, and effort to build up a blog's readership — but there are a lot of simple techniques you can use. One is to write guest posts for other blogs (see Chapter 18) so that you can place your name and message in front of a much larger audience, some of whom will be interested enough to start reading your own blog. An even simpler method is to leave comments on other blogs — add useful material to the conversation, and you'll find that other readers click your name (which links back to your blog) to check out your writing.

If your blog seems to gain no traction despite your best efforts, take a good look at it. Just like an e-book, your blog needs to be attractive and welcoming for readers: The design should look professional, the navigation should be clear and simple to use, and the content should be informative or entertaining (or both). You might want to hire a designer or even an editor to help.

For more assistance with your blog, read *Blogging For Dummies,* by Susannah Gardner and Shane Birley, or *Blogging All-in-One For Dummies,* by Susan Gunelius (both published by Wiley).

I Want to Write My E-Book — Not Market It

For many writers, the best part of their job is the writing — creating a fictional world and populating it with interesting characters or explaining useful information in an easy-to-understand way. The writing part, though, may start to feel like only a fraction of what you do — after your e-book is finished (or even while you're writing it), you also have to think about marketing.

You might start to wish for a traditional book deal, with a publisher who handles all these tasks, but the truth is that you'd still have to do a lot of your own marketing work. Unless you're quite the big-name author, a publisher doesn't have much money to invest in a publicist or marketing team for your book.

Marketing doesn't have to be painful, though. I'm fairly shy when you meet me in person, which is why I focus on online marketing (obviously a good fit for e-books). I actively enjoy writing guest posts to promote my e-books, and I love connecting with readers and writers on Twitter and other social networking sites. Whatever your own personality and preferences, you can find marketing methods that suit you.

If you truly want to stay focused on writing e-books rather than on publicizing them, consider hiring a publicist or paying for advertising. A publicist can do anything from organizing guest posts on your behalf to throwing a Twitter party for your e-book. Paid advertising can range from a slot in a newsletter to a full review on a popular blog.

Keep in mind, too, that if you truly enjoy writing books, you have a single clear marketing advantage: You're likely to place multiple books on the virtual shelves. Many successful e-book authors say that writing a second (or third or fourth) e-book is one of the best things you can do, because the more books you make available, the more readers and sales you'll have.

Chapter 20

Ten Tips for Editing and Proofreading Your E-Book

After you've finished writing the first draft of your e-book, give yourself a well-deserved break. Put aside your manuscript for a week or two, and focus on activities that you neglected while writing — dining out with your significant other or catching up on a favorite TV series, for example. (Or, if you're like me, rediscover the carpet under all the debris in your house.)

Breaking briefly from your writing duties is a helpful way to gain perspective. Many writers find that immediately after completing their first drafts, they simply can't see how and where they might make changes, or they feel tired and dispirited about having to spend even more time on their books. Spending a week or so away from it lets you return newly enthusiastic and brimming with new ideas.

When you're ready to edit, follow the tips in this chapter to help you make efficient progress.

Finding Free Editing Help

The quickest way to edit an e-book to a professional standard is to hire an editor. For many authors, though, this task is prohibitively expensive — especially if the e-book is only in its first draft and is likely to need several rounds of editing.

If you want early feedback on your e-book, you can find it for free in plenty of ways:

✔ Ask for volunteers (often known as *beta-readers*) to read your e-book before it's published, perhaps drawing on your blog or newsletter list for support.

✔ Arrange a manuscript swap with another author — ask whether someone on your Twitter or LinkedIn network has an e-book underway.

✔ Keep an eye out for new freelancers who are just getting started. They might be willing to offer cheap or free editing services in return for your testimonial.

To make life easy for your unpaid army of editors, give them clear instructions on what sort of feedback you're looking for. (If your e-book is only a first draft, for example, you need someone to look at the big picture rather than spot typos.) If you're seeking detailed feedback, split your e-book into sections so that each person reads only one section.

Wherever you end up finding help, offer a form of payment in return. At least give the people who read your manuscript in advance a free copy of your published e-book. Depending on how much editorial help you're asking for, you might also offer other rewards, such as a free consult with you or a signed print version of your book.

Ensuring That Your E-Book Flows from Chapter to Chapter

Readers don't want to be jolted from their enjoyment of your e-book by a jarring break between chapters or a confusing sequence of information. Your first editing task is to ensure that your e-book is working at its broadest level — chapter by chapter. Put aside the draft of your e-book for a week or two and then read it through in its entirety. Then follow these general steps:

1. **Before you begin tinkering with the chapter order, be sure that you have no superfluous or missing chapters.**

   During the drafting process — often over several months or even years — you may have accidentally written repetitive or redundant chapters. You might also recognize that the original scope of your e-book has changed slightly or that you need to add material because your perspective has expanded.

2. **When you're confident that you have all the correct chapters, consider whether you've placed them in the optimum order.**

   Often, you see more than one logical way to arrange your e-book. Your task is to choose the order that best suits your target reader, as in these examples:

   - *An audience of busy executives:* Give quick-to-implement tips in Chapters 1 and 2 and then dig into more in-depth material later.

   - *An academically minded audience:* Give the theoretical side first and then move on to practical implementation.

   - *A novel aimed for a commercial genre:* Follow chronological order from chapter to chapter. A more literary work can use flashbacks or other devices to present the story out of sequence.

   - *A collection of separate essays, short stories, articles, or blog posts:* (You get no free pass.) Consider the overall structure and flow — which might require rearranging the order, creating themed sections, or adding a short introduction before each individual piece. Though readers of print books might dip in and out, readers of e-books are more likely to read sequentially.

Keeping Paragraphs Short and Clear

Unless you're writing literary fiction or an academic textbook, keep paragraphs straightforward and to the point. Your readers may be viewing your e-book on their computer screens (which is more tiring on the eyes than paper is), on small e-reader devices, or even on their mobile phones. Short, clear paragraphs make for easy reading.

When you're editing, keep an eye out for overly long paragraphs, and see whether you can split them in two:

   ✔ In fiction, short paragraphs can help increase the tension, and a paragraph break can indicate a pause or the passage of time.

   ✔ In nonfiction, paragraph breaks help emphasize important points: The first sentence of a paragraph should generally introduce its main point. Read only the first sentence of every paragraph in your manuscript to see whether they provide a rough summary of your e-book; if they do, chances are good that you're starting and stopping your paragraphs in the right places.

Of course, you can go too far with this technique. A string of one-sentence paragraphs might work in a blog post, but in an e-book, it's likely to look odd, and the text may seem to read as disjointed and abrupt. Unless you're writing experimental text or short paragraphs are part of your distinctive style, try to find a happy middle ground. Give the reader an engaging, even immersive, experience — carefully constructed paragraphs help you do that.

Fixing Confusing or Awkward Sentences

After you pass the paragraph level of your manuscript, it's time to consider the sentences. Most authors find that their first drafts have at least a few mangled sentences — ones that have gone grammatically awry or that go on and on or that simply seem clunky and awkward to read. Follow these tips for spotting and fixing these sentences that aren't quite right:

- **Read your manuscript aloud.** If you stumble over a sentence, it's probably a good candidate for a rewrite — start by splitting it into two shorter sentences.

- **Avoid following outdated rules that tie your sentences into knots.** Starting a sentence with *however,* or even *and* or *but,* is fine. You can also split infinitives and end sentences with prepositions; often, they make your words flow much more naturally.

- **Consider a list of bullet points.** If you write a sentence that introduces several points (particularly long ones), see whether it might work better as a series of bullet points. They're much easier for readers to absorb, and they help add visual interest and white space to the page.

Cutting Unnecessary Words

Most authors overwrite on their first drafts, adding unnecessary words and phrases. It's a normal, natural part of the composition process, and it doesn't mean that you're a bad writer. It does mean that you need to look out for text to cut during editing.

Common unnecessary words and phrases include

- **Qualifiers:** Examples are *really, very, quite, mostly,* and *usually.* Sometimes, you need them — and often, you can cut them. The sentence "It was really a very hot day" can be better written as "It was a scorching day."

- **Adjectives:** Examples are *quickly, slowly, happily, quietly,* and *loudly.* A good rule of thumb is to let the verb carry the weight. If you've written "Tom said loudly," "Tom shouted" or "Tom yelled" is a better alternative.

✔ **Personal phrases:** Examples are "In my opinion," "I think," and "I believe." Occasionally, you must clearly distinguish your opinion from objective fact, but you can generally omit these phrases. Readers will understand that your e-book naturally expresses your opinion.

Cutting an unnecessary word or phrase strengthens the surrounding sentence (and paragraph). Rather than get bogged down in words, readers can focus on your message.

Spell-Checking Your E-Book Carefully

However good your spelling is, always check for misspelled words. Everyone makes these occasional *typos,* and they aren't always obvious at a glance.

Your first step is to run an automatic spell checker. Your word processing software should come with one built in, and it may well underline words in red automatically. (While I was working on an early draft of my novel *Lycopolis* in Microsoft Word, a pop-up message alerted me that spelling mistakes would no longer be shown because I'd made so many. Don't reach that point!)

If a word is underlined in red (or green for a grammar correction), check the suggestion first. Don't blindly accept it — spell checkers are far from infallible. If you realize that the correction is indeed correct, accept it. If you're not sure, consult a dictionary, or ask a writer friend.

After you've fixed any typos and mistakes picked up by your spell checker, read the manuscript yourself. Many mistakes won't be spotted because you may have typed a legitimate word or phrase, even if it isn't what you intended. And as anyone who has ever accidentally typed the word *public* without the *l* can tell you, certain undetected spelling mistakes can be embarrassing!

Avoiding Common Spelling Mistakes

As a writing coach, I come across quite a few words that are habitually confused or misspelled. The list in this section is far from exhaustive, but if you can remember these 12 corrections, you'll be well on your way to a typo-free e-book.

A lot is two separate words. (Compare with *a few.*)

Affect is usually a verb, and *effect* is usually a noun. (Note, though, that you can effect a change.)

Conscious means "awake." Your *conscience* makes you feel guilty about doing something wrong.

Its means "belonging to it." (Compare with *his* and *hers*.) *It's* means "it is." (Compare with *he's* and *she's*.) If you've used *it's*, and you're unsure whether (ahem) it's what you want, try replacing it with *it is*. Does the sentence still make sense?

Lose is when you don't win. *Loose* isn't tight.

Principals are in charge of schools. *Principles* are rules.

Set and *sit* are different words. Some dialects say "set down" for "sit down," but unless you're writing dialogue, you should use the correct word in writing.

Stationary means "not moving." *Stationery* is what you write on.

Their means "belonging to them." *They're* means "they are." *There* means "over there."

Yeah is a slang term for "yes." *Yea* is an archaic form of "yes" and is now used only in the context of voting ("yea" or "nay").

Your means "belonging to you," and *you're* means "you are." Most people know the difference, but it's easy to make mistakes when you're writing in a hurry.

Weird defies the *i before e* rule for "ee" sounds.

Printing Your E-Book Before Proofreading

The final editing task to complete your e-book manuscript is to proofread it to catch any last errors. When you've worked on the same material for months or years, though, it can be almost impossible to spot your own typos. Though your eyes know what you meant to write, they skim over the words on the page.

One simple trick for improving your ability to proofread is to print your manuscript. You'll see it in a different way, and it's easier on your eyes than reading on a computer screen. You can easily circle words or phrases on a printed version of your book, too — you don't have to make corrections in the manuscript as you're proofing.

You can either print your e-book on your home printer or use a print-on-demand service to create a single copy of your book, for your own use. I've done this several times via www.lulu.com, and it usually costs around $10 for a full-length novel.

When you proof, go slowly, and have a pen or highlighter in your hand. Look out for these common errors:

- **Misspellings and confusing words:** Double-check any of your habitual trouble spots.

- **Missing punctuation:** Especially scrutinize closing quotation marks and closing parentheses.

- **Grammatical mistakes:** They often creep in during editing.

The proofing stage isn't the place to edit for flow or voice. If you spot a jarring error, fix it — but resist the urge to rewrite paragraph after paragraph of your manuscript. At this point, you're only focusing on eliminating errors in spelling, grammar, or punctuation.

Hiring a Professional Editor or Proofreader

Perhaps you're an excellent writer, but you're also busy: You absolutely don't want to spend hours and hours reviewing your e-book to hunt down every typo. Or maybe you have great content, but you know that your writing skills could be improved — and you want to get professional support.

As an independent author, you can easily hire a freelance editor or proofreader to help you, and I highly recommend it. Yes, it's an investment, but it makes a significant difference in the quality of your finished e-book.

If you can't afford to have your whole manuscript edited, look for an editor to take on a shorter section — perhaps the first three chapters. Review these edits carefully, and look for patterns in the errors you make. For example, if you have a lot of misplaced (or missing) apostrophes, look out for them in the rest of your e-book.

All editors and proofreaders do their jobs a little differently, but you can generally expect editors to make suggestions about flow, style, and organization and proofreaders to concentrate on typos and punctuation. Before you sign a contract or hand over money, specify what you expect your editor or proofreader to do.

When you're looking for a good editor or proofreader, ask around for recommendations — you want to hire someone who's reliable and who delivers quality work at a fair price. If you don't know anyone who can give you a good recommendation, look at several different editors' websites. Review the services they offer, the prices they charge, and their previous clients' testimonials. You can even ask to contact former clients so that you can ask their opinions directly.

Letting Go of Editing to Make the Leap to Publishing

The editing process can take months or years. If you've been working on your e-book for a long time, you might find it difficult to let go and complete the project. After all, there's always another chapter that you can add or a couple of paragraphs that might work better in a different order or a few words that can be tweaked.

If you want your e-book to ever end up on the virtual shelves of a bookstore, you need to eventually stop editing. Your manuscript may still have imperfections — but every book does. If you've edited the big picture, honed the sentences, and proofread carefully, your e-book is ready to be sent out into the world.

Chapter 21

Ten Ways to Enhance Your E-Book Sales — or Your Career

In This Chapter

▶ Adding extra value to your e-book

▶ Using your e-book to support a writing career

▶ Turning your e-book into a new product

*A*fter you've been bitten by the e-book-writing bug, you might find yourself in a curious situation: You not only have become a published author, but have also taken a stride into the world of business by producing and selling your own product.

Whether you want to further your writing mission or begin a whole new career, your e-book can be a useful starting point for new and exciting projects. In this chapter, I walk you through ten activities to consider. Some require skills you've already developed, such as writing a sequel to your e-book, and others help you advance new skills, such as experimenting with audio or video creation or teaching an online course.

Updating Your E-Book After Receiving Feedback

One simple way to take your e-book further is to release a new edition. Six months or a year after its publication, you might realize that you've gained new knowledge or that readers have suggested changes or additional chapters.

When you receive feedback on your e-book, whether it's positive or negative, record it somewhere safe. Save all related e-mail messages and Amazon reviews, for example. Don't act on every piece of feedback immediately — there's no point in adding five extra chapters simply on the request of a lone reader. Schedule time to review the feedback systematically.

Consider inserting extra material (perhaps in the form of an appendix) or making changes to help the reader engage with the material you've written. For example, if you've written an in-depth time management guide that gives lots of advice, include a few quick-start bullet points to help readers start saving time immediately.

When you update your e-book, let past customers know. If possible, graciously let them have the updated version for free, to encourage them to buy from you again. If you're selling your e-book from your own website, or via E-junkie (see Chapter 12) or a similar site, you can easily supply everyone who has bought the previous version with a link to download the new one. If you don't have the e-mail addresses of readers who bought your e-book via Amazon or another store, you can announce the new edition on your blog, Twitter feed, or Facebook page, for example. Amazon now sends updated editions to readers who request them, so let those readers know to contact customer service.

Writing a Sequel to Your First E-Book

One easy way to encourage past customers to buy again is to write a sequel. In a fiction e-book, you would use the same characters that your readers already know and love; in nonfiction, you would tackle a new (but related) topic area in a familiar way. It's no accident that many of the best-selling independent authors have trilogies or series of novels, not separate books.

For a fiction series or trilogy, examine the reviews and feedback from the first e-book to see which aspects resonate with readers. For example, if a minor character has proved especially popular, you may give that character a greater role in your next novel.

Let readers of your first e-book know about the sequel — an active blog, Twitter feed, or Facebook page can help you get the word out. (If you sell your e-book on your own site via E-junkie, you can send purchasers an e-mail about the sequel.) People who've already bought and enjoyed your first e-book are likely to buy again.

Your sequel isn't good only for repeat business, though — you'll also pick up new customers, who may well buy your first e-book, too. After you've written several e-books, you can package them in a bundle and offer a discount to encourage readers to buy all (rather than only one) of your e-books.

Creating Audio and Print Versions of Your E-Book

Not all readers enjoy reading text on a display screen, such as on an e-reader or a computer, so consider producing alternative versions of your e-book. One useful option, the *audiobook,* lets readers enjoy listening to your writing while they're driving, working, or exercising, for example.

Producing an audiobook isn't especially complicated: You simply record yourself reading the text of your book. Use a microphone of decent quality, and record in a quiet location. You can download free Audacity software (`http://audacity.sourceforge.net`) to record yourself speaking and then edit the recording. If you stumble over your words, repeat a line and then edit out the mistake.

If you aren't confident about creating your own audio file, pay a professional to record your e-book for you. First survey your audience to gauge interest in the audio version of your e-book, to avoid paying for a professional recording that only one person will buy.

Like the text version of your e-book, an audiobook, in the form of a file in MP3 format, can easily be sold online for downloading from your own website. You can also sell your e-book as a CD or an MP3 download via CreateSpace (an Amazon company, at `www.createspace.com`), CDBaby (`www.cdbaby.com` — enter *audiobook* in the Search box at the top of the page), or Kunaki (`www.kunaki.com`). These sites offer varying options and pricing, so shop around before choosing one. You can also burn your audiobook onto DVDs to sell at live events.

The print version of an e-book appeals to readers who prefer "real" (physical) books over electronic books. Again, you may be able to sell yours at live events — book launches or conferences, for example. I prefer Lulu (www.lulu.com) and CreateSpace for creating print books; LightningSource (www.lightningsource.com) is popular, but it has a steeper learning curve and an initial setup fee.

Using print-on-demand services eliminates the need to order hundreds or thousands of copies of your book — the site produces and ships a copy whenever a reader purchases one.

Major print-on-demand sites offer comprehensive guidance to help you produce your print book — be sure to follow it. Before you make your print book publicly available, order a physical proof copy (don't rely on the PDF version) to ensure that it looks the way you want.

Launching a New Career As a Coach or Consultant

If you've written a nonfiction e-book, you may already have strong qualifications and considerable experience in your field. (And you've probably even enhanced your skills while researching your book.) If so, consider setting yourself up as a coach or consultant.

Coaches work with individuals in all sorts of areas. You can find life coaches and business coaches and specialists in nutrition, parenting, and even writing. You need no specific qualifications to call yourself a coach, though you can affiliate yourself with training courses and organizations. The word *mentor* is sometimes used in place of *coach*.

Consultants work with companies, often to help with specific projects by offering expert advice. Consultants usually have no direct authority to make changes within the company. You need no specific qualifications to consult, though companies normally expect you to have a significant amount of demonstrable experience.

To get started as a coach or consultant, simply let potential clients know that you're available by setting up a website (or adding a page to your existing site) and explaining your services. If you'll be working as a consultant, you may have testimonials from former employers or line managers; if you'll be coaching, you might work with a few individuals for free in return for feedback and testimonials.

Approaching Agents (Or Publishers) to Represent Your E-Book

Some self-publishing authors haven't ruled out the possibility of making traditional print deals. In fact, they may well have published in e-book format to build an initial audience and to prove that a market for the book exists.

If your e-book has sold reasonably well (a few hundred copies), you may be ready to approach agents and publishers. In the past, the publishing industry was reluctant to handle material that had already been released online — but that resistance is changing fast. By demonstrating that your book has appeal and that you have a strong author platform, you gain an edge over other authors in the slush pile.

You should, obviously, follow any guidelines set out by the agents or publishers you're approaching. Most post information on their websites, so check to see, for example, their preferences for e-mail or snail-mail (postal mail) contact, manuscript formatting in your sample chapter, and query letters. If you find scant (or nonexistent) submission guidelines, follow the standard use of double-spaced type, in 12-point Times New Roman or Courier font, on plain white paper with 1-inch margins.

Even if your e-book is selling well, a print deal can help it reach a much wider audience. Though a print deal doesn't necessarily result in a great deal more money from book sales (after all, your royalty cut is much lower), you gain greater credibility and visibility within your field.

Using Your E-Book As the Basis of a Digital Product

Your e-book is already a stand-alone product, but if you want, you can easily add new elements to create an expanded — and, potentially, higher-priced — product. Authors commonly enhance their nonfiction (rather than fiction) products, though if you're a novelist, you can create a package of novels, short stories, audio, and even videos related to your fiction.

Digital products can contain any element produced in digital format: text, audio, graphics, video content, or even software. You can add to your e-book several text worksheets or a spreadsheet that readers can download, or include audio files that you've recorded with experts in your field. If your e-book teaches a computer-related topic, such as how to set up your own website, include code or graphics to help readers get up to speed quickly.

If you're selling audio and video content, your download is undoubtedly large. You may want to host videos on a password-protected website so that readers don't need to download them all one huge package.

Partnering with Another Writer to Sell E-Books Together

For some e-book authors, partnering with other writers makes great business sense. By combining your strengths with someone else's, you can make much faster progress in writing, publishing, and marketing your e-book.

This arrangement works well in a couple of situations:

- ✔ **You're an excellent writer, but you lack knowledge about the subject matter.** Work with someone who's an expert in the field but who has little time or inclination to write a book on his or her own.

- ✔ **You write well and are knowledgeable about the subject matter, but you have no online platform.** Partner with someone who maintains a large blog or newsletter list (with perhaps tens of thousands of subscribers) to produce an e-book — you do most of the work, and the other person's name helps sell your collaboration.

Don't assume that a partnership requires much less work than writing an e-book on your own. It may well *more* work — though the rewards are often correspondingly greater. Clarify up front how the process will work, particularly the royalty split (50-50 or otherwise), writing and publication time scales, and division of responsibilities.

Choose a partner whom you already know well, perhaps someone you've worked with in the past. Pick a reliable person whom you can trust to deliver their share of the work on time, and be sure that you have compatible working styles. Before committing to a full-length e-book, work on a small, collaborative project together, such as a blog post or a short e-book.

Becoming a Freelance E-Book Writer

Perhaps you enjoyed the experience of writing your nonfiction e-book, but you didn't enjoy the publishing process, or you struggled with marketing your book. Take a look at writing e-books as a freelancer, to produce written material for individuals, businesses, or companies who want a book but need for someone else to write it.

If you choose this route, you'll likely work as a *ghostwriter,* someone who writes content under the name of another person (or a company). You can expect to write fairly specialized material, usually for businesses that sell books directly to customers rather than via Amazon.

As with any sort of freelancing work, writing e-books in this way has benefits and drawbacks. If you enjoy the researching and writing process, or if you want a guaranteed return on the time you invest, freelancing should suit you well. However, if your e-book is successful — perhaps selling thousands of copies — keep in mind that you still receive only the pay that you agreed on up front. (You can still try to negotiate a flat fee plus a percentage of royalties.)

Setting a rate for freelance work can be difficult. Freelancers commonly quote by project cost rather than by hourly rate. Clients care about the total project cost, not the number of hours you work. Hone your skill in accurately estimating the time you spend researching, writing, and editing, and be sure to allow for revisions and margin of error.

Creating Merchandise Based on Your E-Book

Certain e-books lend themselves well to physical products, or *merchandise.* Plenty of sites on the Internet let you create your own products, such as T-shirts, mugs, stationery, and other items from CafePress (www.cafe press.com), or greeting cards and other photo-printed items from PhotoBox (www.photobox.com).

You can produce merchandise for promotional purposes, such as your e-book's cover, title, and blurb printed on T-shirts to wear at conferences or on postcards to mail. You can also make merchandise that you plan to sell directly to customers. (Sites such as CafePress work similarly to print-on-demand publishing, so you don't need to stock up on supplies initially.)

If individuals have helped you by serving as beta (advance) readers or even by helping fund your e-book, you can thank them by sending them T-shirts, mugs, or other gifts you've designed.

Unless your e-book has an extremely loyal or extremely large fan base, you're unlikely to get rich selling merchandise — so don't invest large sums of money in design or manufacturing unless you're sure of a good return. Survey your audience before creating products to find out what might be popular.

Turning Your Nonfiction E-Book into an Online Course

If you're anything like me, you own books packed with helpful advice that you've read (maybe even more than once) but that you've never put into action. Most readers struggle to engage fully with the material in an e-book — we skim it, or we nod along with good ideas but struggle to implement them in a meaningful way.

By converting your e-book into an online course, you create a win-win scenario: You can charge a much higher price, and your customers are far more likely to take action on what they learn.

Teaching an online course requires no complex technology. All you need is a way for people to pay you and a way for you to deliver course materials daily or weekly. For a simple way to accept payment, use PayPal (www.paypal.com), and add your course members to a mailing list so that you can send the course directly to their inboxes. If you want to create a website for logging in, search for *membership site software* at your favorite search engine, and ask for recommendations from other authors who've created similar methods.

Your online course can follow a structure similar to your table of contents. Don't simply copy and paste your words into a new format, though — include interactive elements (such as one-to-one coaching, group forums, or a weekly live webinar) to help people engage with the material. At the end of every lesson or section, give your course members clear instructions on what to do next, perhaps in the form of an exercise or an assignment.

Index